STAR WARS®

AGENT OF THE EMPIRE

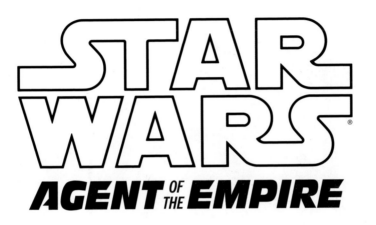

Illustration by » **STÉPHANE ROUX**

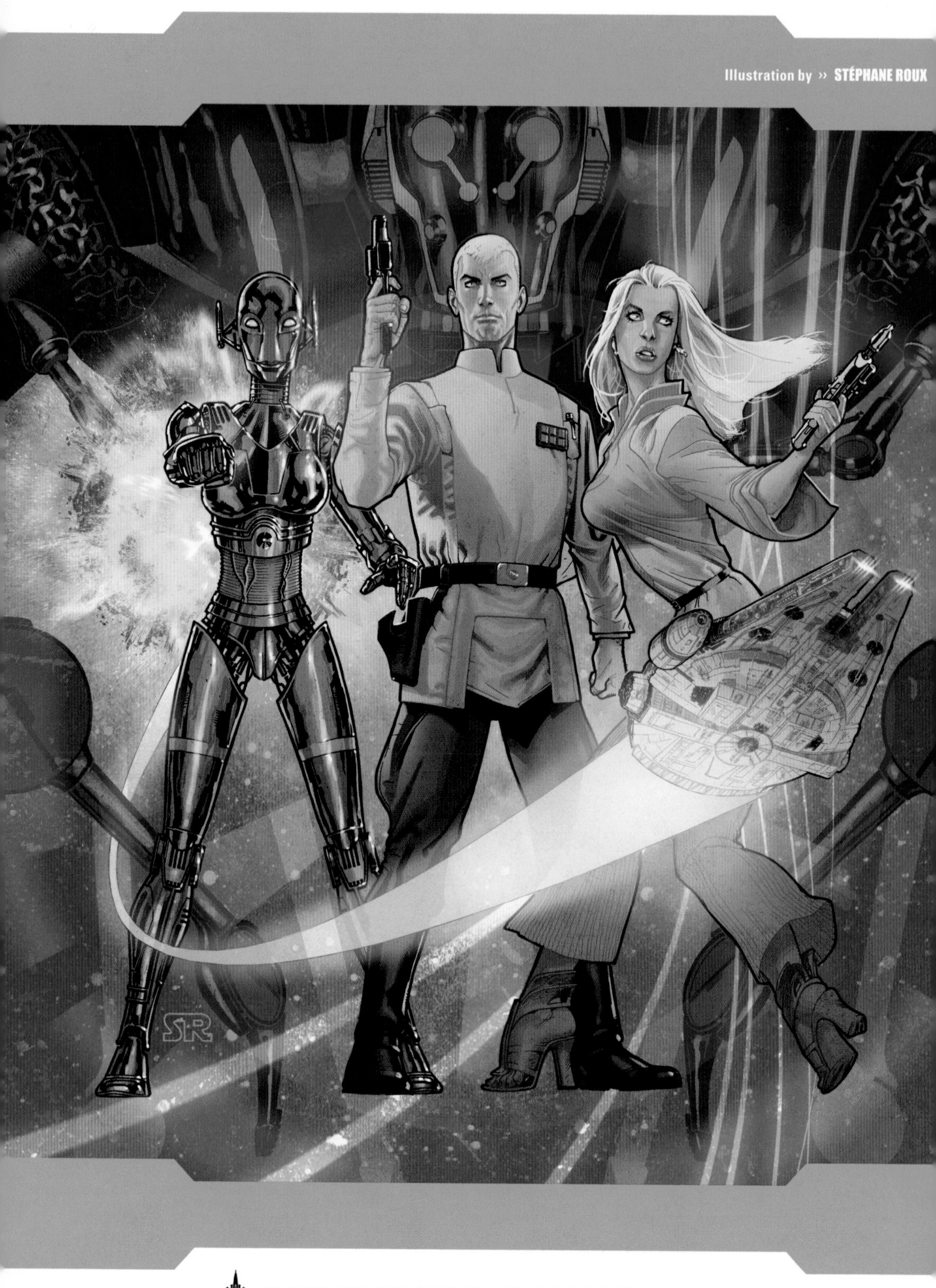

SR

THE RISE OF THE EMPIRE (1,000–0 YEARS BEFORE THE BATTLE OF YAVIN)

After the seeming final defeat of the Sith, the Republic enters a state of complacency. In the waning years of the Republic, the Senate rife with corruption, the ambitious Senator Palpatine causes himself to be elected Supreme Chancellor. This is the era of the prequel trilogy.

The events in this story take place approximately three years before the events in Star Wars: Episode IV—A New Hope.

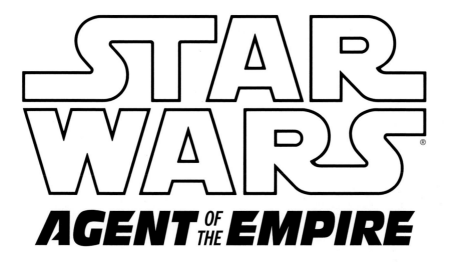

STAR WARS®

AGENT OF THE EMPIRE

VOLUME ONE

IRON ECLIPSE

Script
JOHN OSTRANDER

Pencils
STÉPHANE ROUX (pages 7–50 & 95–115)
STÉPHANE CRÉTY (pages 51–94)

Inks
JULIEN HUGONNARD-BERT

Colors
WES DZIOBA

Lettering
MICHAEL HEISLER

Cover Art
STÉPHANE ROUX

DARK HORSE BOOKS
LUCAS BOOKS

president and publisher
MIKE RICHARDSON

collection designer
TINA ALESSI

editor
RANDY STRADLEY

assistant editor
FREDDYE LINS

Special thanks to **JENNIFER HEDDLE, LELAND CHEE, TROY ALDERS, CAROL ROEDER, JANN MOORHEAD**, and **DAVID ANDERMAN** at Lucas Licensing.

NEIL HANKERSON Executive Vice President TOM WEDDLE Chief Financial Officer RANDY STRADLEY Vice President of Publishing MICHAEL MARTENS Vice President of Book Trade Sales ANITA NELSON Vice President of Business Affairs DAVID SCROGGY Vice President of Product Development DALE LAFOUNTAIN Vice President of Information Technology DARLENE VOGEL Senior Director of Print, Design, and Production KEN LIZZI General Counsel MATT PARKINSON Senior Director of Marketing DAVEY ESTRADA Editorial Director SCOTT ALLIE Senior Managing Editor CHRIS WARNER Senior Books Editor DIANA SCHUTZ Executive Editor CARY GRAZZINI Director of Print and Development LIA RIBACCHI Art Director CARA NIECE Director of Scheduling

STAR WARS®: AGENT OF THE EMPIRE Volume 1—IRON ECLIPSE

This volume collects issues #1–#5 of the Dark Horse comic-book series *Star Wars: Agent of the Empire—Iron Eclipse*.

Published by Dark Horse Books, a division of Dark Horse Comics, Inc.
10956 SE Main Street, Milwaukie, OR 97222

DarkHorse.com
StarWars.com

To find a comics shop in your area, call the Comic Shop Locator Service toll-free at 1-888-266-4226

LIBRARY OF CONGRESS CATALOGING-IN-PUBLICATION DATA

Ostrander, John.
Star wars, agent of the empire. Volume 1, Iron eclipse / script, John Ostrander ; pencils, Stéphane Roux and Stephane Crety ; inks, Julien Hugonnard-Bert ; colors, Wes Dzioba ; lettering, Michael Heisler ; cover art, Stephane Roux. -- 1st ed.
    p. cm.
Summary: "Secret agent for the Galactic Empire Jahan Cross investigates the Stark family and their secret droid project"--Provided by publisher.
ISBN 978-1-59582-950-4
1. Star Wars fiction. 2. Graphic novels. I. Roux, Stéphane. II. Crety, Stephane. III. Hugonnard-Bert, Julien. IV. Title. V. Title: Iron eclipse.
PN6728.S73O83 2012
741.5'973--dc23

                    2012016663

First edition: October 2012
ISBN 978-1-59582-950-4

10 9 8 7 6 5 4 3 2 1
Printed at Midas Printing International, Ltd., Huizhou, China

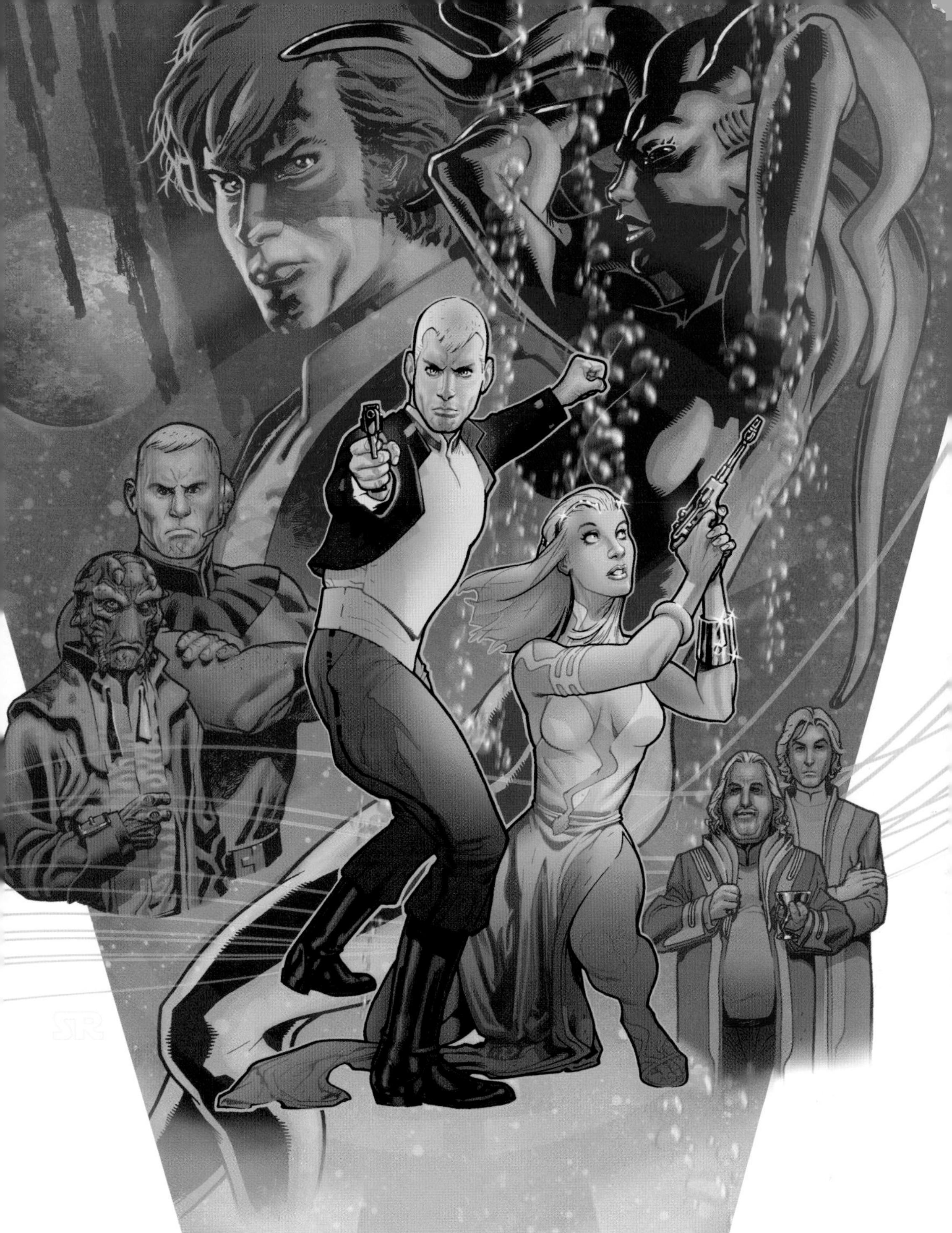

Illustration by » **STÉPHANE ROUX**

THE **GALACTIC EMPIRE** maintains peace and order in a galaxy rife with chaos and corruption. Always quick to deal with treachery or hints of intrigue, the Emperor has many ways to enforce his will.

Darth Vader is the Emperor's face of fear, whose mere presence can quell an uprising . . .

The stormtrooper legions and fleets of Star Destroyers are the Emperor's hammer, for when an application of force is necessary . . .

But a finer tool is required when situations call for delicacy—or even for the hand of power to go undetected. In those cases, the Emperor calls for his scalpel . . . Imperial Agent Jahan Cross.

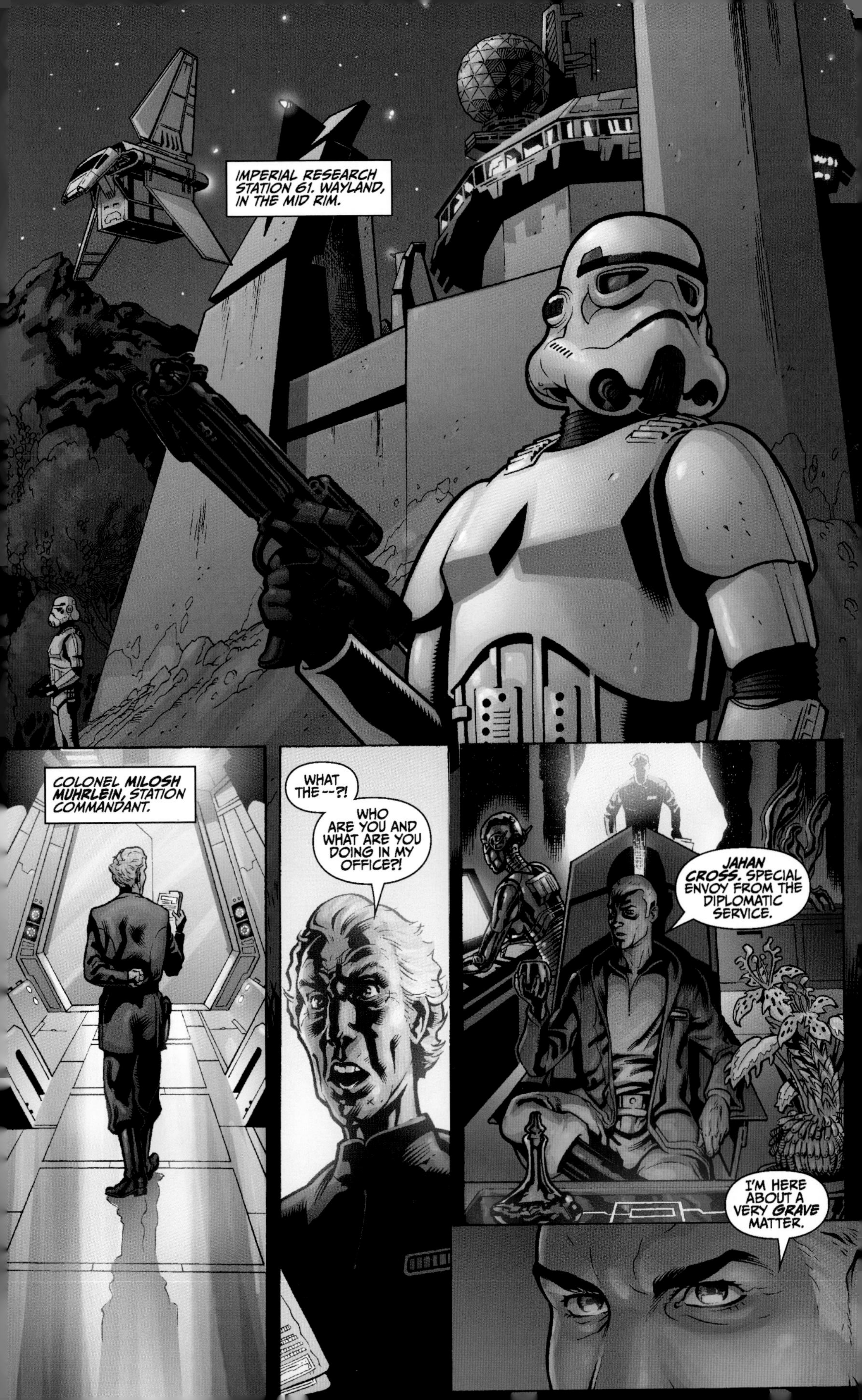
IMPERIAL RESEARCH STATION 61. WAYLAND, IN THE MID RIM.
COLONEL MILOSH MUHRLEIN, STATION COMMANDANT.
WHAT THE--?!
WHO ARE YOU AND WHAT ARE YOU DOING IN MY OFFICE?!
JAHAN CROSS. SPECIAL ENVOY FROM THE DIPLOMATIC SERVICE.
I'M HERE ABOUT A VERY GRAVE MATTER.

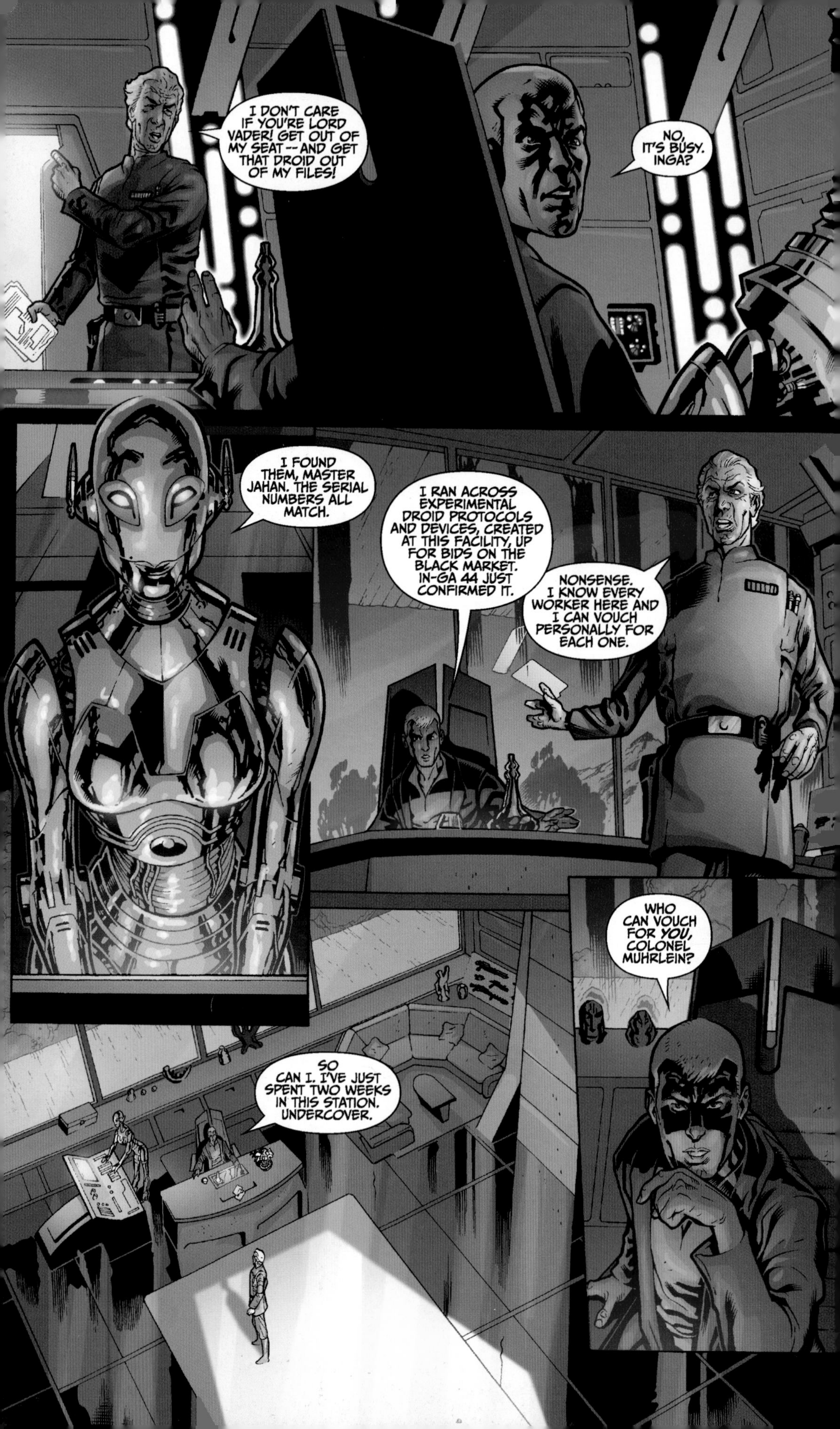
I DON'T CARE IF YOU'RE LORD VADER! GET OUT OF MY SEAT -- AND GET THAT DROID OUT OF MY FILES!
NO, IT'S BUSY. INGA?
I FOUND THEM, MASTER JAHAN. THE SERIAL NUMBERS ALL MATCH.
I RAN ACROSS EXPERIMENTAL DROID PROTOCOLS AND DEVICES, CREATED AT THIS FACILITY, UP FOR BIDS ON THE BLACK MARKET. IN-GA 44 JUST CONFIRMED IT.
NONSENSE. I KNOW EVERY WORKER HERE AND I CAN VOUCH PERSONALLY FOR EACH ONE.
WHO CAN VOUCH FOR *YOU*, COLONEL MUHRLEIN?
SO CAN I. I'VE JUST SPENT TWO WEEKS IN THIS STATION. UNDERCOVER.

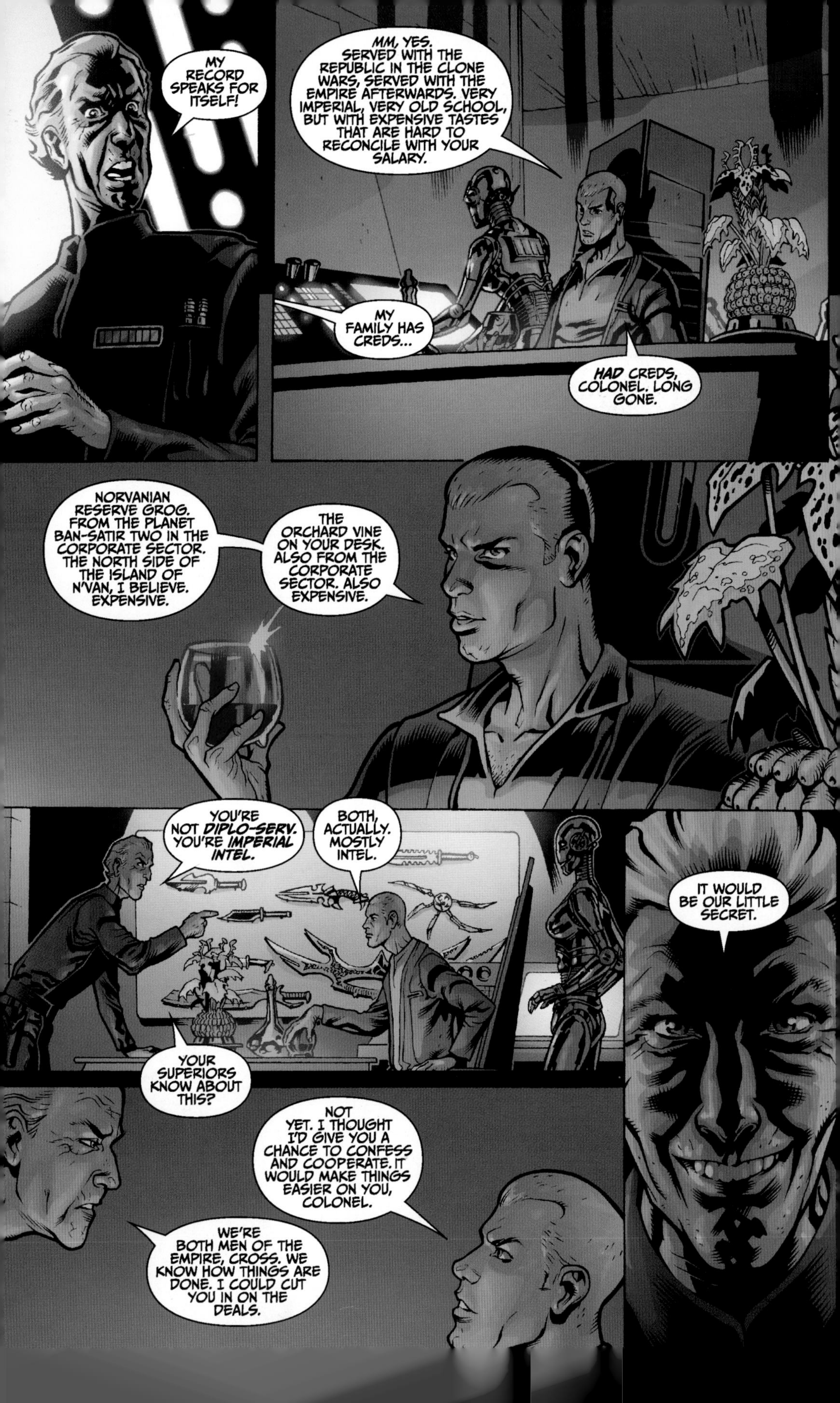
MY RECORD SPEAKS FOR ITSELF!
MM, YES. SERVED WITH THE REPUBLIC IN THE CLONE WARS, SERVED WITH THE EMPIRE AFTERWARDS. VERY IMPERIAL, VERY OLD SCHOOL, BUT WITH EXPENSIVE TASTES THAT ARE HARD TO RECONCILE WITH YOUR SALARY.
MY FAMILY HAS CREDS...
HAD CREDS, COLONEL. LONG GONE.
NORVANIAN RESERVE GROG. FROM THE PLANET BAN-SATIR TWO IN THE CORPORATE SECTOR. THE NORTH SIDE OF THE ISLAND OF N'VAN, I BELIEVE. EXPENSIVE.
THE ORCHARD VINE ON YOUR DESK. ALSO FROM THE CORPORATE SECTOR. ALSO EXPENSIVE.
YOU'RE NOT DIPLO-SERV. YOU'RE IMPERIAL INTEL.
BOTH, ACTUALLY. MOSTLY INTEL.
YOUR SUPERIORS KNOW ABOUT THIS?
NOT YET. I THOUGHT I'D GIVE YOU A CHANCE TO CONFESS AND COOPERATE. IT WOULD MAKE THINGS EASIER ON YOU, COLONEL.
WE'RE BOTH MEN OF THE EMPIRE, CROSS. WE KNOW HOW THINGS ARE DONE. I COULD CUT YOU IN ON THE DEALS.
IT WOULD BE OUR LITTLE SECRET.

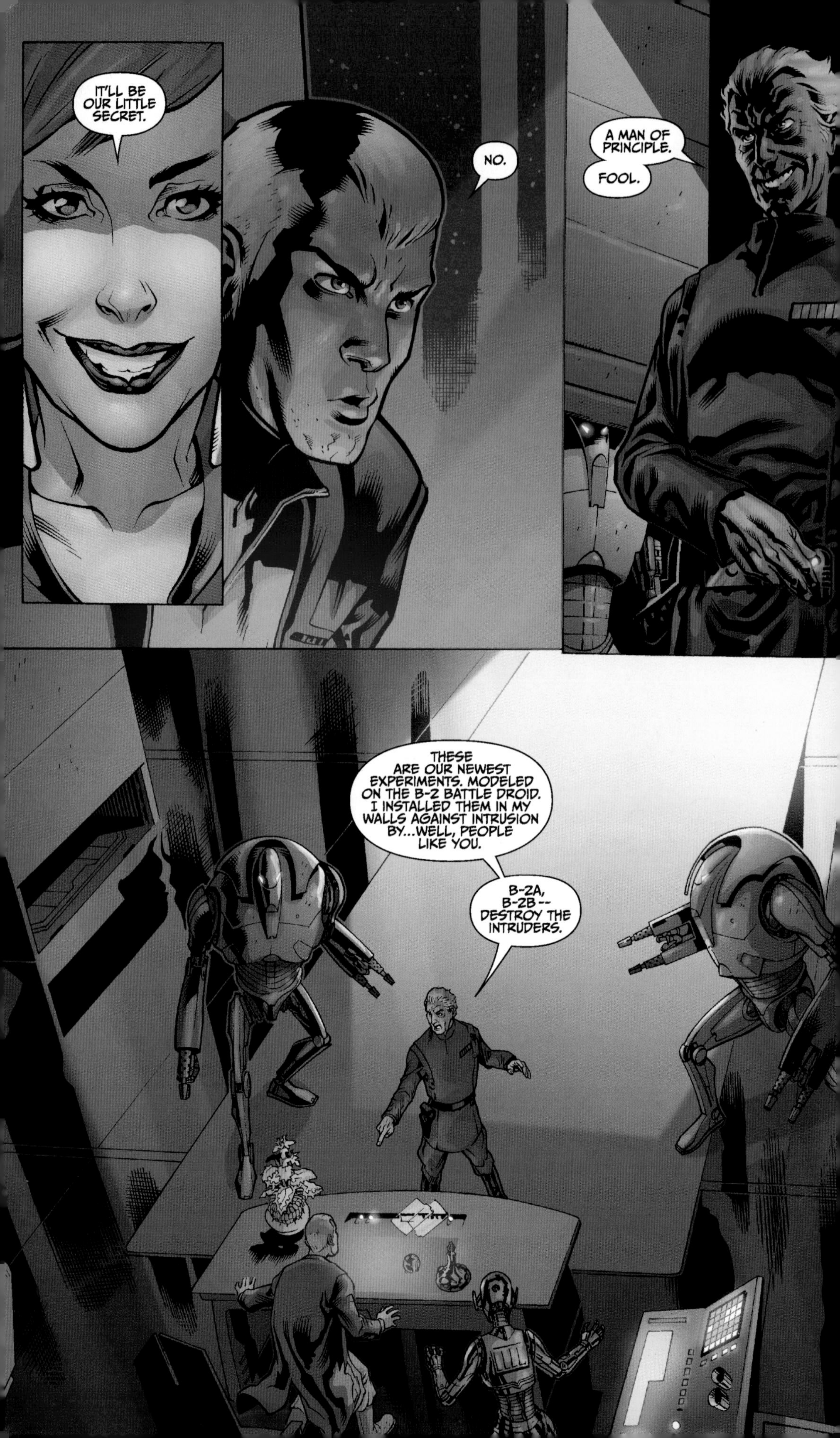

IT'LL BE OUR LITTLE SECRET.
NO.
A MAN OF PRINCIPLE.
FOOL.
THESE ARE OUR NEWEST EXPERIMENTS. MODELED ON THE B-2 BATTLE DROID. I INSTALLED THEM IN MY WALLS AGAINST INTRUSION BY...WELL, PEOPLE LIKE YOU.
B-2A, B-2B-- DESTROY THE INTRUDERS.

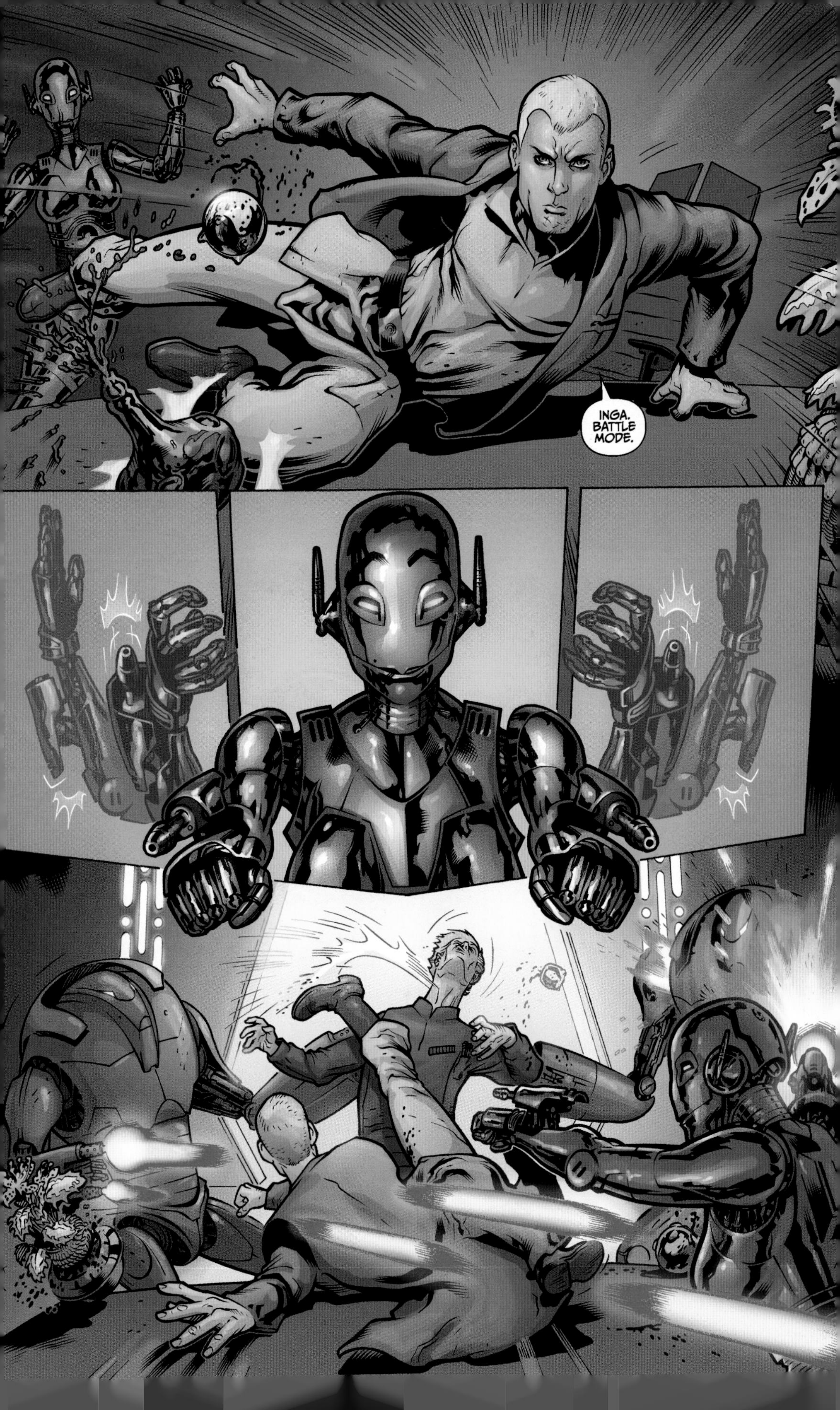
INGA. BATTLE MODE.

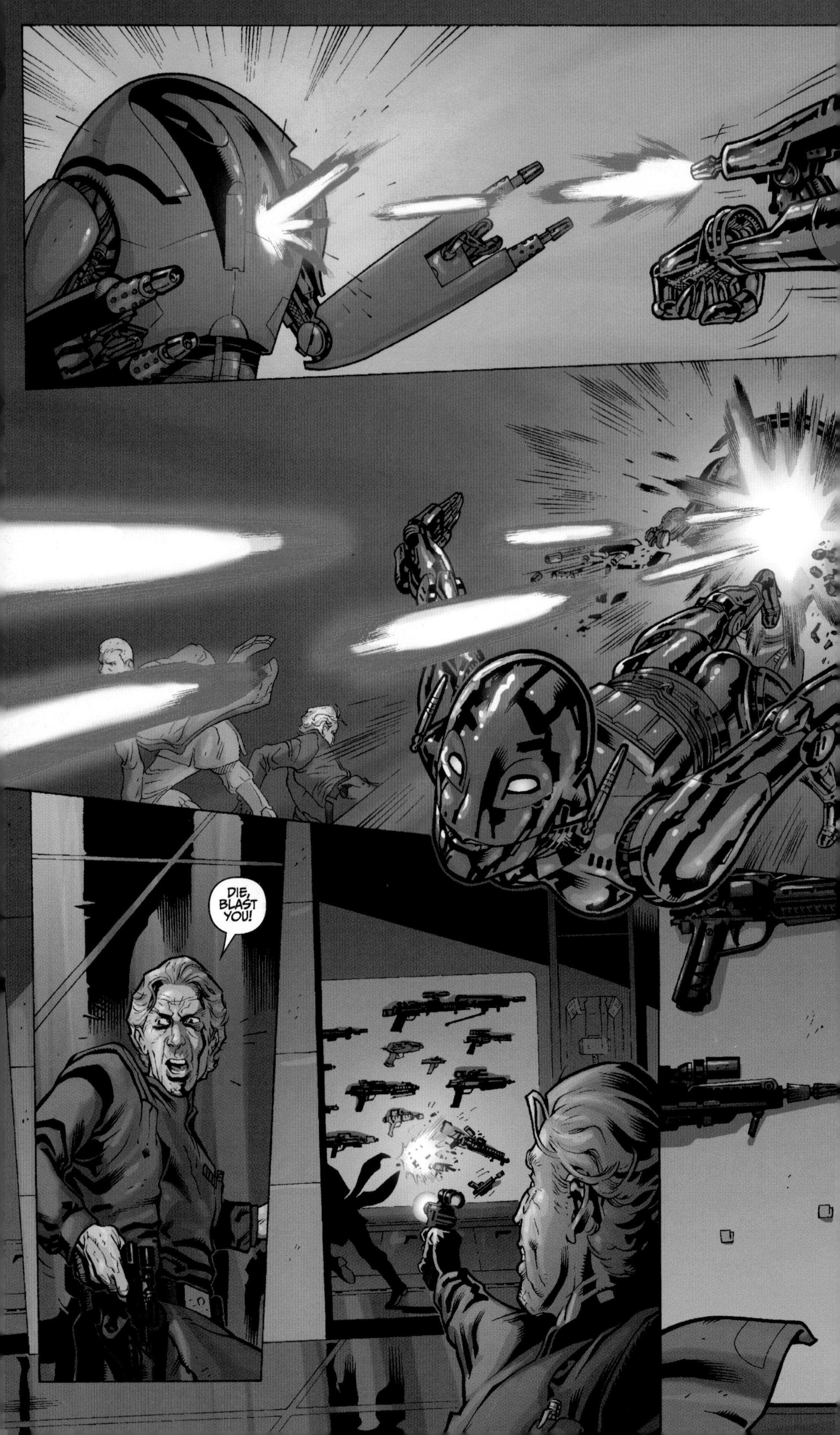
DIE, BLAST YOU!

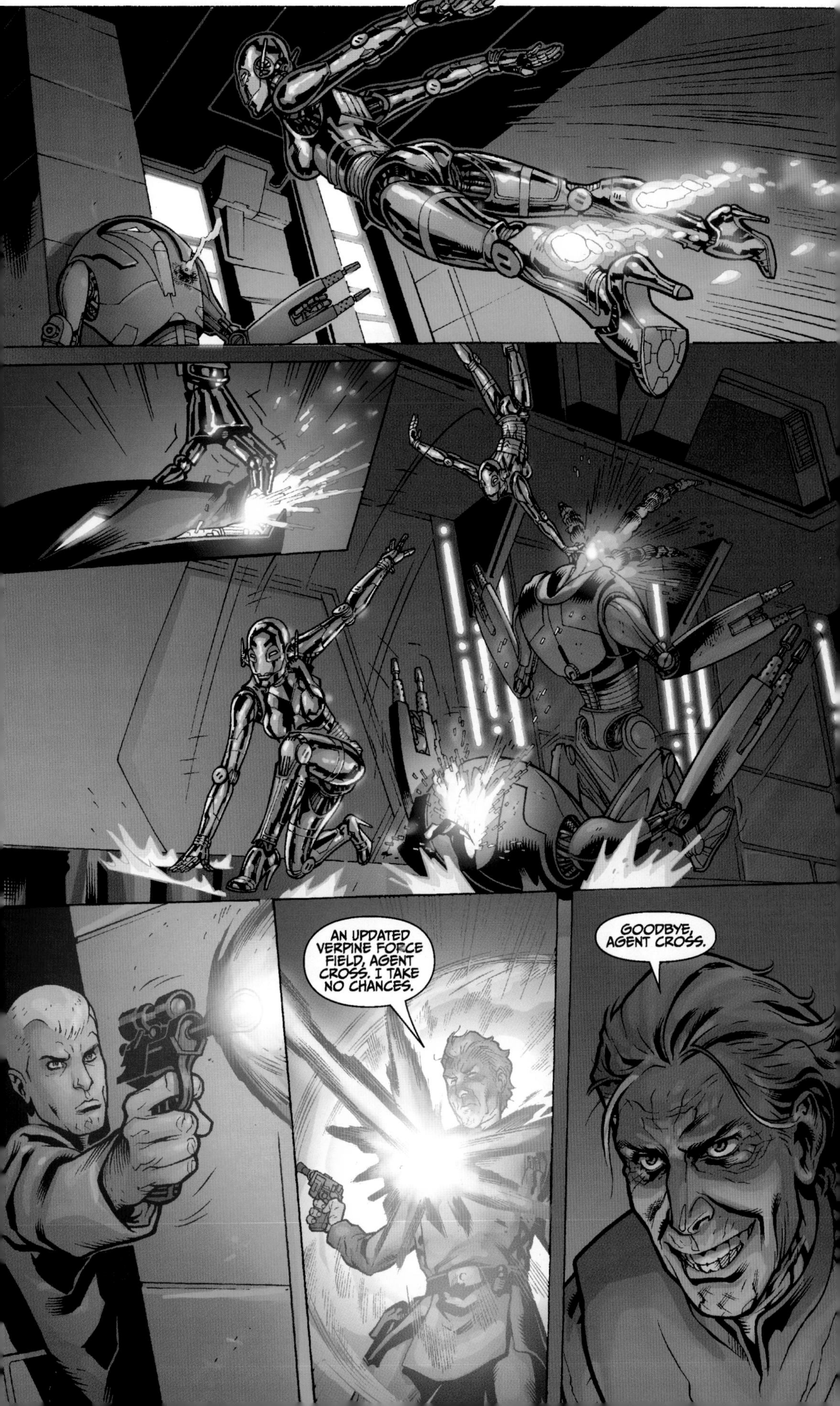
AN UPDATED VERPINE FORCE FIELD, AGENT CROSS. I TAKE NO CHANCES.
GOODBYE, AGENT CROSS.

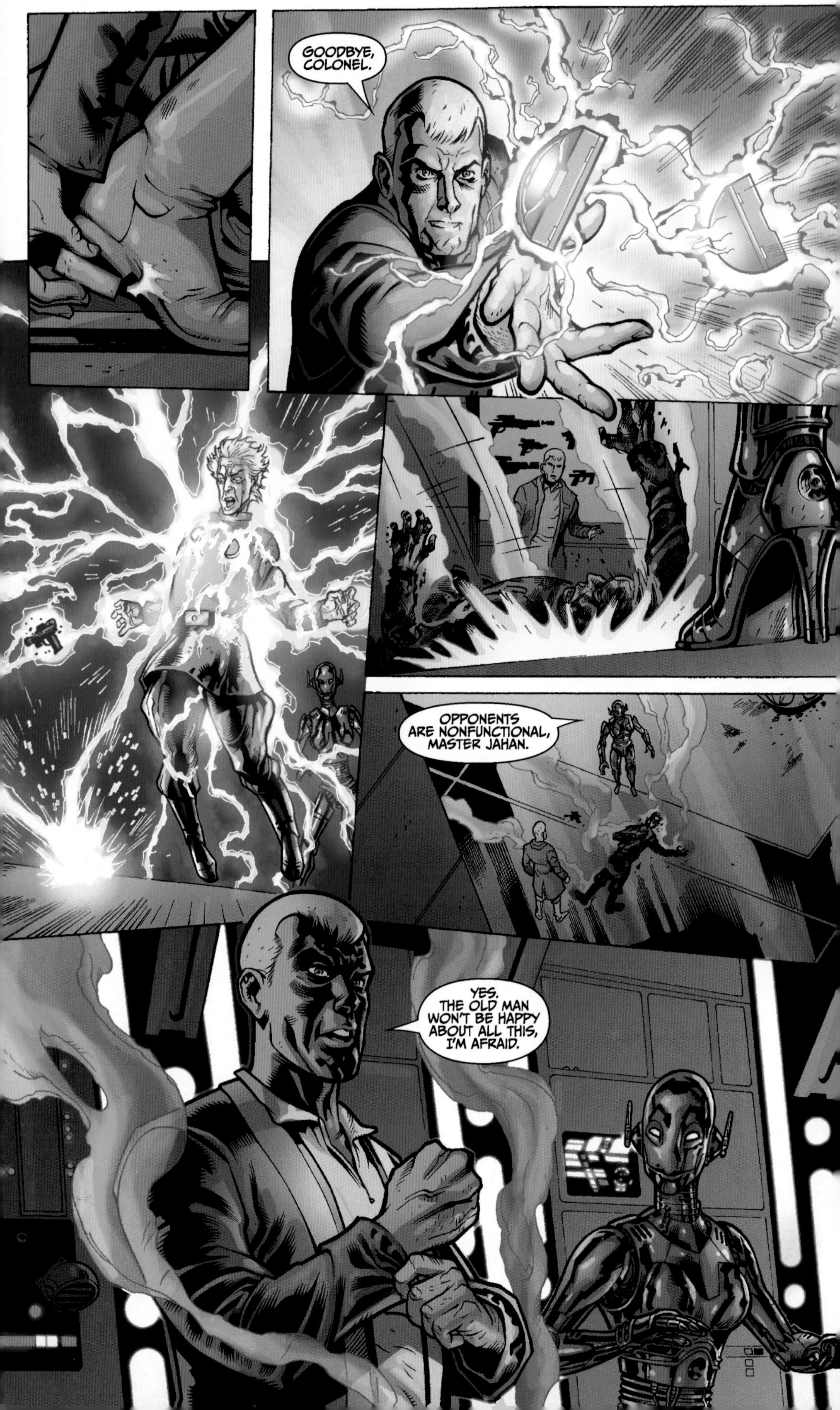
GOODBYE, COLONEL.
OPPONENTS ARE NONFUNCTIONAL, MASTER JAHAN.
YES. THE OLD MAN WON'T BE HAPPY ABOUT ALL THIS, I'M AFRAID.

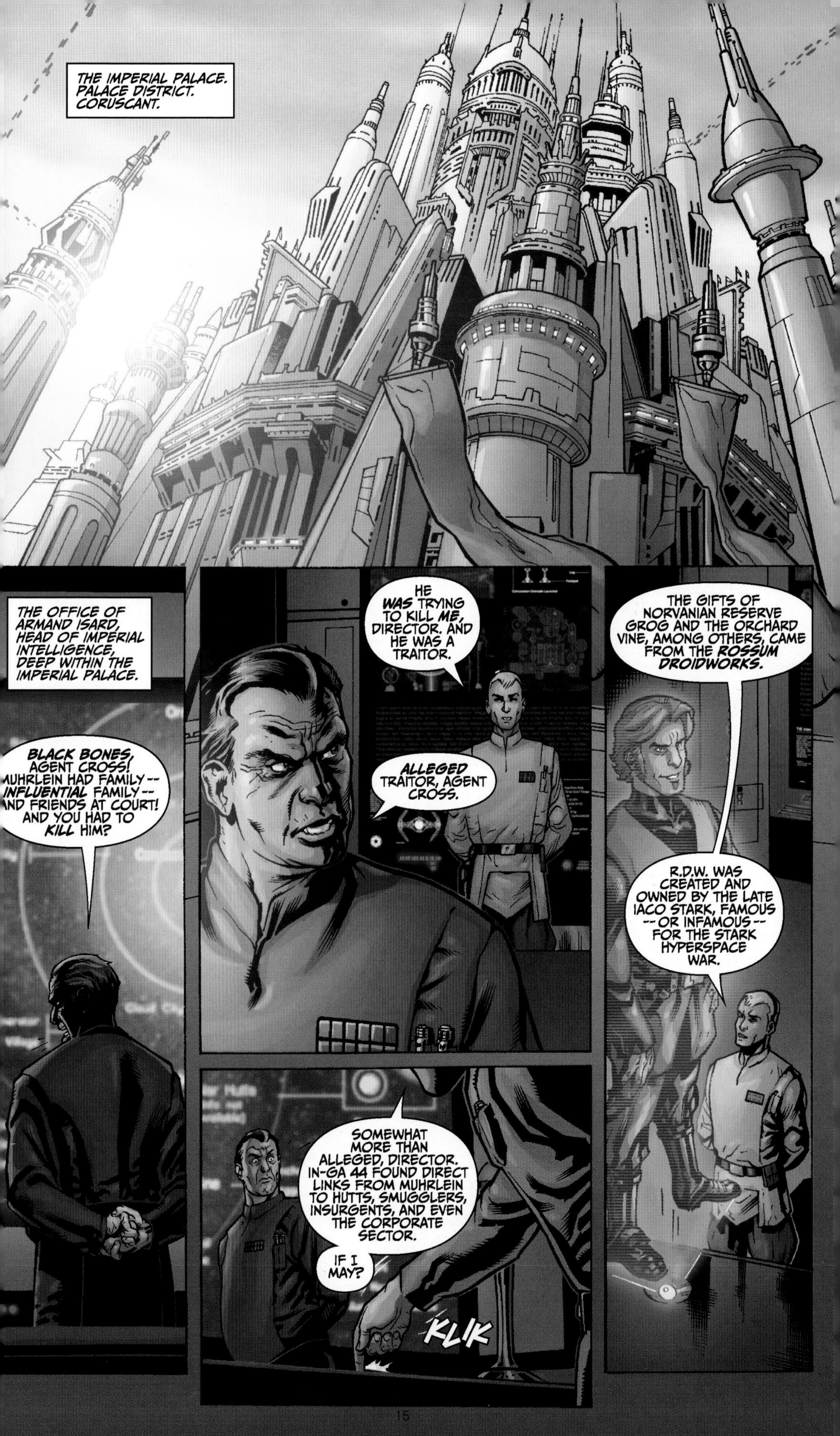
THE IMPERIAL PALACE. PALACE DISTRICT. CORUSCANT.
THE OFFICE OF ARMAND ISARD, HEAD OF IMPERIAL INTELLIGENCE, DEEP WITHIN THE IMPERIAL PALACE.
BLACK BONES, AGENT CROSS! MUHRLEIN HAD FAMILY-- INFLUENTIAL FAMILY-- AND FRIENDS AT COURT! AND YOU HAD TO KILL HIM?
HE WAS TRYING TO KILL ME, DIRECTOR. AND HE WAS A TRAITOR.
ALLEGED TRAITOR, AGENT CROSS.
SOMEWHAT MORE THAN ALLEGED, DIRECTOR. IN-GA 44 FOUND DIRECT LINKS FROM MUHRLEIN TO HUTTS, SMUGGLERS, INSURGENTS, AND EVEN THE CORPORATE SECTOR.
IF I MAY?
KLIK
THE GIFTS OF NORVANIAN RESERVE GROG AND THE ORCHARD VINE, AMONG OTHERS, CAME FROM THE ROSSUM DROIDWORKS.
R.D.W. WAS CREATED AND OWNED BY THE LATE IACO STARK, FAMOUS --OR INFAMOUS-- FOR THE STARK HYPERSPACE WAR.

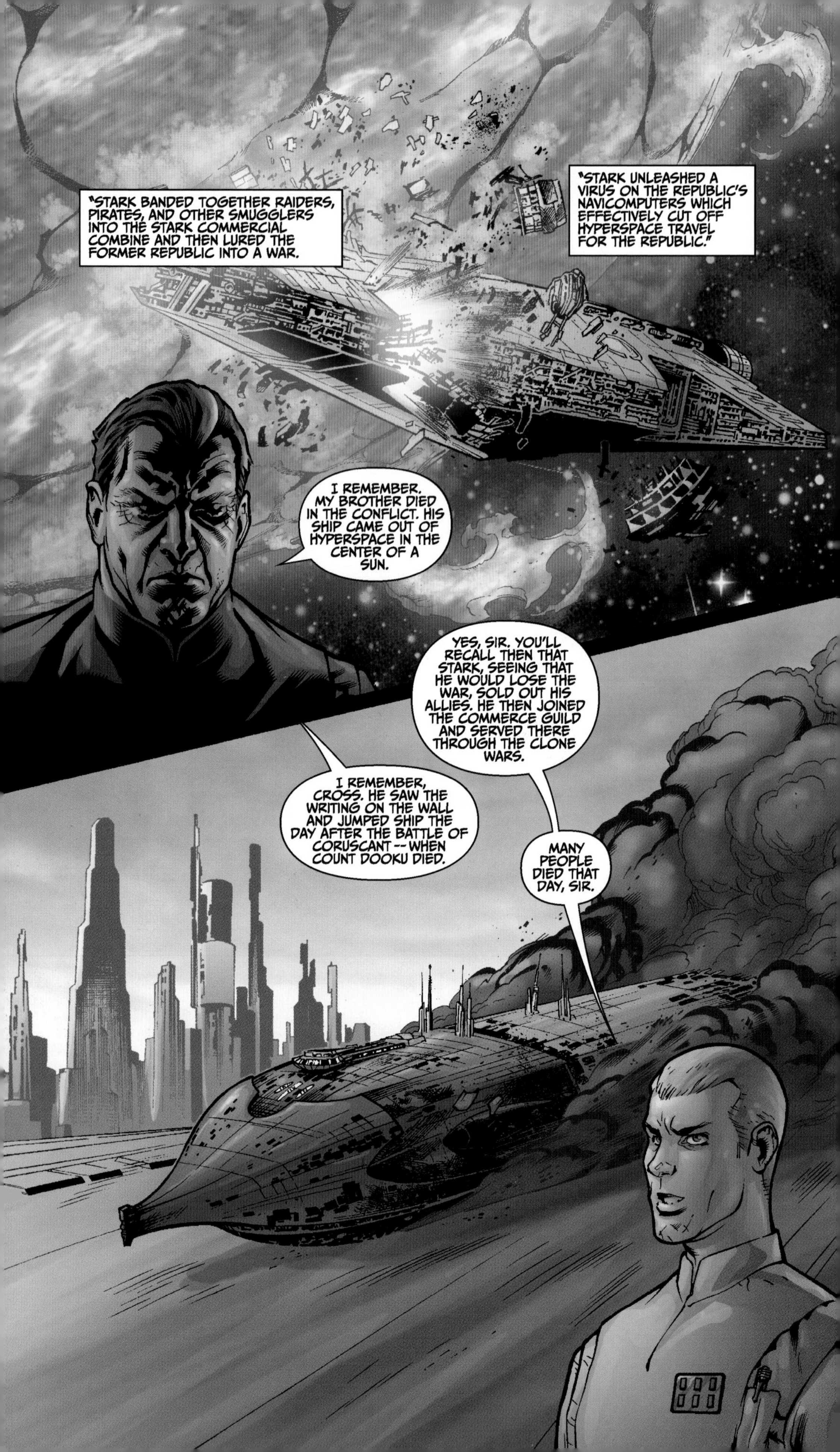
"STARK BANDED TOGETHER RAIDERS, PIRATES, AND OTHER SMUGGLERS INTO THE STARK COMMERCIAL COMBINE AND THEN LURED THE FORMER REPUBLIC INTO A WAR.
"STARK UNLEASHED A VIRUS ON THE REPUBLIC'S NAVICOMPUTERS WHICH EFFECTIVELY CUT OFF HYPERSPACE TRAVEL FOR THE REPUBLIC."
I REMEMBER. MY BROTHER DIED IN THE CONFLICT. HIS SHIP CAME OUT OF HYPERSPACE IN THE CENTER OF A SUN.
YES, SIR. YOU'LL RECALL THEN THAT STARK, SEEING THAT HE WOULD LOSE THE WAR, SOLD OUT HIS ALLIES. HE THEN JOINED THE COMMERCE GUILD AND SERVED THERE THROUGH THE CLONE WARS.
I REMEMBER, CROSS. HE SAW THE WRITING ON THE WALL AND JUMPED SHIP THE DAY AFTER THE BATTLE OF CORUSCANT -- WHEN COUNT DOOKU DIED.
MANY PEOPLE DIED THAT DAY, SIR.

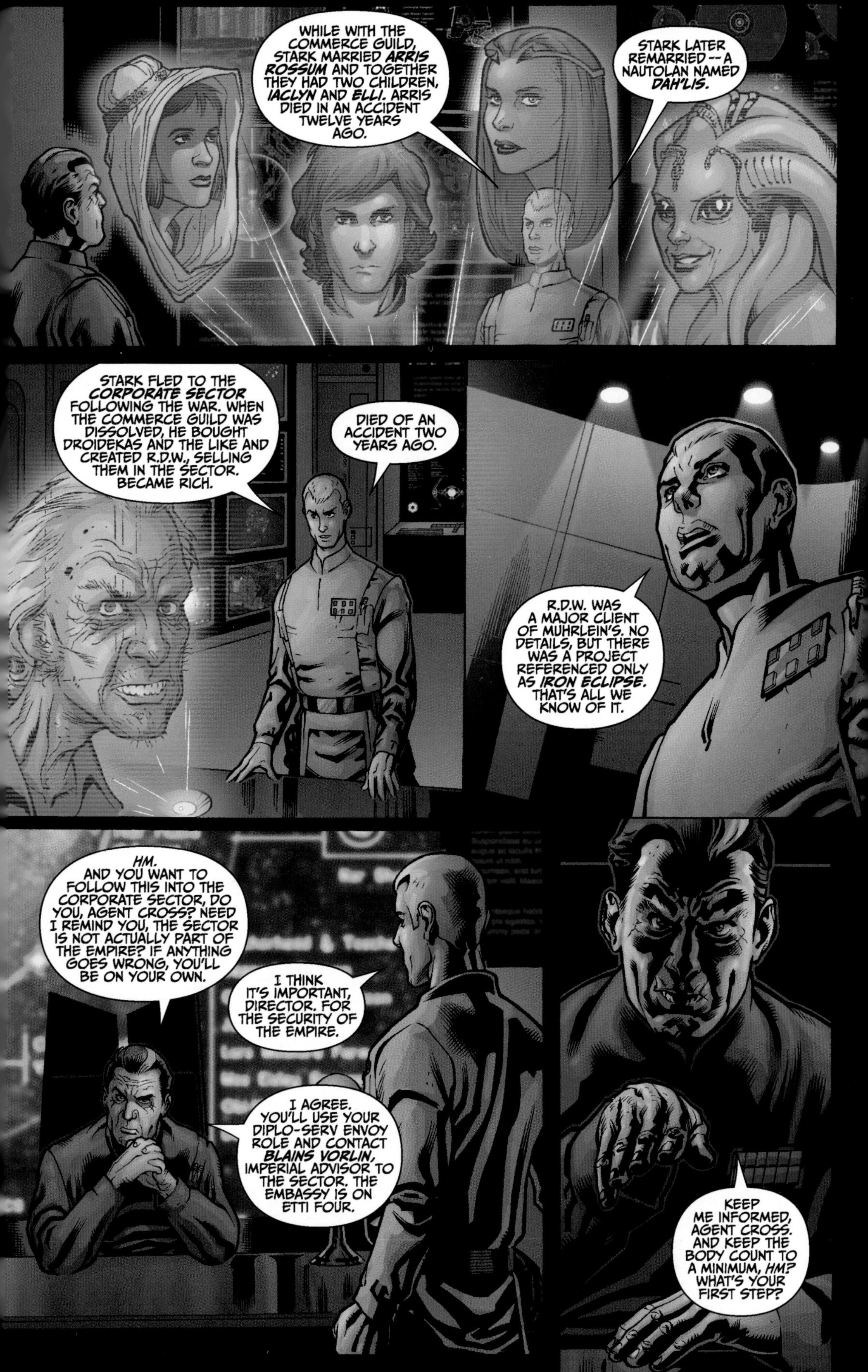

WHILE WITH THE COMMERCE GUILD, STARK MARRIED ARRIS ROSSUM AND TOGETHER THEY HAD TWO CHILDREN, IACLYN AND ELLI. ARRIS DIED IN AN ACCIDENT TWELVE YEARS AGO.
STARK LATER REMARRIED -- A NAUTOLAN NAMED DAH'LIS.
STARK FLED TO THE CORPORATE SECTOR FOLLOWING THE WAR. WHEN THE COMMERCE GUILD WAS DISSOLVED, HE BOUGHT DROIDEKAS AND THE LIKE AND CREATED R.D.W., SELLING THEM IN THE SECTOR. BECAME RICH.
DIED OF AN ACCIDENT TWO YEARS AGO.
R.D.W. WAS A MAJOR CLIENT OF MUHRLEIN'S. NO DETAILS, BUT THERE WAS A PROJECT REFERENCED ONLY AS IRON ECLIPSE. THAT'S ALL WE KNOW OF IT.
HM. AND YOU WANT TO FOLLOW THIS INTO THE CORPORATE SECTOR, DO YOU, AGENT CROSS? NEED I REMIND YOU, THE SECTOR IS NOT ACTUALLY PART OF THE EMPIRE? IF ANYTHING GOES WRONG, YOU'LL BE ON YOUR OWN.
I THINK IT'S IMPORTANT, DIRECTOR. FOR THE SECURITY OF THE EMPIRE.
I AGREE. YOU'LL USE YOUR DIPLO-SERV ENVOY ROLE AND CONTACT BLAINS VORLIN, IMPERIAL ADVISOR TO THE SECTOR. THE EMBASSY IS ON ETTI FOUR.
KEEP ME INFORMED, AGENT CROSS. AND KEEP THE BODY COUNT TO A MINIMUM, HM? WHAT'S YOUR FIRST STEP?

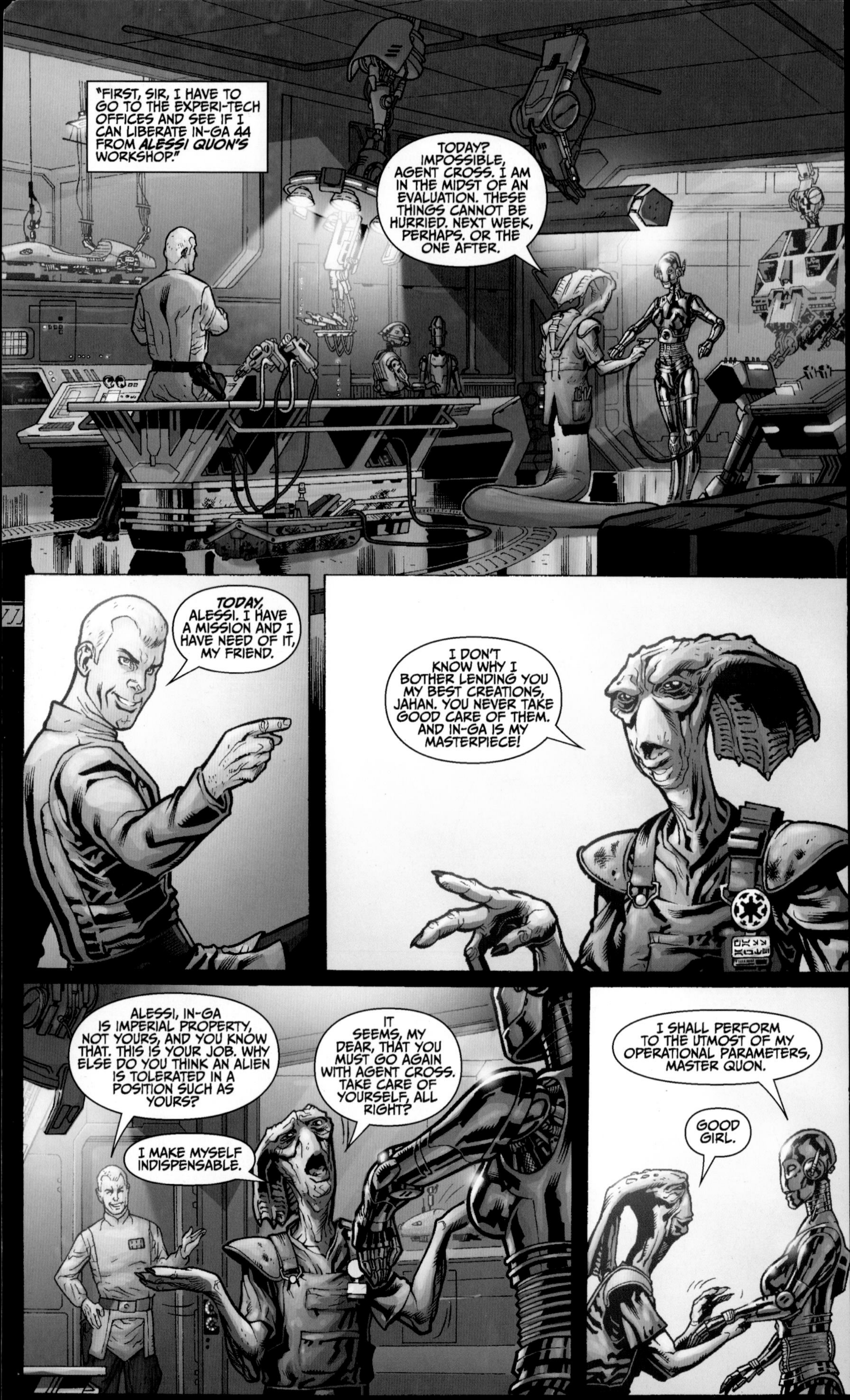
"FIRST, SIR, I HAVE TO GO TO THE EXPERI-TECH OFFICES AND SEE IF I CAN LIBERATE IN-GA 44 FROM *ALESSI QUON'S* WORKSHOP."
TODAY? IMPOSSIBLE, AGENT CROSS. I AM IN THE MIDST OF AN EVALUATION. THESE THINGS CANNOT BE HURRIED. NEXT WEEK, PERHAPS. OR THE ONE AFTER.
TODAY, ALESSI. I HAVE A MISSION AND I HAVE NEED OF IT, MY FRIEND.
I DON'T KNOW WHY I BOTHER LENDING YOU MY BEST CREATIONS, JAHAN. YOU NEVER TAKE GOOD CARE OF THEM. AND IN-GA IS MY MASTERPIECE!
ALESSI, IN-GA IS IMPERIAL PROPERTY, NOT YOURS, AND YOU KNOW THAT. THIS IS YOUR JOB. WHY ELSE DO YOU THINK AN ALIEN IS TOLERATED IN A POSITION SUCH AS YOURS?
I MAKE MYSELF INDISPENSABLE.
IT SEEMS, MY DEAR, THAT YOU MUST GO AGAIN WITH AGENT CROSS. TAKE CARE OF YOURSELF, ALL RIGHT?
I SHALL PERFORM TO THE UTMOST OF MY OPERATIONAL PARAMETERS, MASTER QUON.
GOOD GIRL.

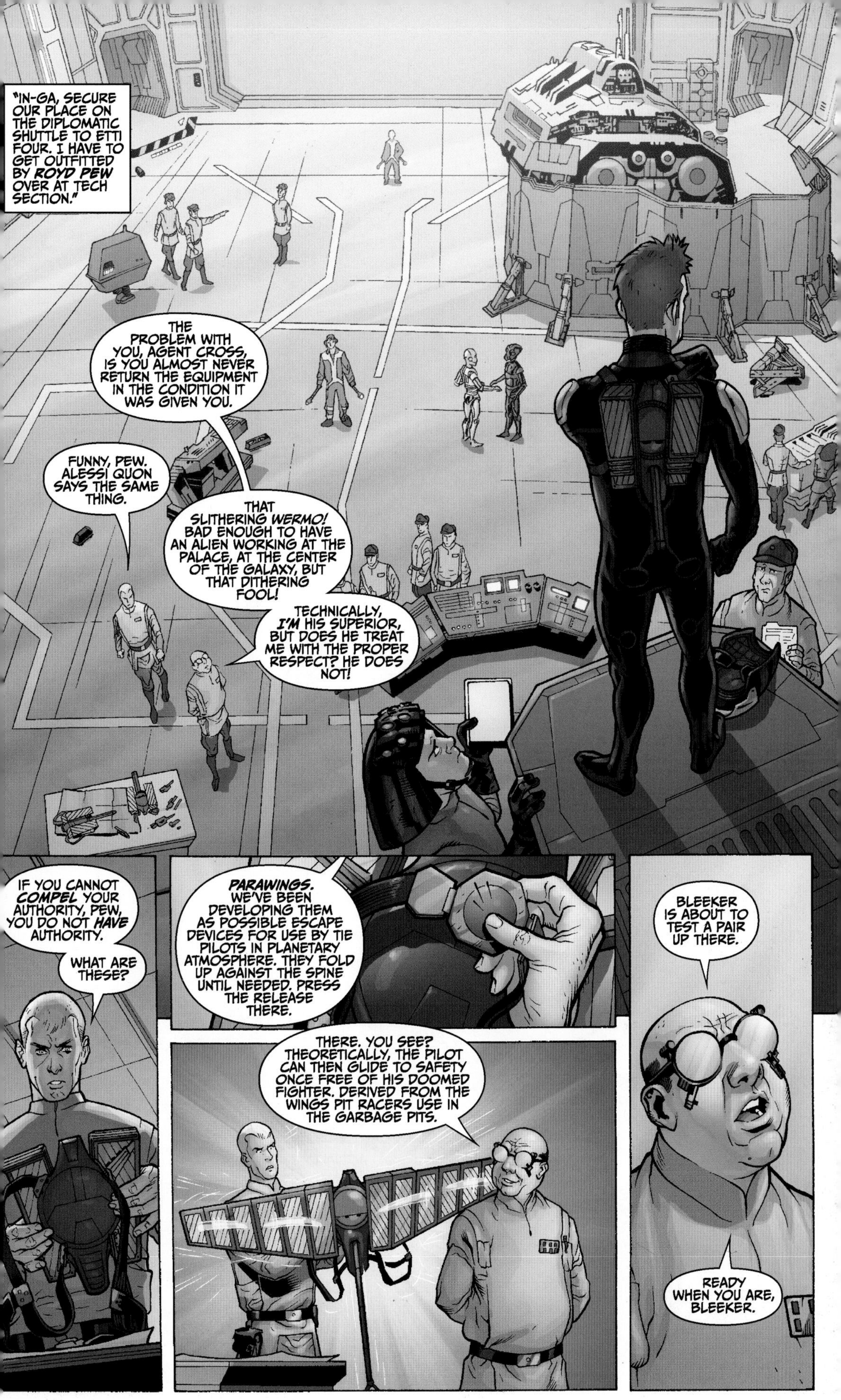
"IN-GA, SECURE OUR PLACE ON THE DIPLOMATIC SHUTTLE TO ETTI FOUR. I HAVE TO GET OUTFITTED BY ROYD PEW OVER AT TECH SECTION."
THE PROBLEM WITH YOU, AGENT CROSS, IS YOU ALMOST NEVER RETURN THE EQUIPMENT IN THE CONDITION IT WAS GIVEN YOU.
FUNNY, PEW. ALESSI QUON SAYS THE SAME THING.
THAT SLITHERING WERMO! BAD ENOUGH TO HAVE AN ALIEN WORKING AT THE PALACE, AT THE CENTER OF THE GALAXY, BUT THAT DITHERING FOOL!
TECHNICALLY, I'M HIS SUPERIOR, BUT DOES HE TREAT ME WITH THE PROPER RESPECT? HE DOES NOT!
IF YOU CANNOT COMPEL YOUR AUTHORITY, PEW, YOU DO NOT HAVE AUTHORITY.
WHAT ARE THESE?
PARAWINGS. WE'VE BEEN DEVELOPING THEM AS POSSIBLE ESCAPE DEVICES FOR USE BY TIE PILOTS IN PLANETARY ATMOSPHERE. THEY FOLD UP AGAINST THE SPINE UNTIL NEEDED. PRESS THE RELEASE THERE.
THERE. YOU SEE? THEORETICALLY, THE PILOT CAN THEN GLIDE TO SAFETY ONCE FREE OF HIS DOOMED FIGHTER. DERIVED FROM THE WINGS PIT RACERS USE IN THE GARBAGE PITS.
BLEEKER IS ABOUT TO TEST A PAIR UP THERE.
READY WHEN YOU ARE, BLEEKER.

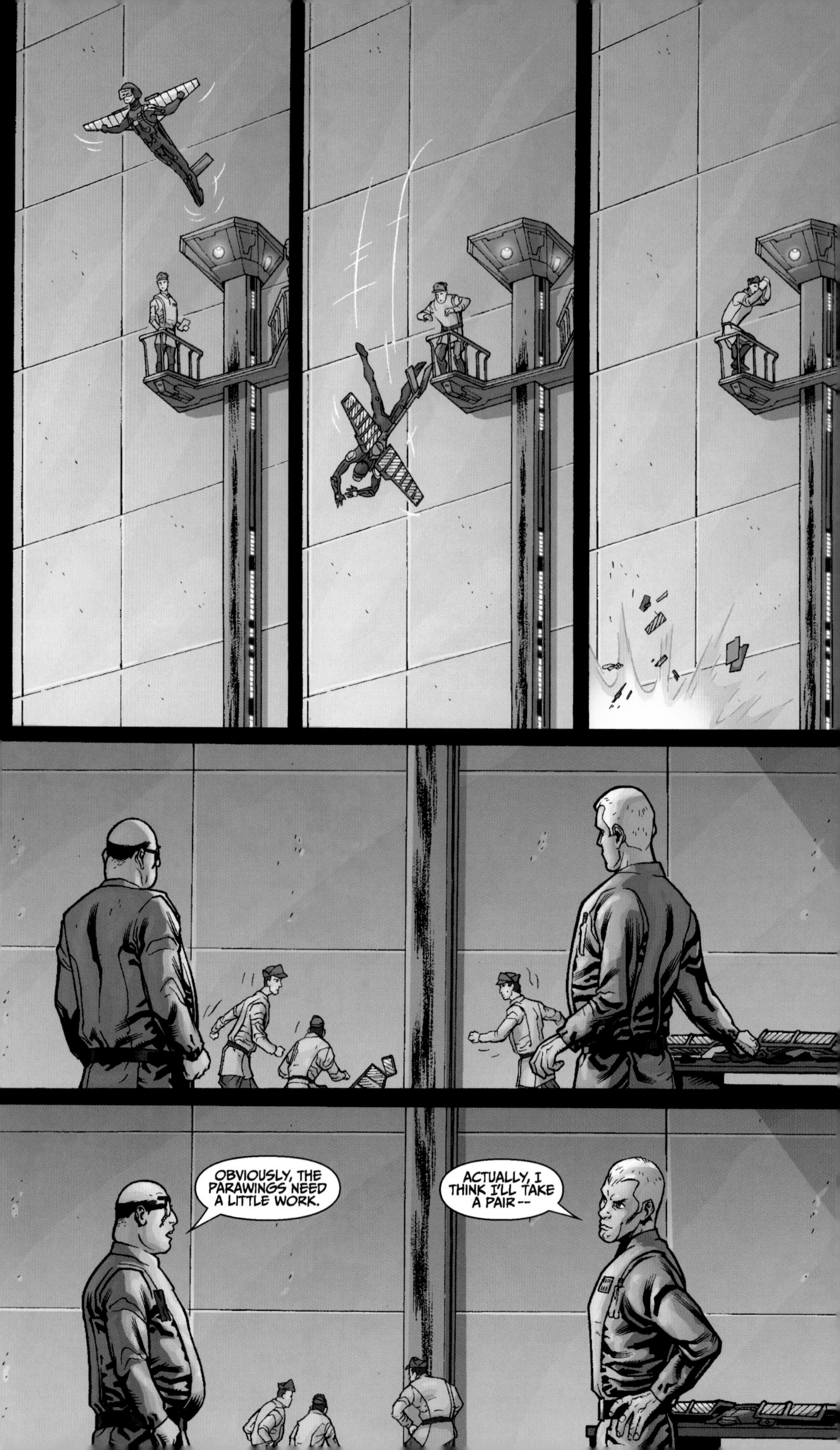
OBVIOUSLY, THE PARAWINGS NEED A LITTLE WORK.
ACTUALLY, I THINK I'LL TAKE A PAIR--

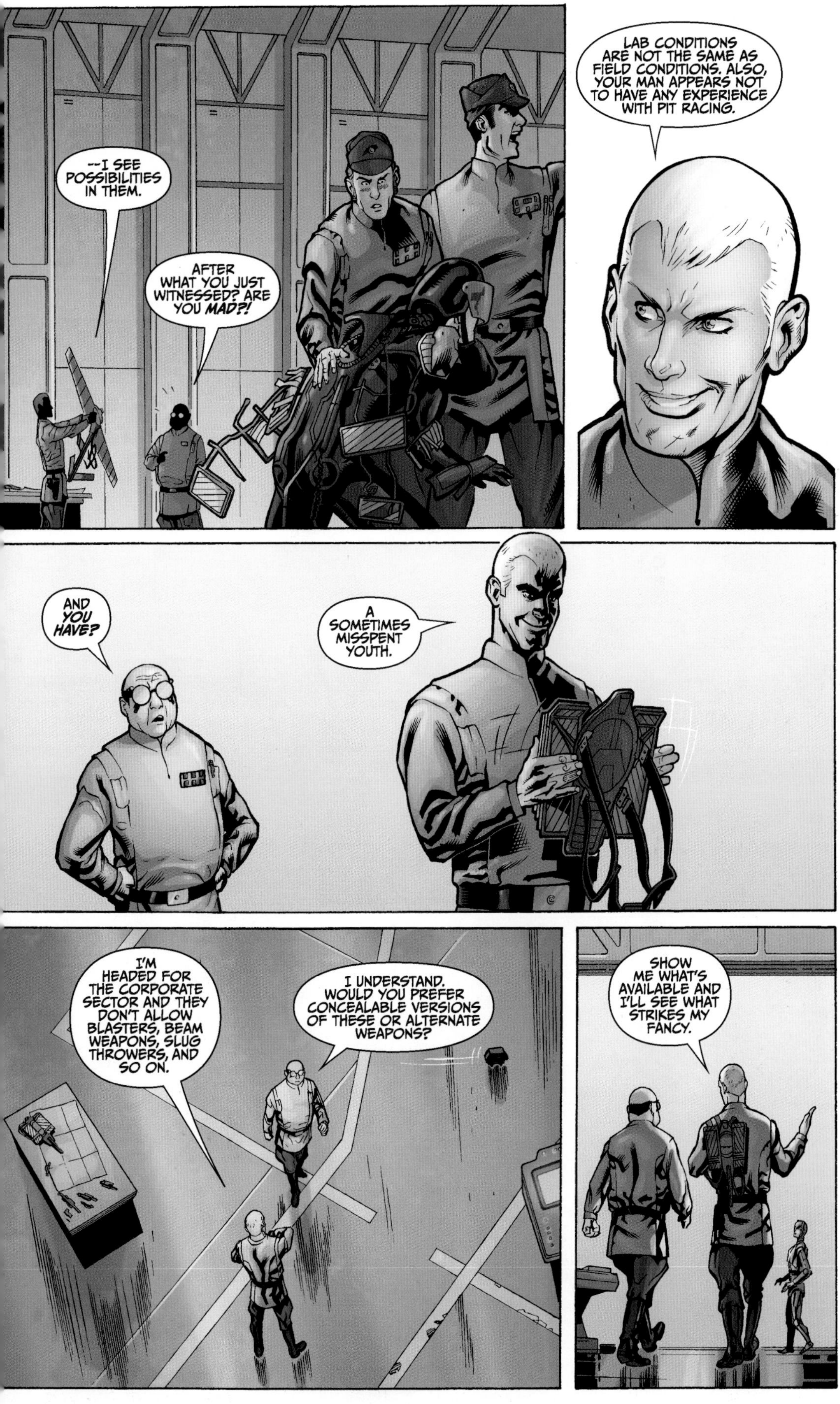
--I SEE POSSIBILITIES IN THEM.
AFTER WHAT YOU JUST WITNESSED? ARE YOU *MAD?!*
LAB CONDITIONS ARE NOT THE SAME AS FIELD CONDITIONS. ALSO, YOUR MAN APPEARS NOT TO HAVE ANY EXPERIENCE WITH PIT RACING.
AND *YOU HAVE?*
A SOMETIMES MISSPENT YOUTH.
I'M HEADED FOR THE CORPORATE SECTOR AND THEY DON'T ALLOW BLASTERS, BEAM WEAPONS, SLUG THROWERS, AND SO ON.
I UNDERSTAND. WOULD YOU PREFER CONCEALABLE VERSIONS OF THESE OR ALTERNATE WEAPONS?
SHOW ME WHAT'S AVAILABLE AND I'LL SEE WHAT STRIKES MY FANCY.

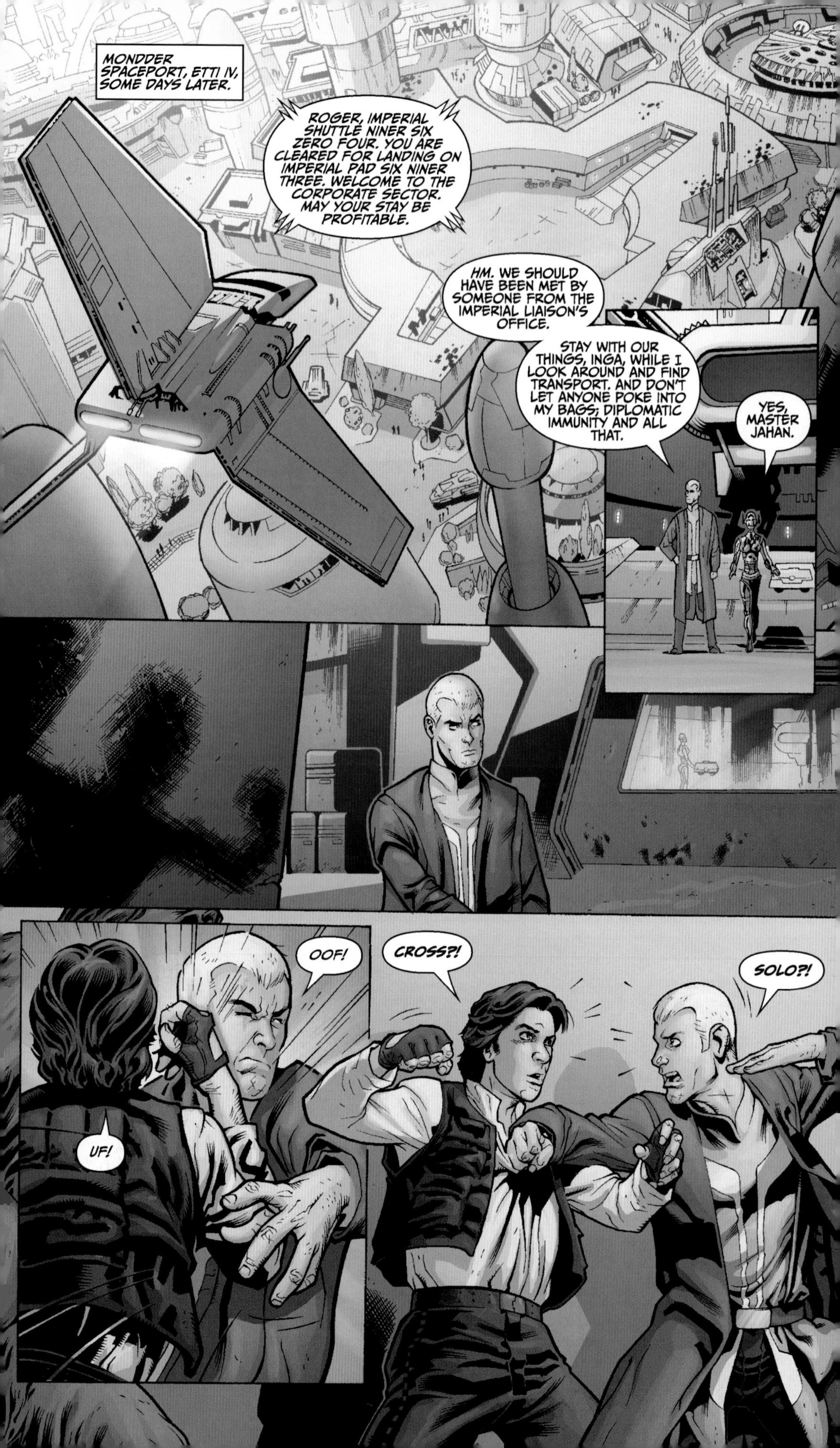
MONDDER SPACEPORT, ETTI IV, SOME DAYS LATER.
ROGER, IMPERIAL SHUTTLE NINER SIX ZERO FOUR. YOU ARE CLEARED FOR LANDING ON IMPERIAL PAD SIX NINER THREE. WELCOME TO THE CORPORATE SECTOR. MAY YOUR STAY BE PROFITABLE.
HM. WE SHOULD HAVE BEEN MET BY SOMEONE FROM THE IMPERIAL LIAISON'S OFFICE.
STAY WITH OUR THINGS, INGA, WHILE I LOOK AROUND AND FIND TRANSPORT. AND DON'T LET ANYONE POKE INTO MY BAGS; DIPLOMATIC IMMUNITY AND ALL THAT.
YES, MASTER JAHAN.
OOF!
UF!
CROSS?!
SOLO?!

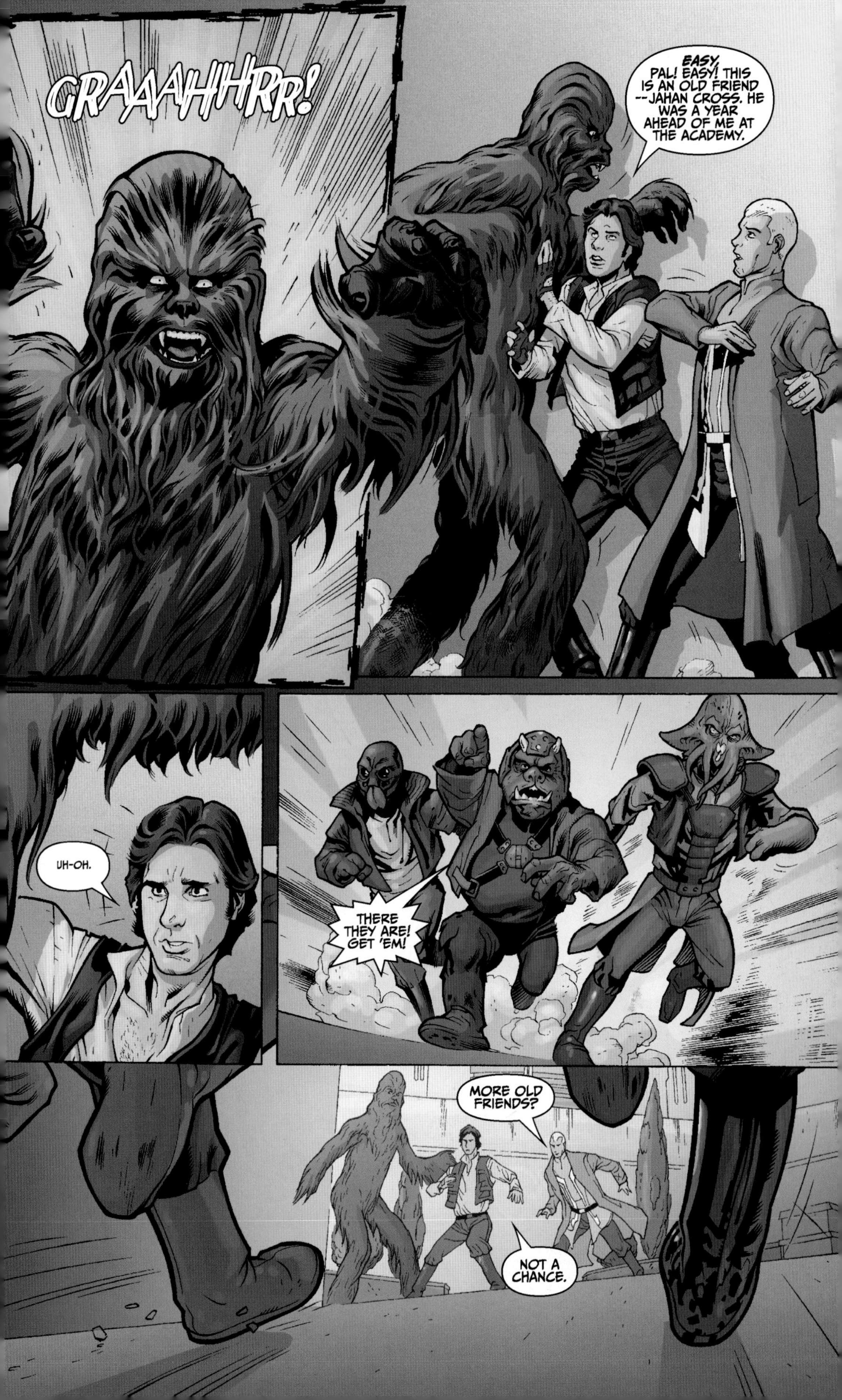
GRAAAHHRR!
EASY, PAL! EASY! THIS IS AN OLD FRIEND --JAHAN CROSS. HE WAS A YEAR AHEAD OF ME AT THE ACADEMY.
UH-OH.
THERE THEY ARE! GET 'EM!
MORE OLD FRIENDS?
NOT A CHANCE.

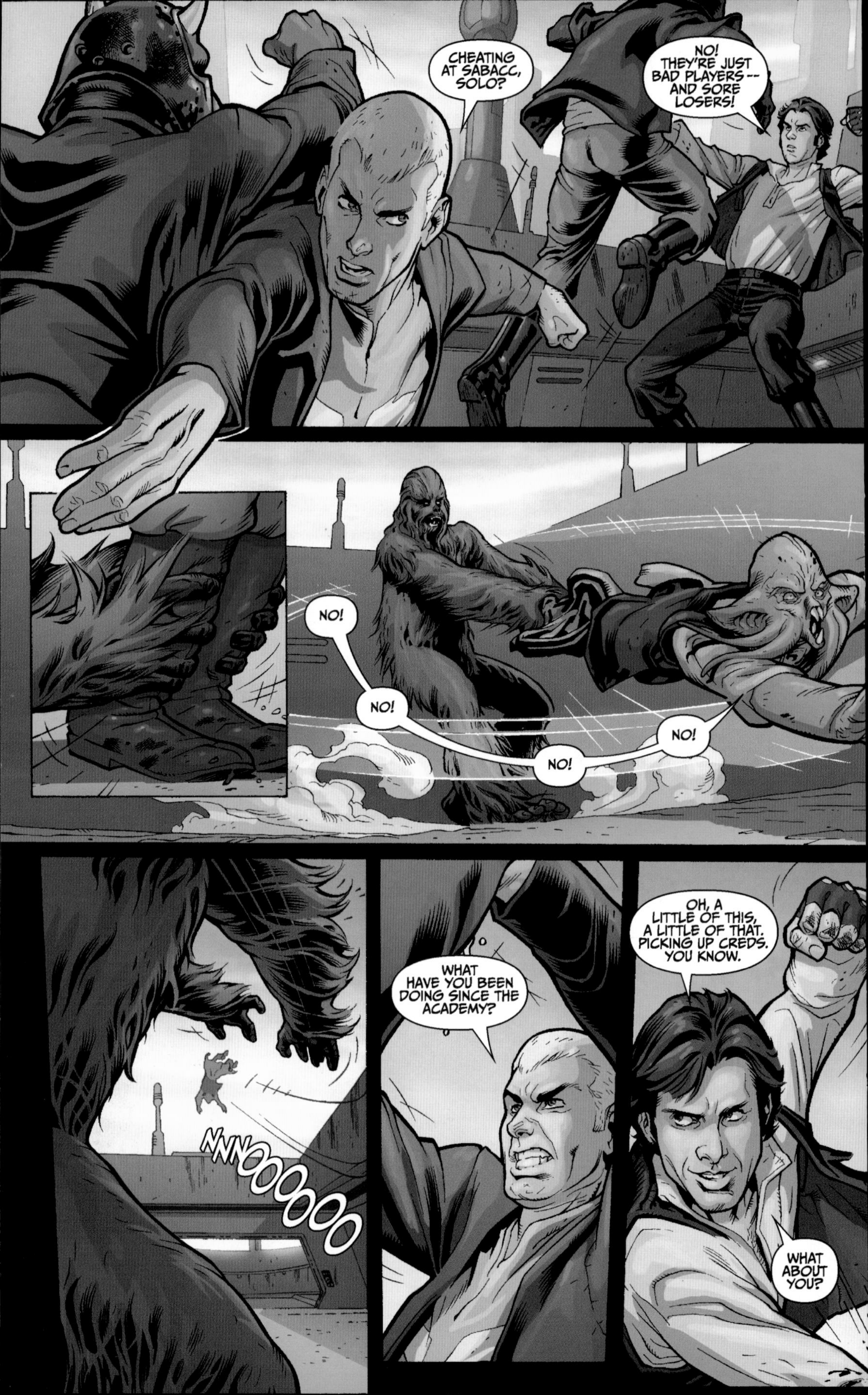
CHEATING AT SABACC, SOLO?
NO! THEY'RE JUST BAD PLAYERS -- AND SORE LOSERS!
NO!
NO!
NO!
NO!
NNNOOOOOO
WHAT HAVE YOU BEEN DOING SINCE THE ACADEMY?
OH, A LITTLE OF THIS, A LITTLE OF THAT. PICKING UP CREDS. YOU KNOW.
WHAT ABOUT YOU?

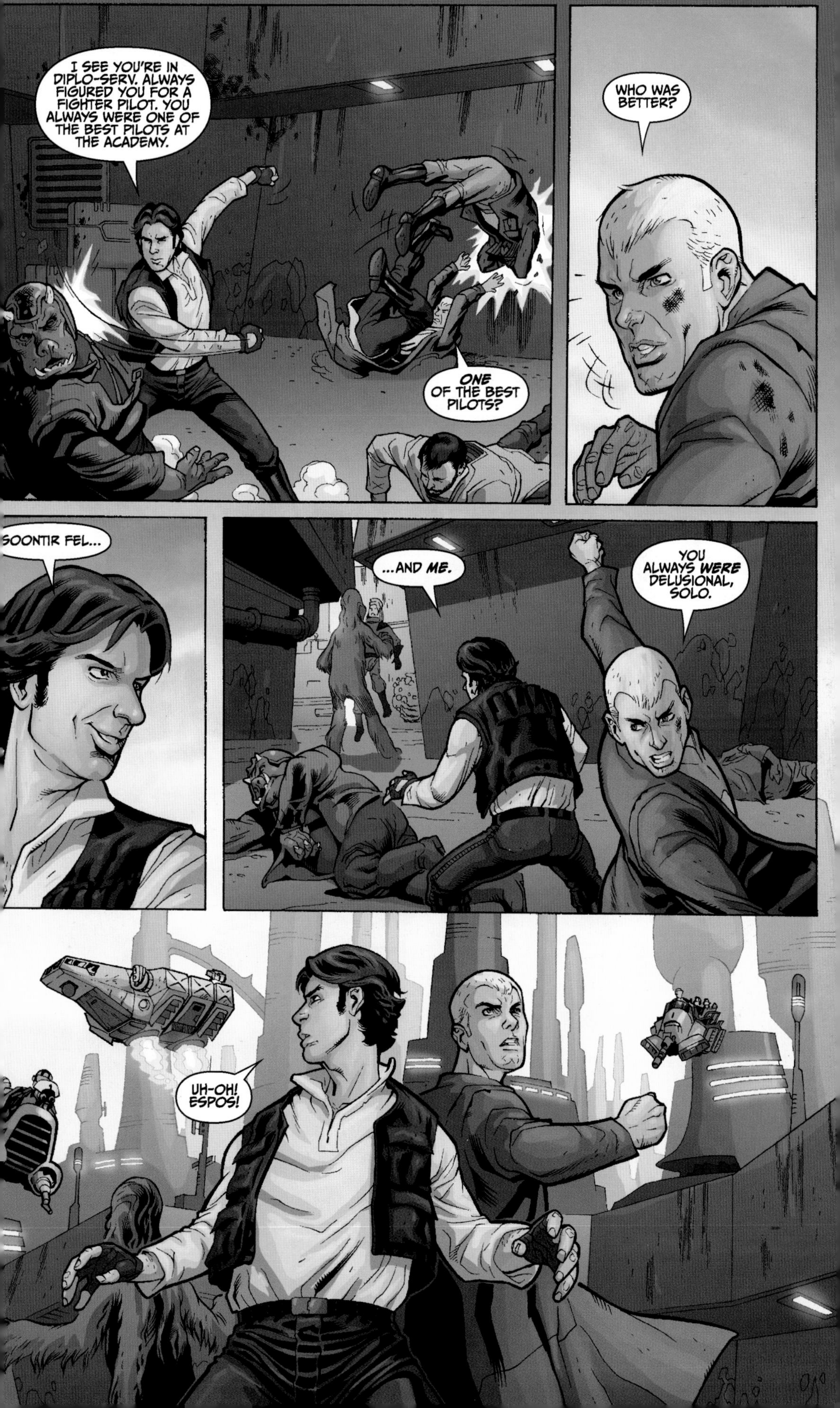
I SEE YOU'RE IN DIPLO-SERV. ALWAYS FIGURED YOU FOR A FIGHTER PILOT. YOU ALWAYS WERE ONE OF THE BEST PILOTS AT THE ACADEMY.
ONE OF THE BEST PILOTS?
WHO WAS BETTER?
SOONTIR FEL...
...AND ME.
YOU ALWAYS WERE DELUSIONAL, SOLO.
UH-OH! ESPOS!

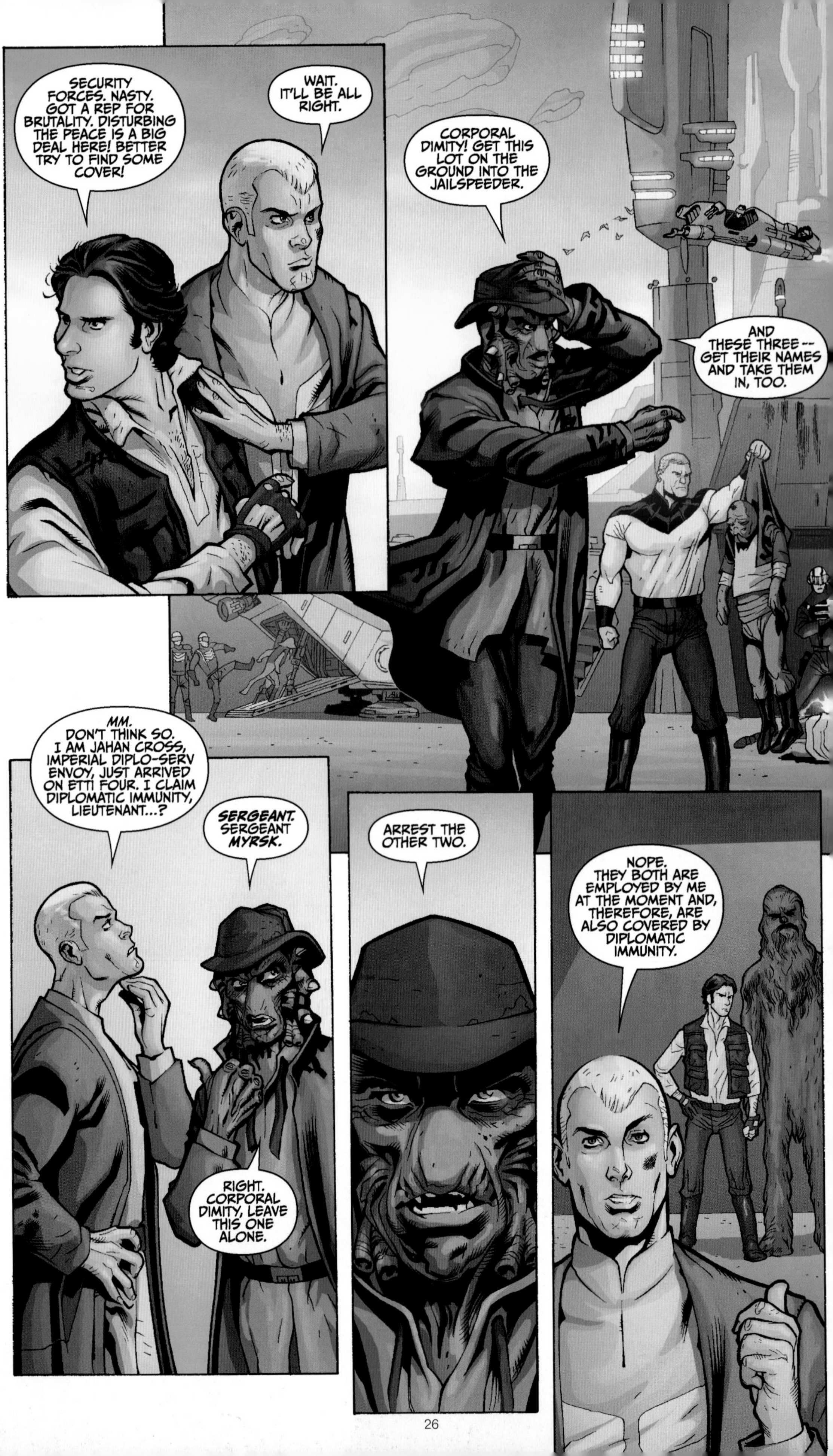
SECURITY FORCES. NASTY. GOT A REP FOR BRUTALITY. DISTURBING THE PEACE IS A BIG DEAL HERE! BETTER TRY TO FIND SOME COVER!
WAIT. IT'LL BE ALL RIGHT.
CORPORAL DIMITY! GET THIS LOT ON THE GROUND INTO THE JAILSPEEDER.
AND THESE THREE -- GET THEIR NAMES AND TAKE THEM IN, TOO.
MM. DON'T THINK SO. I AM JAHAN CROSS, IMPERIAL DIPLO-SERV ENVOY, JUST ARRIVED ON ETTI FOUR. I CLAIM DIPLOMATIC IMMUNITY, LIEUTENANT...?
SERGEANT. SERGEANT MYRSK.
RIGHT. CORPORAL DIMITY, LEAVE THIS ONE ALONE.
ARREST THE OTHER TWO.
NOPE. THEY BOTH ARE EMPLOYED BY ME AT THE MOMENT AND, THEREFORE, ARE ALSO COVERED BY DIPLOMATIC IMMUNITY.

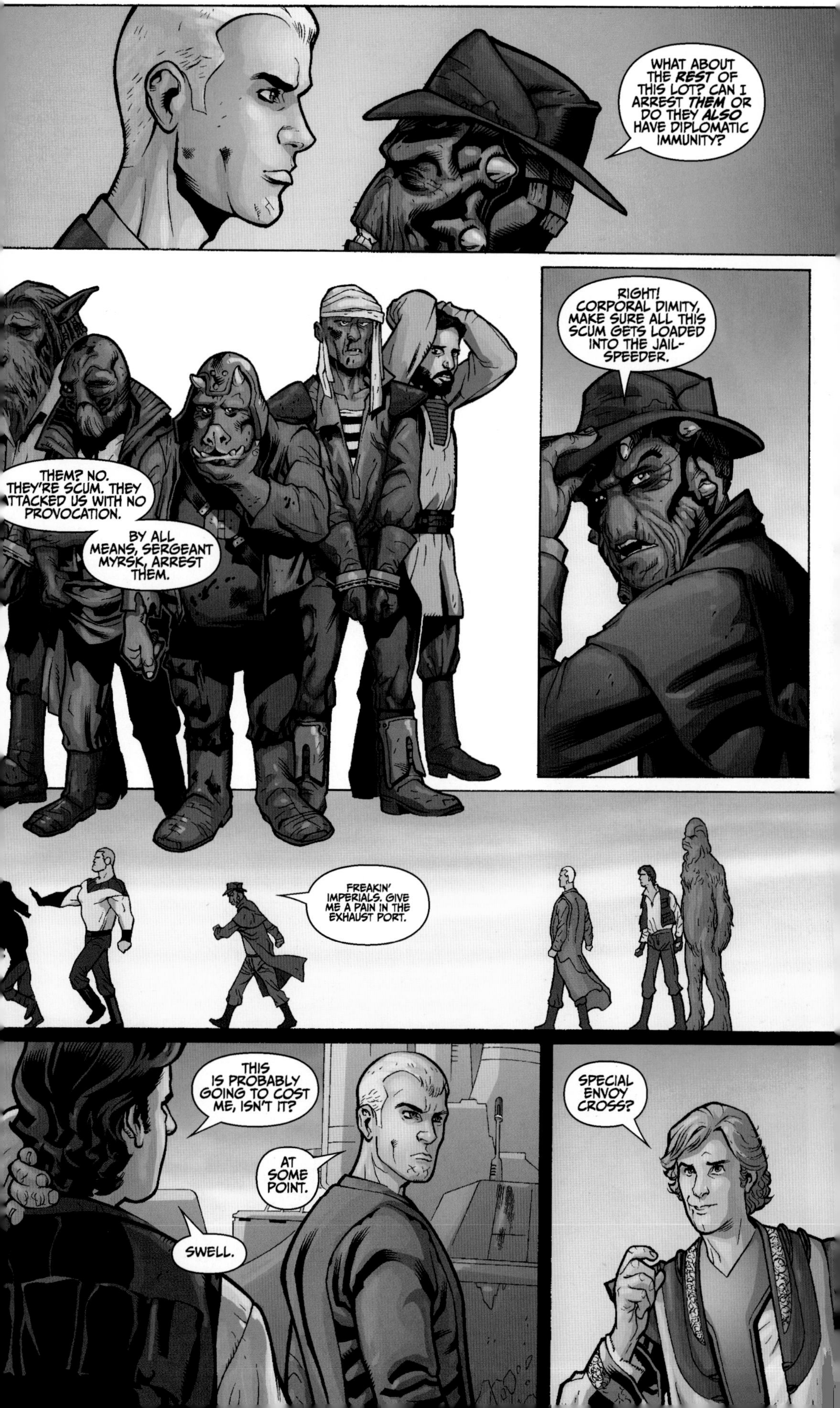
WHAT ABOUT THE REST OF THIS LOT? CAN I ARREST THEM OR DO THEY ALSO HAVE DIPLOMATIC IMMUNITY?
THEM? NO. THEY'RE SCUM. THEY ATTACKED US WITH NO PROVOCATION.
BY ALL MEANS, SERGEANT MYRSK, ARREST THEM.
RIGHT! CORPORAL DIMITY, MAKE SURE ALL THIS SCUM GETS LOADED INTO THE JAIL-SPEEDER.
FREAKIN' IMPERIALS. GIVE ME A PAIN IN THE EXHAUST PORT.
THIS IS PROBABLY GOING TO COST ME, ISN'T IT?
AT SOME POINT.
SWELL.
SPECIAL ENVOY CROSS?

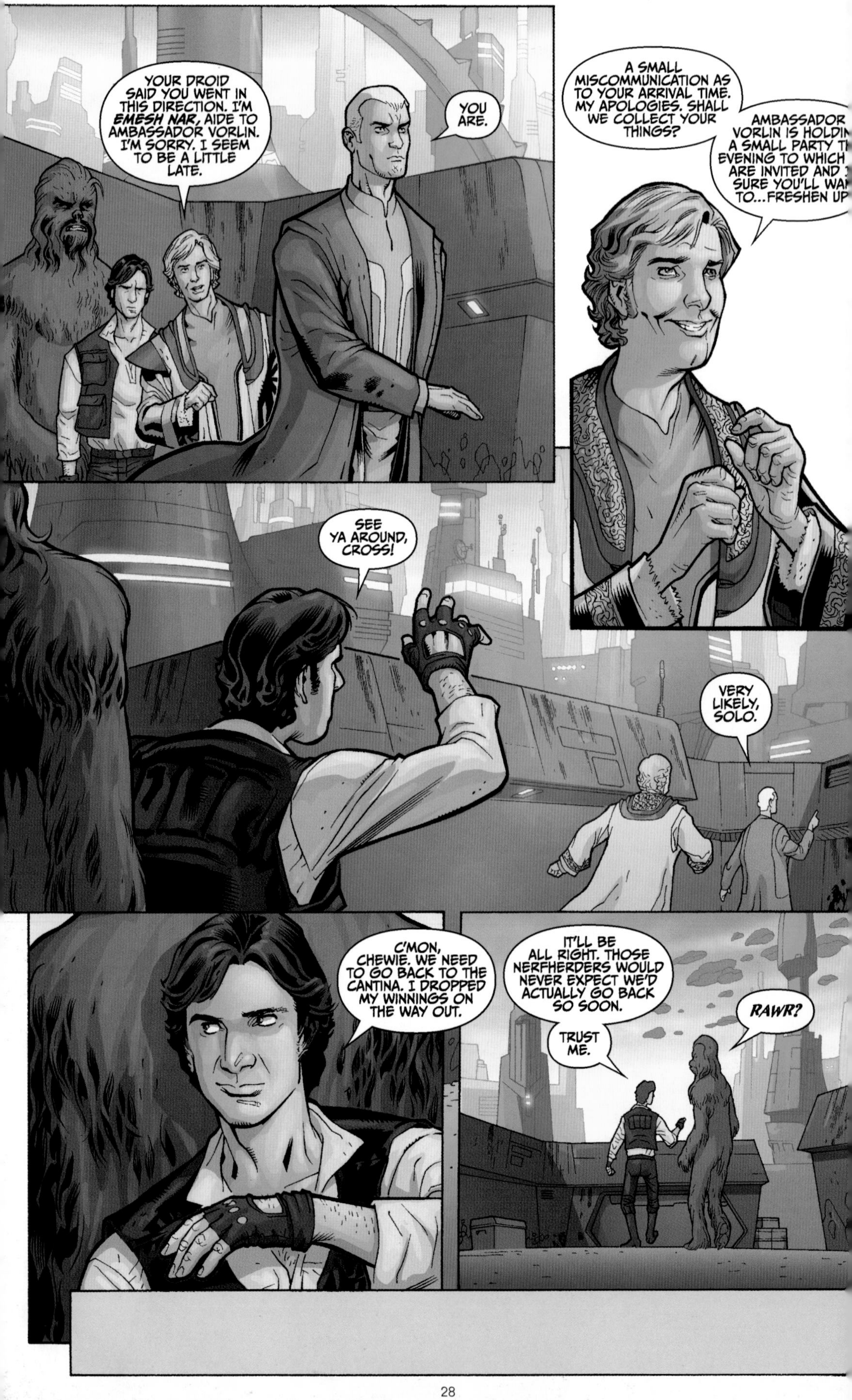

YOUR DROID SAID YOU WENT IN THIS DIRECTION. I'M *EMESH NAR*, AIDE TO AMBASSADOR VORLIN. I'M SORRY. I SEEM TO BE A LITTLE LATE.
YOU ARE.
A SMALL MISCOMMUNICATION AS TO YOUR ARRIVAL TIME. MY APOLOGIES. SHALL WE COLLECT YOUR THINGS?
AMBASSADOR VORLIN IS HOLDIN A SMALL PARTY T EVENING TO WHICH ARE INVITED AND SURE YOU'LL WA TO...FRESHEN UP
SEE YA AROUND, CROSS!
VERY LIKELY, SOLO.
C'MON, CHEWIE. WE NEED TO GO BACK TO THE CANTINA. I DROPPED MY WINNINGS ON THE WAY OUT.
IT'LL BE ALL RIGHT. THOSE NERFHERDERS WOULD NEVER EXPECT WE'D ACTUALLY GO BACK SO SOON.
TRUST ME.
RAWR?

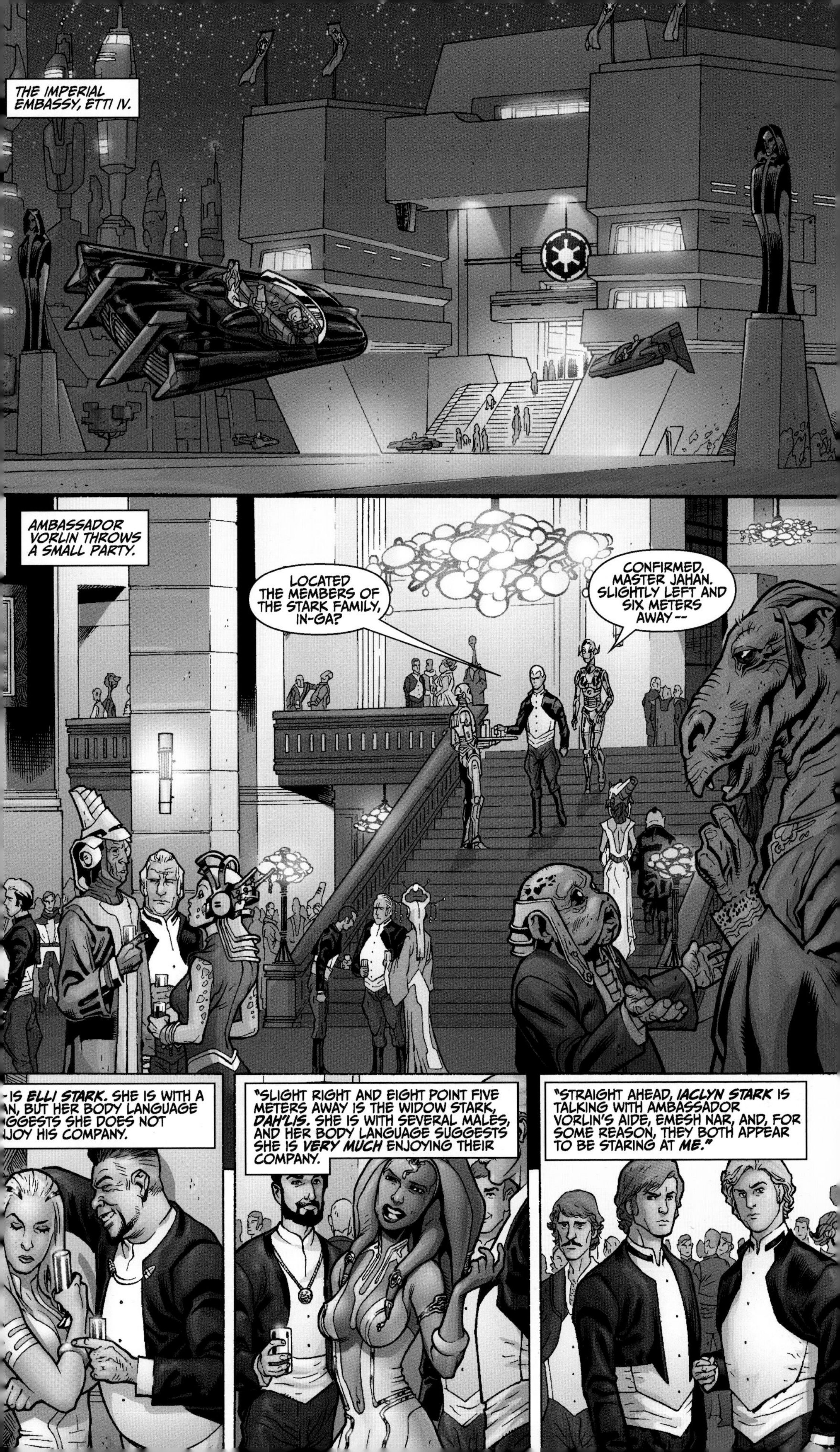
THE IMPERIAL EMBASSY, ETTI IV.
AMBASSADOR VORLIN THROWS A SMALL PARTY.
LOCATED THE MEMBERS OF THE STARK FAMILY, IN-GA?
CONFIRMED, MASTER JAHAN. SLIGHTLY LEFT AND SIX METERS AWAY --
-- IS ELLI STARK. SHE IS WITH A AN, BUT HER BODY LANGUAGE UGGESTS SHE DOES NOT NJOY HIS COMPANY.
"SLIGHT RIGHT AND EIGHT POINT FIVE METERS AWAY IS THE WIDOW STARK, DAH'LIS. SHE IS WITH SEVERAL MALES, AND HER BODY LANGUAGE SUGGESTS SHE IS VERY MUCH ENJOYING THEIR COMPANY.
"STRAIGHT AHEAD, IACLYN STARK IS TALKING WITH AMBASSADOR VORLIN'S AIDE, EMESH NAR, AND, FOR SOME REASON, THEY BOTH APPEAR TO BE STARING AT ME."

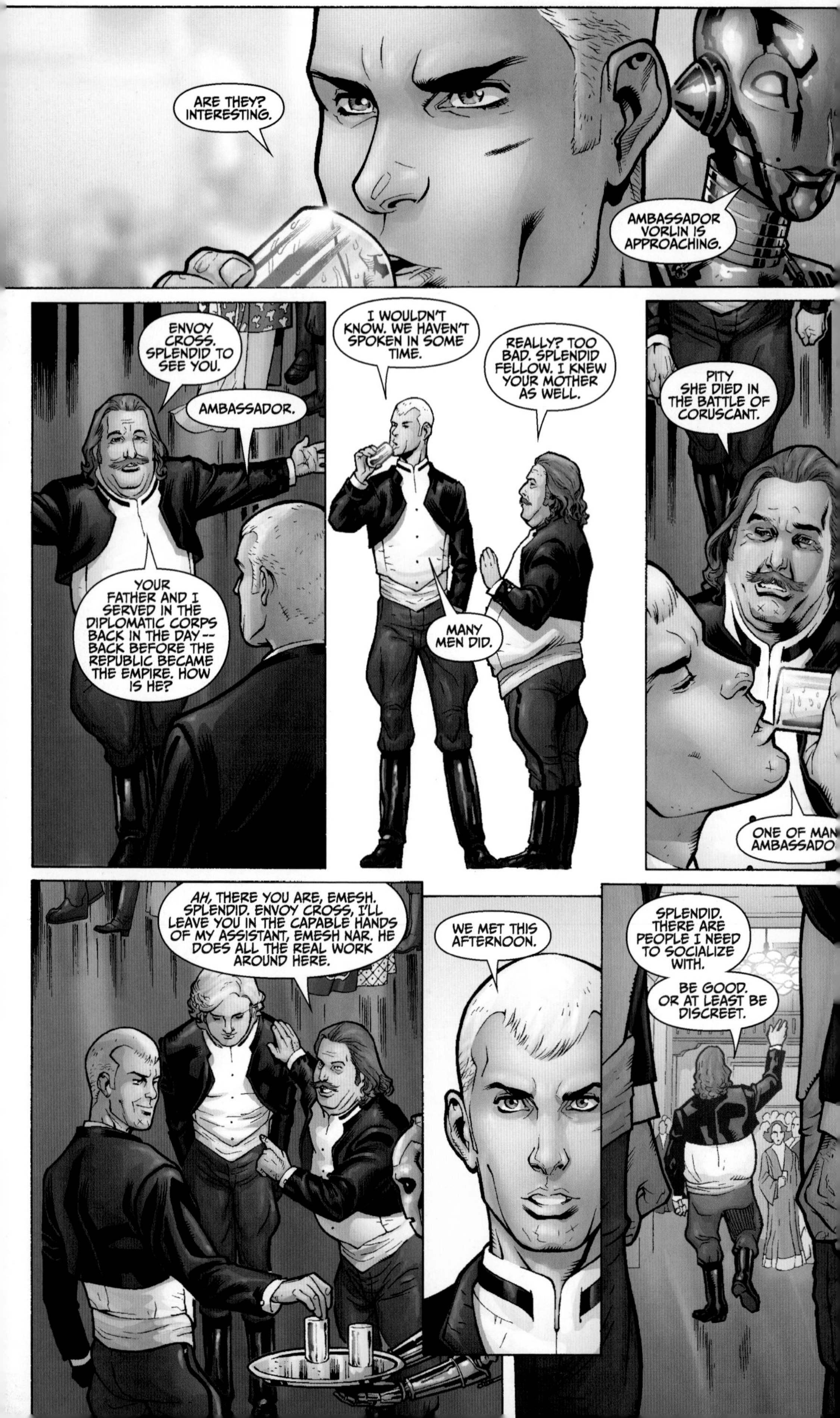
ARE THEY? INTERESTING.
AMBASSADOR VORLIN IS APPROACHING.
ENVOY CROSS. SPLENDID TO SEE YOU.
AMBASSADOR.
YOUR FATHER AND I SERVED IN THE DIPLOMATIC CORPS BACK IN THE DAY-- BACK BEFORE THE REPUBLIC BECAME THE EMPIRE. HOW IS HE?
I WOULDN'T KNOW. WE HAVEN'T SPOKEN IN SOME TIME.
REALLY? TOO BAD. SPLENDID FELLOW. I KNEW YOUR MOTHER AS WELL.
MANY MEN DID.
PITY SHE DIED IN THE BATTLE OF CORUSCANT.
AH, THERE YOU ARE, EMESH. SPLENDID. ENVOY CROSS, I'LL LEAVE YOU IN THE CAPABLE HANDS OF MY ASSISTANT, EMESH NAR. HE DOES ALL THE REAL WORK AROUND HERE.
WE MET THIS AFTERNOON.
SPLENDID. THERE ARE PEOPLE I NEED TO SOCIALIZE WITH.
BE GOOD. OR AT LEAST BE DISCREET.

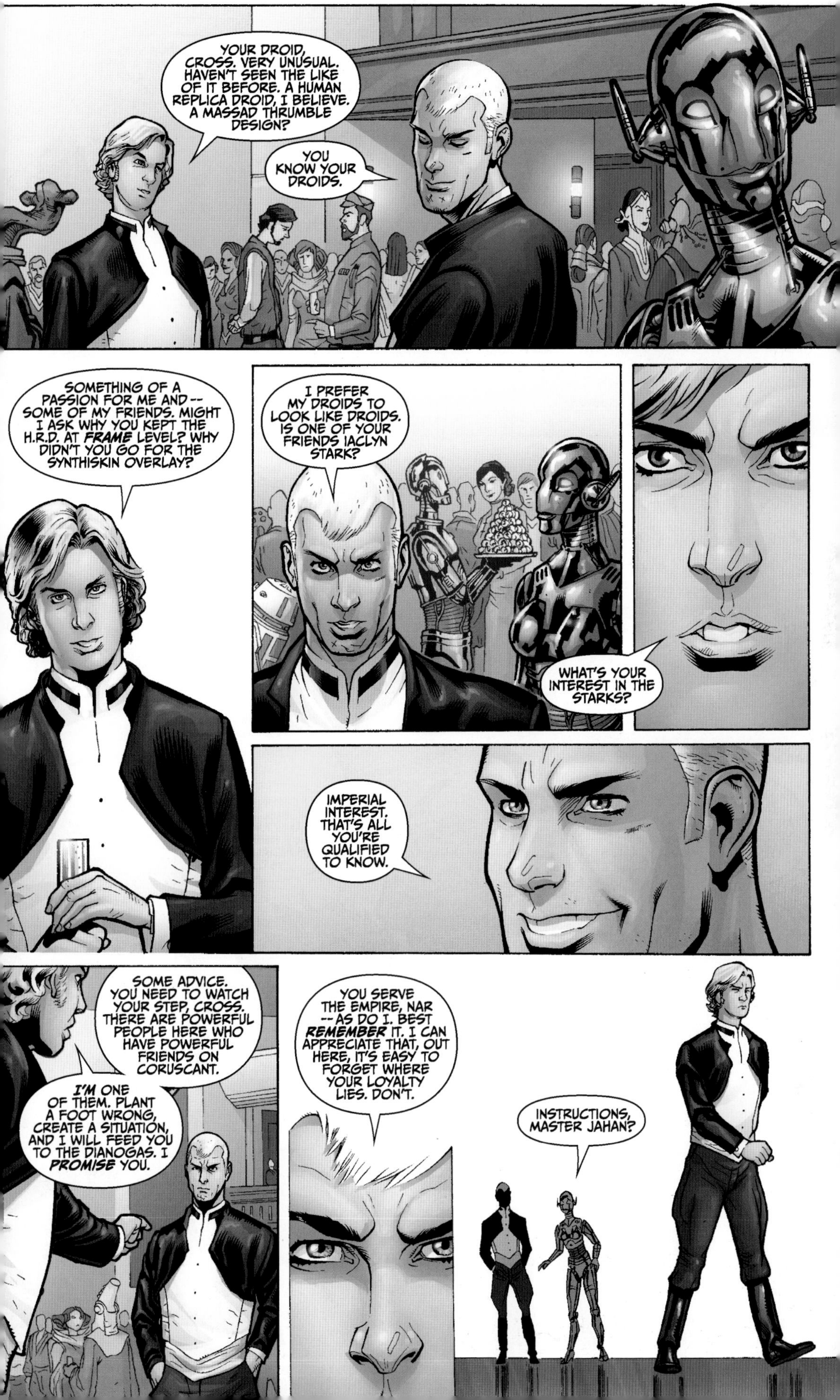
YOUR DROID, CROSS. VERY UNUSUAL. HAVEN'T SEEN THE LIKE OF IT BEFORE. A HUMAN REPLICA DROID, I BELIEVE. A MASSAD THRUMBLE DESIGN?
YOU KNOW YOUR DROIDS.
SOMETHING OF A PASSION FOR ME AND -- SOME OF MY FRIENDS. MIGHT I ASK WHY YOU KEPT THE H.R.D. AT FRAME LEVEL? WHY DIDN'T YOU GO FOR THE SYNTHISKIN OVERLAY?
I PREFER MY DROIDS TO LOOK LIKE DROIDS. IS ONE OF YOUR FRIENDS IACLYN STARK?
WHAT'S YOUR INTEREST IN THE STARKS?
IMPERIAL INTEREST. THAT'S ALL YOU'RE QUALIFIED TO KNOW.
SOME ADVICE. YOU NEED TO WATCH YOUR STEP, CROSS. THERE ARE POWERFUL PEOPLE HERE WHO HAVE POWERFUL FRIENDS ON CORUSCANT.
I'M ONE OF THEM. PLANT A FOOT WRONG, CREATE A SITUATION, AND I WILL FEED YOU TO THE DIANOGAS. I PROMISE YOU.
YOU SERVE THE EMPIRE, NAR -- AS DO I. BEST REMEMBER IT. I CAN APPRECIATE THAT, OUT HERE, IT'S EASY TO FORGET WHERE YOUR LOYALTY LIES. DON'T.
INSTRUCTIONS, MASTER JAHAN?

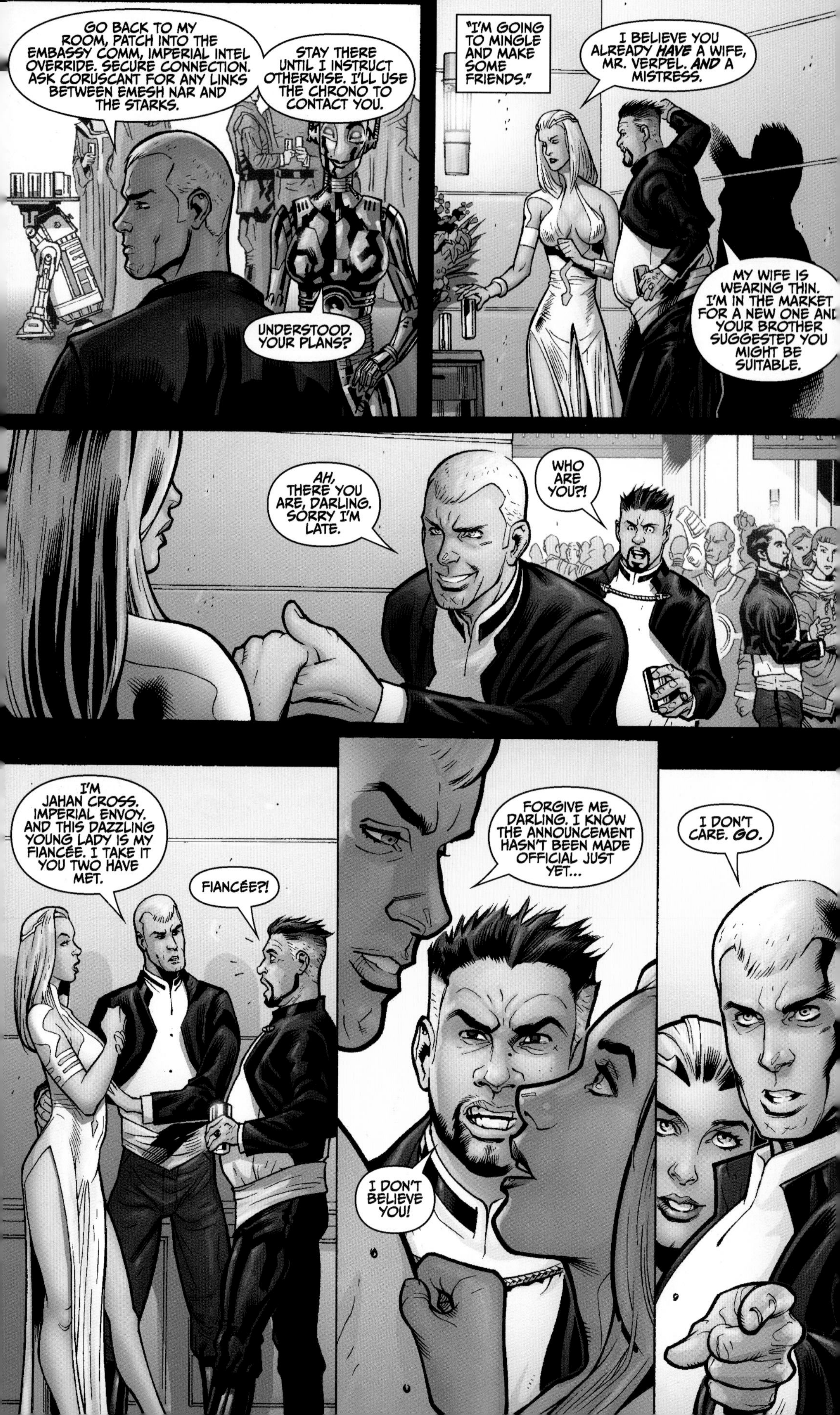
GO BACK TO MY ROOM, PATCH INTO THE EMBASSY COMM, IMPERIAL INTEL OVERRIDE. SECURE CONNECTION. ASK CORUSCANT FOR ANY LINKS BETWEEN EMESH NAR AND THE STARKS.
STAY THERE UNTIL I INSTRUCT OTHERWISE. I'LL USE THE CHRONO TO CONTACT YOU.
UNDERSTOOD. YOUR PLANS?
"I'M GOING TO MINGLE AND MAKE SOME FRIENDS."
I BELIEVE YOU ALREADY HAVE A WIFE, MR. VERPEL. AND A MISTRESS.
MY WIFE IS WEARING THIN. I'M IN THE MARKET FOR A NEW ONE AND YOUR BROTHER SUGGESTED YOU MIGHT BE SUITABLE.
AH, THERE YOU ARE, DARLING. SORRY I'M LATE.
WHO ARE YOU?!
I'M JAHAN CROSS. IMPERIAL ENVOY. AND THIS DAZZLING YOUNG LADY IS MY FIANCÉE. I TAKE IT YOU TWO HAVE MET.
FIANCÉE?!
FORGIVE ME, DARLING. I KNOW THE ANNOUNCEMENT HASN'T BEEN MADE OFFICIAL JUST YET...
I DON'T BELIEVE YOU!
I DON'T CARE. GO.

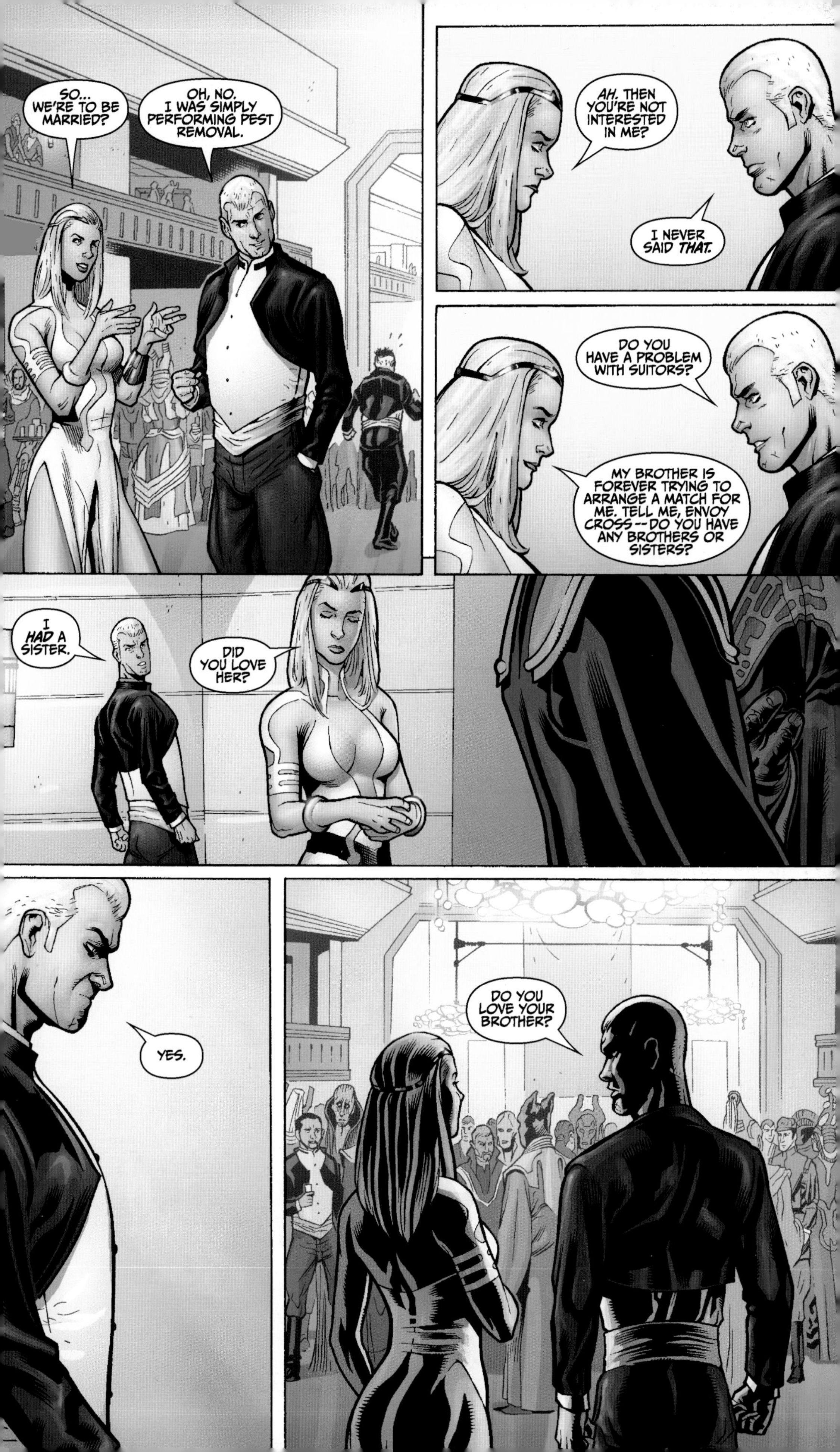
SO... WE'RE TO BE MARRIED?
OH, NO. I WAS SIMPLY PERFORMING PEST REMOVAL.
AH. THEN YOU'RE NOT INTERESTED IN ME?
I NEVER SAID THAT.
DO YOU HAVE A PROBLEM WITH SUITORS?
MY BROTHER IS FOREVER TRYING TO ARRANGE A MATCH FOR ME. TELL ME, ENVOY CROSS--DO YOU HAVE ANY BROTHERS OR SISTERS?
I HAD A SISTER.
DID YOU LOVE HER?
YES.
DO YOU LOVE YOUR BROTHER?

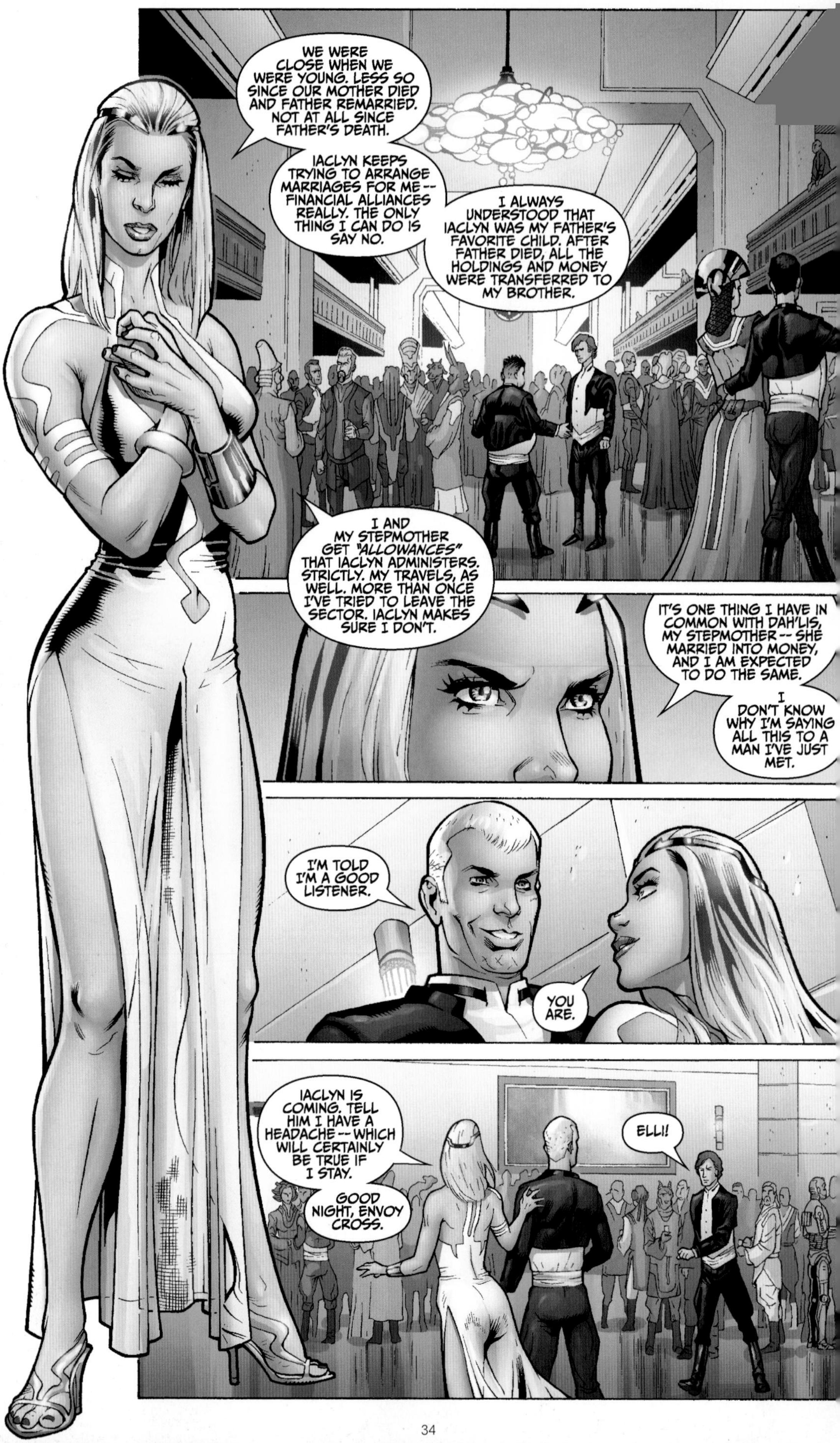
WE WERE CLOSE WHEN WE WERE YOUNG. LESS SO SINCE OUR MOTHER DIED AND FATHER REMARRIED. NOT AT ALL SINCE FATHER'S DEATH.
IACLYN KEEPS TRYING TO ARRANGE MARRIAGES FOR ME -- FINANCIAL ALLIANCES REALLY. THE ONLY THING I CAN DO IS SAY NO.
I ALWAYS UNDERSTOOD THAT IACLYN WAS MY FATHER'S FAVORITE CHILD. AFTER FATHER DIED, ALL THE HOLDINGS AND MONEY WERE TRANSFERRED TO MY BROTHER.
I AND MY STEPMOTHER GET "ALLOWANCES" THAT IACLYN ADMINISTERS. STRICTLY. MY TRAVELS, AS WELL. MORE THAN ONCE I'VE TRIED TO LEAVE THE SECTOR. IACLYN MAKES SURE I DON'T.
IT'S ONE THING I HAVE IN COMMON WITH DAH'LIS, MY STEPMOTHER -- SHE MARRIED INTO MONEY, AND I AM EXPECTED TO DO THE SAME.
I DON'T KNOW WHY I'M SAYING ALL THIS TO A MAN I'VE JUST MET.
I'M TOLD I'M A GOOD LISTENER.
YOU ARE.
IACLYN IS COMING. TELL HIM I HAVE A HEADACHE -- WHICH WILL CERTAINLY BE TRUE IF I STAY.
GOOD NIGHT, ENVOY CROSS.
ELLI!

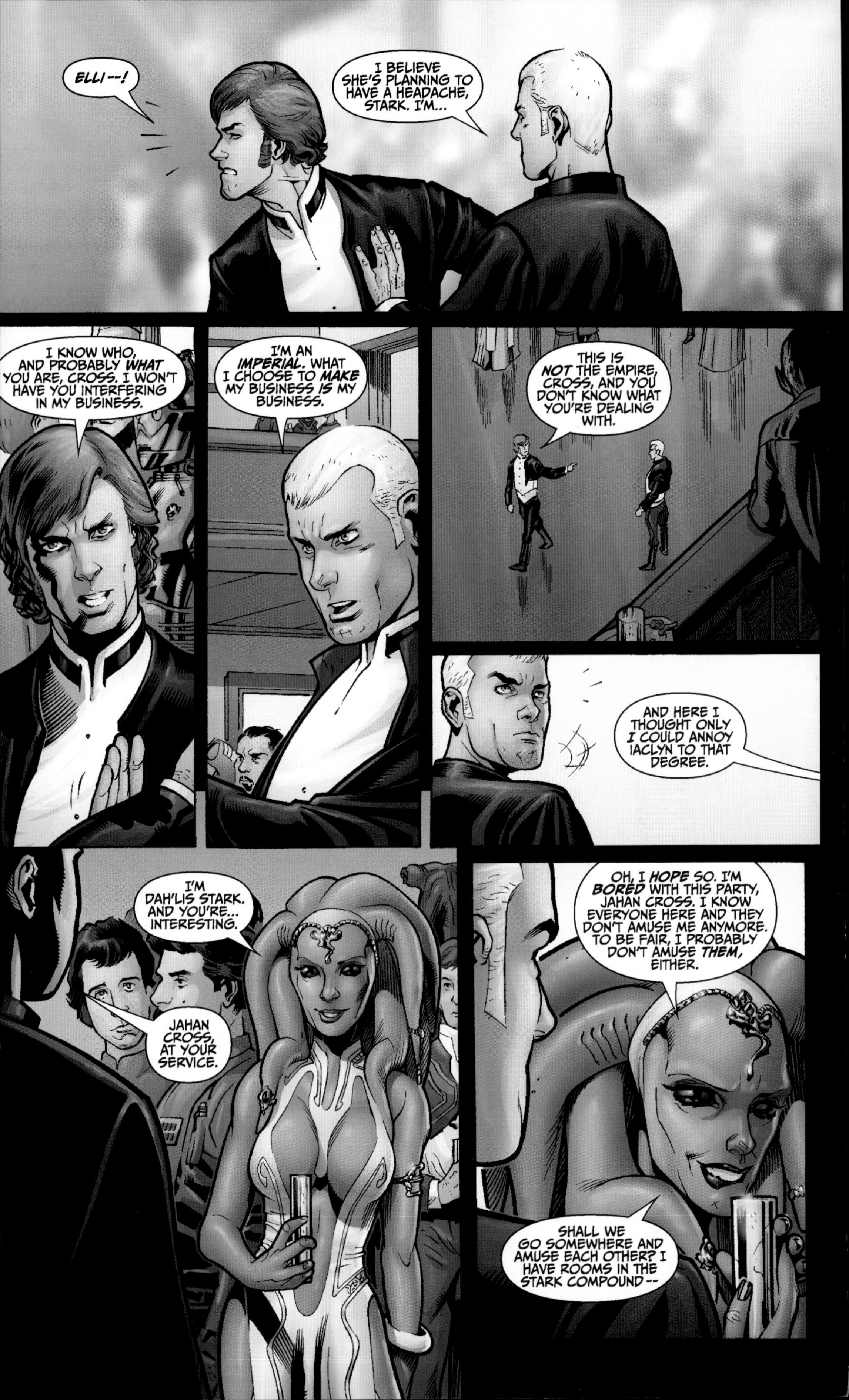
ELLI--!
I BELIEVE SHE'S PLANNING TO HAVE A HEADACHE, STARK. I'M...
I KNOW WHO, AND PROBABLY *WHAT* YOU ARE, CROSS. I WON'T HAVE YOU INTERFERING IN MY BUSINESS.
I'M AN *IMPERIAL*. WHAT I CHOOSE TO *MAKE* MY BUSINESS *IS* MY BUSINESS.
THIS IS *NOT* THE EMPIRE, CROSS, AND YOU DON'T KNOW WHAT YOU'RE DEALING WITH.
AND HERE I THOUGHT ONLY *I* COULD ANNOY IACLYN TO THAT DEGREE.
I'M DAH'LIS STARK. AND YOU'RE... INTERESTING.
JAHAN CROSS, AT YOUR SERVICE.
OH, I *HOPE* SO. I'M *BORED* WITH THIS PARTY, JAHAN CROSS. I KNOW EVERYONE HERE AND THEY DON'T AMUSE ME ANYMORE. TO BE FAIR, I PROBABLY DON'T AMUSE *THEM*, EITHER.
SHALL WE GO SOMEWHERE AND AMUSE EACH OTHER? I HAVE ROOMS IN THE STARK COMPOUND--

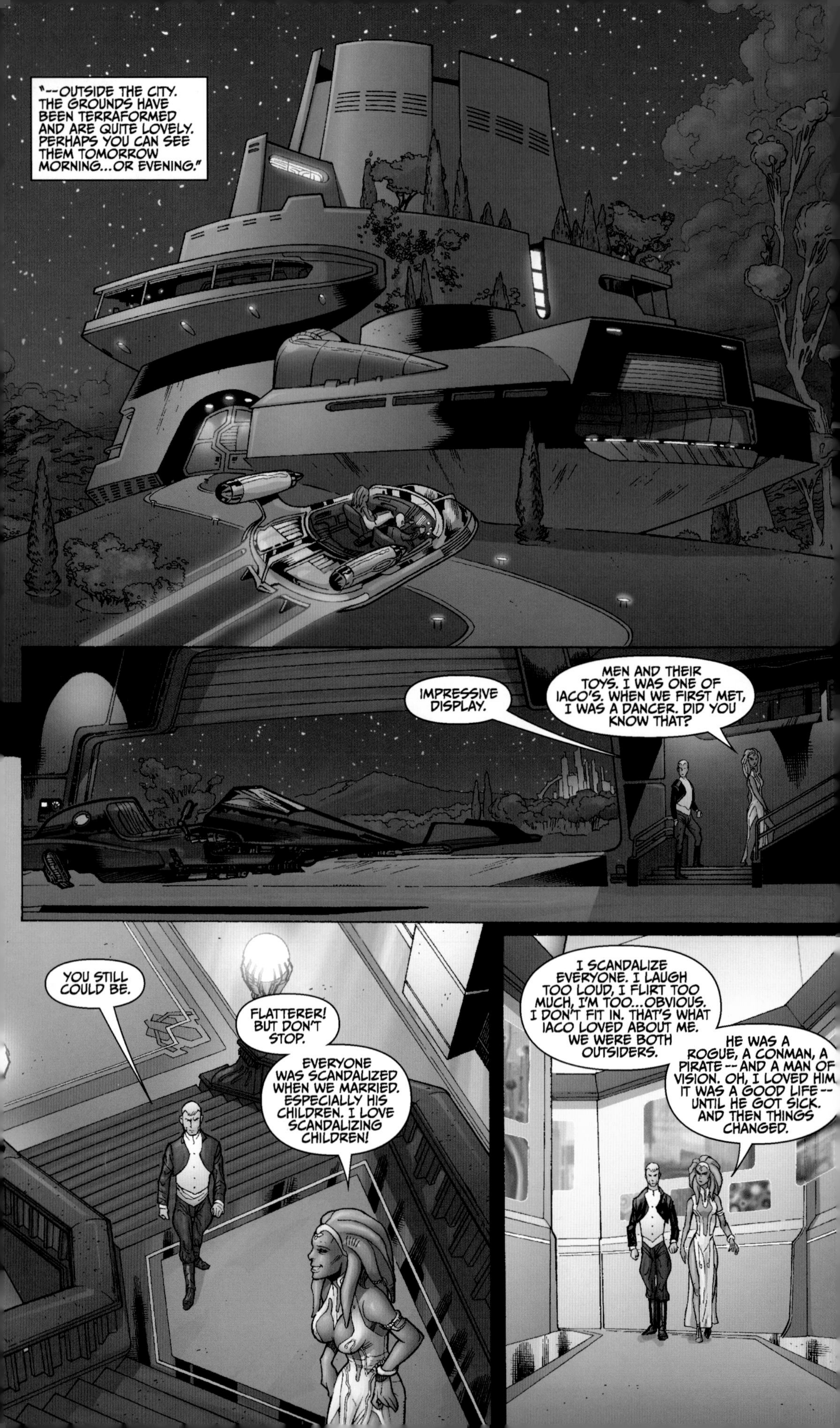
"--OUTSIDE THE CITY. THE GROUNDS HAVE BEEN TERRAFORMED AND ARE QUITE LOVELY. PERHAPS YOU CAN SEE THEM TOMORROW MORNING...OR EVENING."
IMPRESSIVE DISPLAY.
MEN AND THEIR TOYS. I WAS ONE OF IACO'S. WHEN WE FIRST MET, I WAS A DANCER. DID YOU KNOW THAT?
YOU STILL COULD BE.
FLATTERER! BUT DON'T STOP.
EVERYONE WAS SCANDALIZED WHEN WE MARRIED. ESPECIALLY HIS CHILDREN. I LOVE SCANDALIZING CHILDREN!
I SCANDALIZE EVERYONE. I LAUGH TOO LOUD, I FLIRT TOO MUCH, I'M TOO...OBVIOUS. I DON'T FIT IN. THAT'S WHAT IACO LOVED ABOUT ME. WE WERE BOTH OUTSIDERS.
HE WAS A ROGUE, A CONMAN, A PIRATE--AND A MAN OF VISION. OH, I LOVED HIM. IT WAS A GOOD LIFE--UNTIL HE GOT SICK. AND THEN THINGS CHANGED.

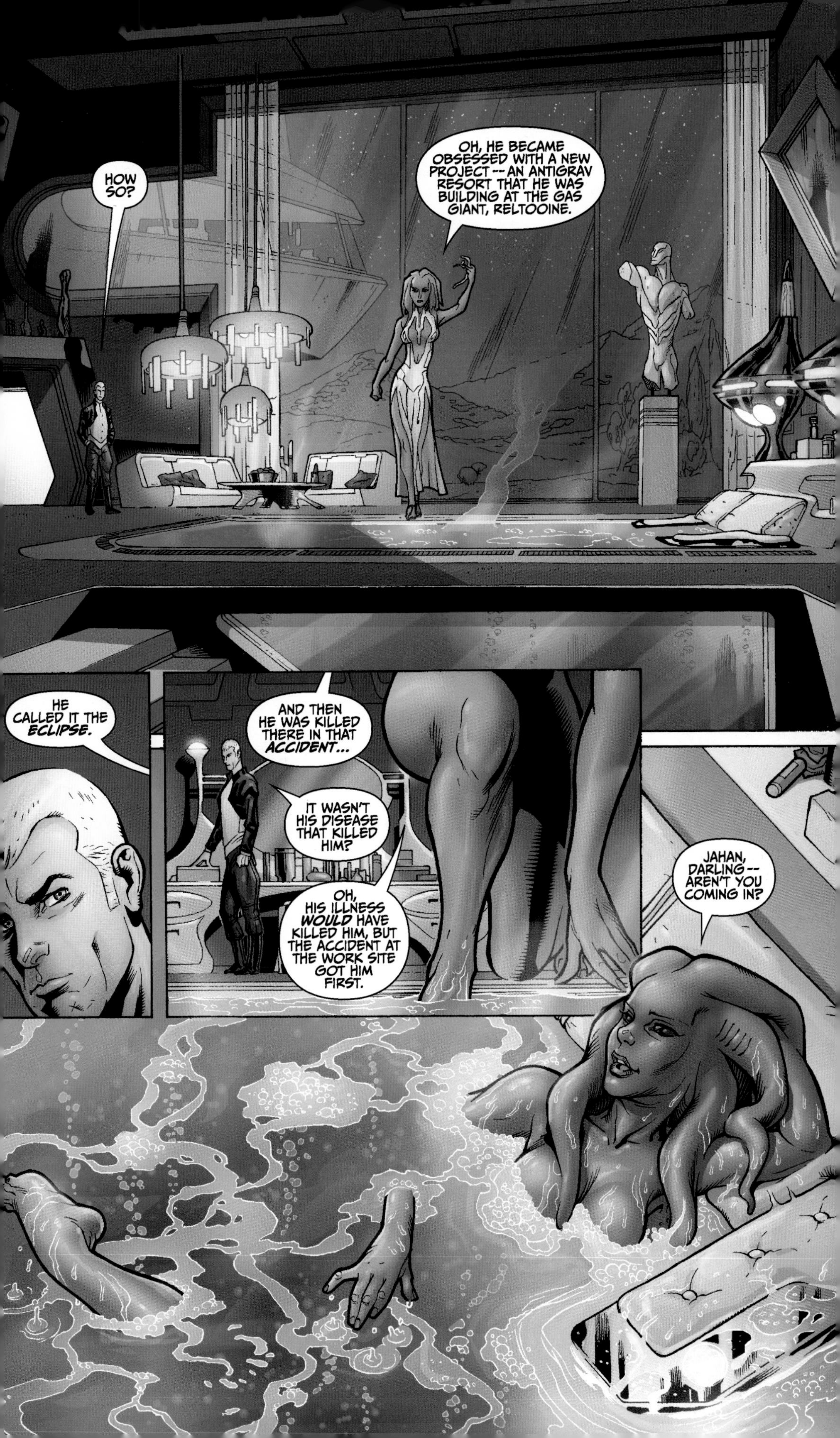
HOW SO?
OH, HE BECAME OBSESSED WITH A NEW PROJECT--AN ANTIGRAV RESORT THAT HE WAS BUILDING AT THE GAS GIANT, RELTOOINE.
HE CALLED IT THE *ECLIPSE.*
AND THEN HE WAS KILLED THERE IN THAT *ACCIDENT...*
IT WASN'T HIS DISEASE THAT KILLED HIM?
OH, HIS ILLNESS *WOULD* HAVE KILLED HIM, BUT THE ACCIDENT AT THE WORK SITE GOT HIM FIRST.
JAHAN, DARLING--AREN'T YOU COMING IN?

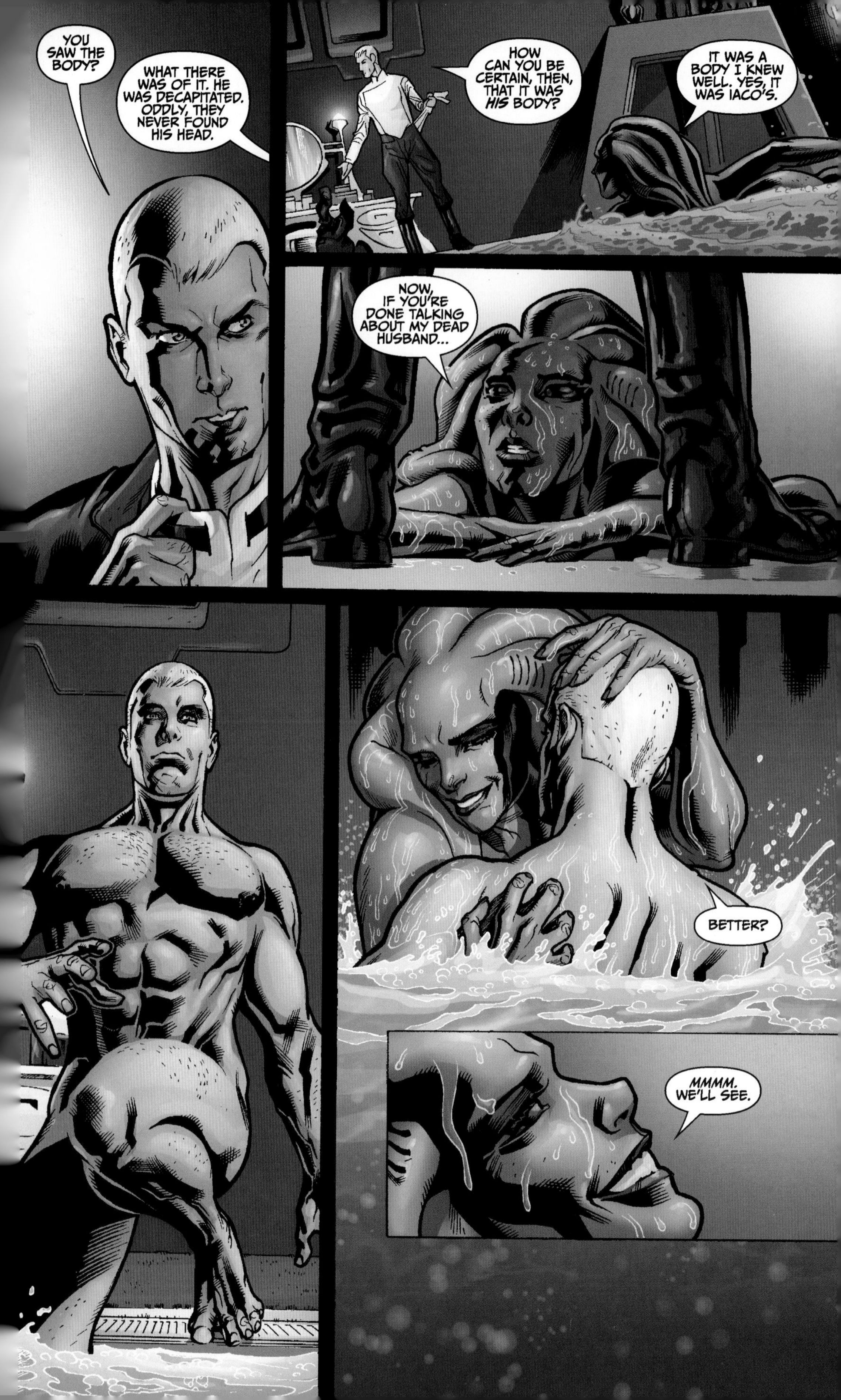
YOU SAW THE BODY?
WHAT THERE WAS OF IT. HE WAS DECAPITATED. ODDLY, THEY NEVER FOUND HIS HEAD.
HOW CAN YOU BE CERTAIN, THEN, THAT IT WAS *HIS* BODY?
IT WAS A BODY I KNEW WELL. YES, IT WAS IACO'S.
NOW, IF YOU'RE DONE TALKING ABOUT MY DEAD HUSBAND...
BETTER?
MMMM. WE'LL SEE.

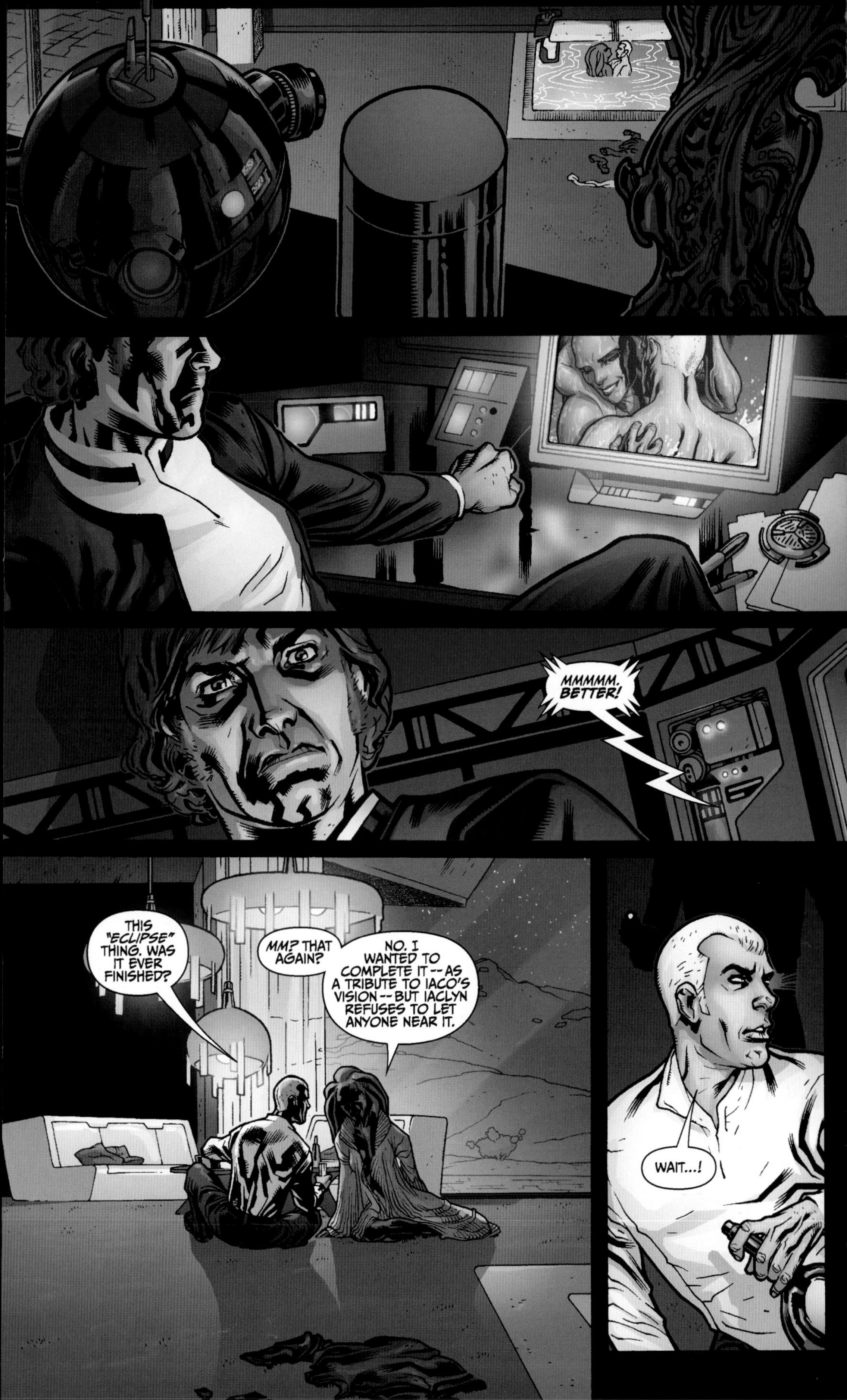
MMMMM. BETTER!
THIS "ECLIPSE" THING. WAS IT EVER FINISHED?
MM? THAT AGAIN?
NO. I WANTED TO COMPLETE IT--AS A TRIBUTE TO IACO'S VISION--BUT IACLYN REFUSES TO LET ANYONE NEAR IT.
WAIT...!

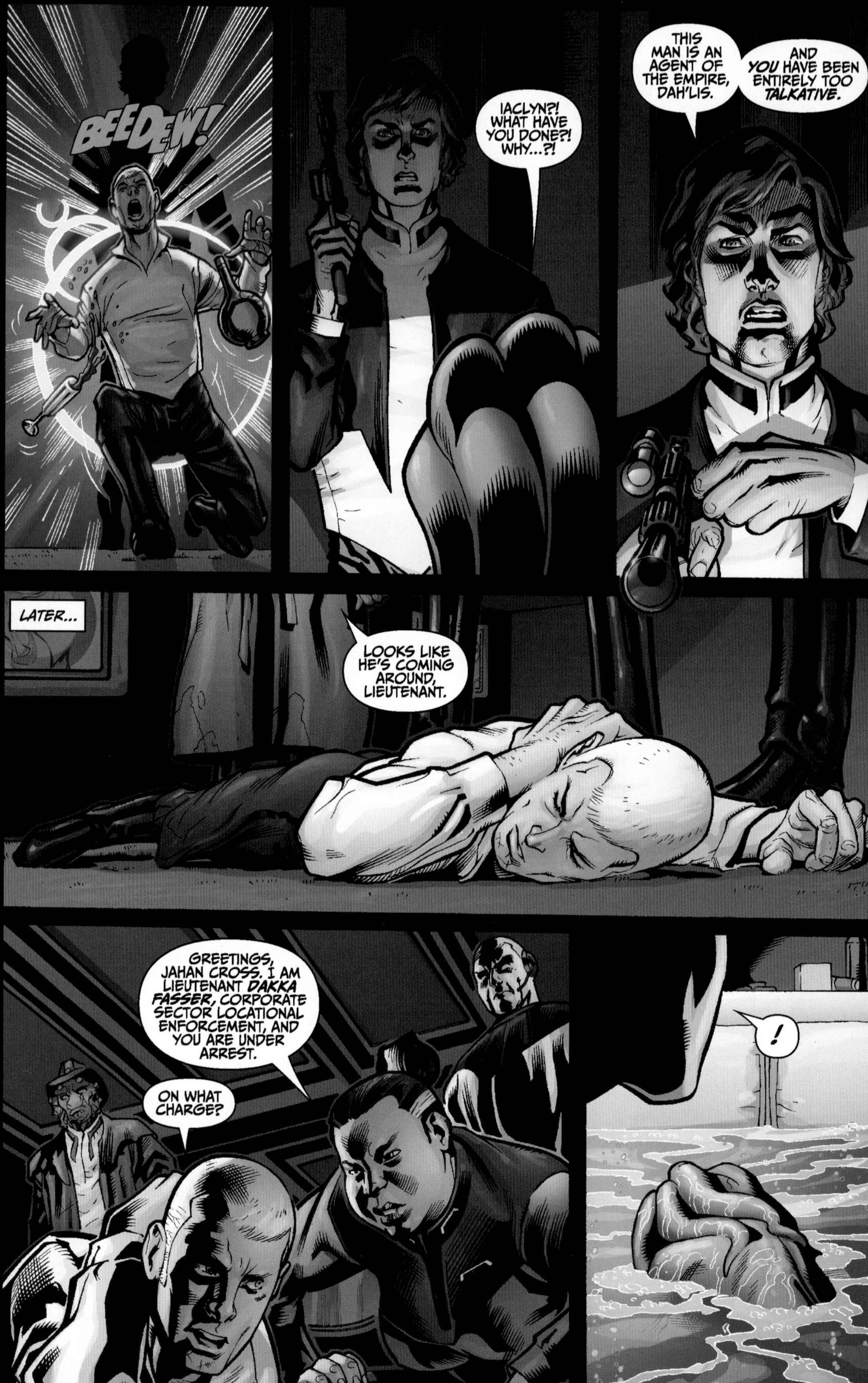
BEEDEW!
IACLYN?! WHAT HAVE YOU DONE?! WHY...?!
THIS MAN IS AN AGENT OF THE EMPIRE, DAH'LIS.
AND YOU HAVE BEEN ENTIRELY TOO TALKATIVE.
LATER...
LOOKS LIKE HE'S COMING AROUND, LIEUTENANT.
GREETINGS, JAHAN CROSS. I AM LIEUTENANT DAKKA FASSER, CORPORATE SECTOR LOCATIONAL ENFORCEMENT, AND YOU ARE UNDER ARREST.
ON WHAT CHARGE?
!

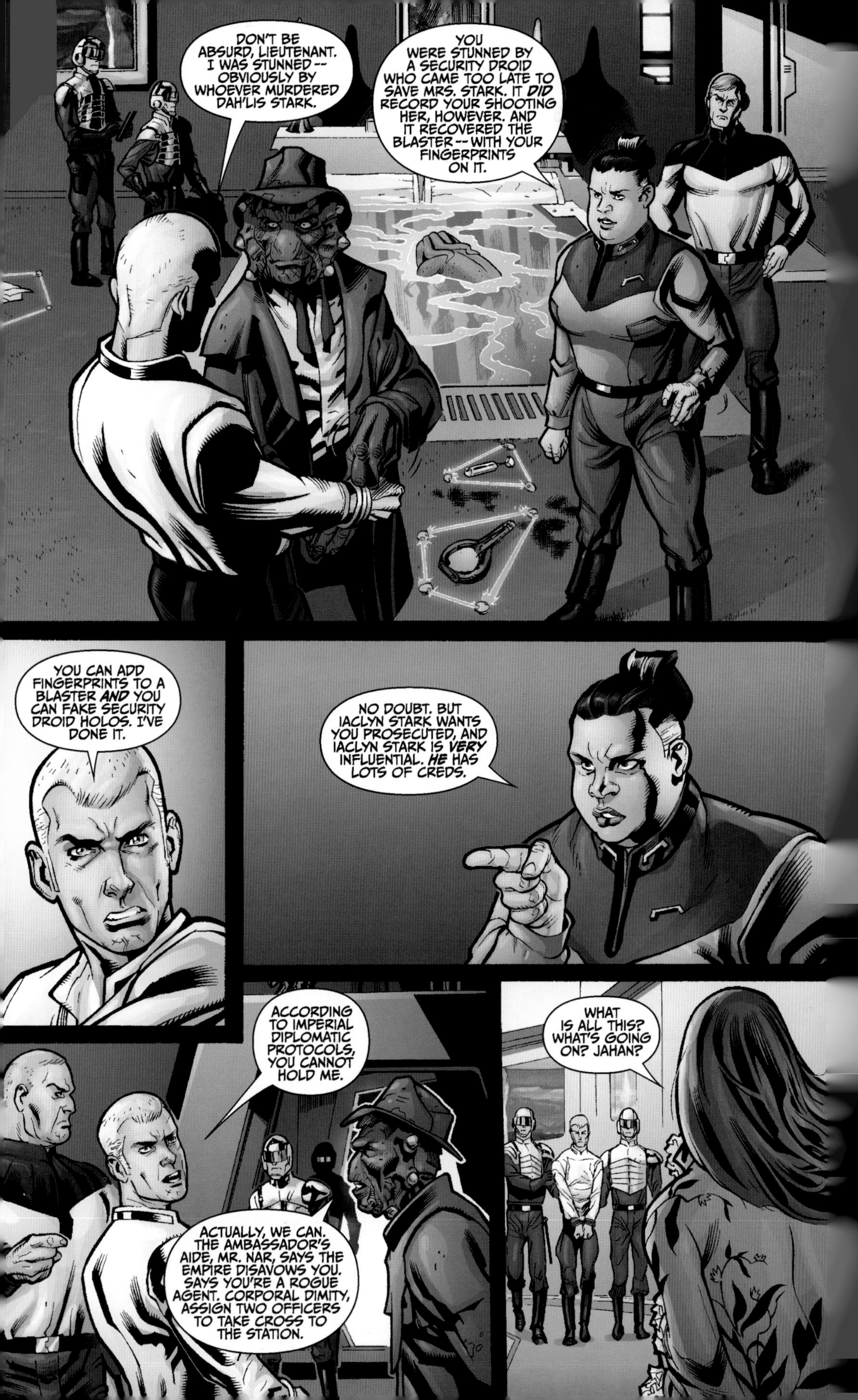
DON'T BE ABSURD, LIEUTENANT. I WAS STUNNED -- OBVIOUSLY BY WHOEVER MURDERED DAH'LIS STARK.
YOU WERE STUNNED BY A SECURITY DROID WHO CAME TOO LATE TO SAVE MRS. STARK. IT *DID* RECORD YOUR SHOOTING HER, HOWEVER. AND IT RECOVERED THE BLASTER -- WITH YOUR FINGERPRINTS ON IT.
YOU CAN ADD FINGERPRINTS TO A BLASTER ***AND*** YOU CAN FAKE SECURITY DROID HOLOS. I'VE DONE IT.
NO DOUBT. BUT IACLYN STARK WANTS YOU PROSECUTED, AND IACLYN STARK IS ***VERY*** INFLUENTIAL. ***HE*** HAS LOTS OF CREDS.
ACCORDING TO IMPERIAL DIPLOMATIC PROTOCOLS, YOU CANNOT HOLD ME.
ACTUALLY, WE CAN. THE AMBASSADOR'S AIDE, MR. NAR, SAYS THE EMPIRE DISAVOWS YOU. SAYS YOU'RE A ROGUE AGENT. CORPORAL DIMITY, ASSIGN TWO OFFICERS TO TAKE CROSS TO THE STATION.
WHAT IS ALL THIS? WHAT'S GOING ON? JAHAN?

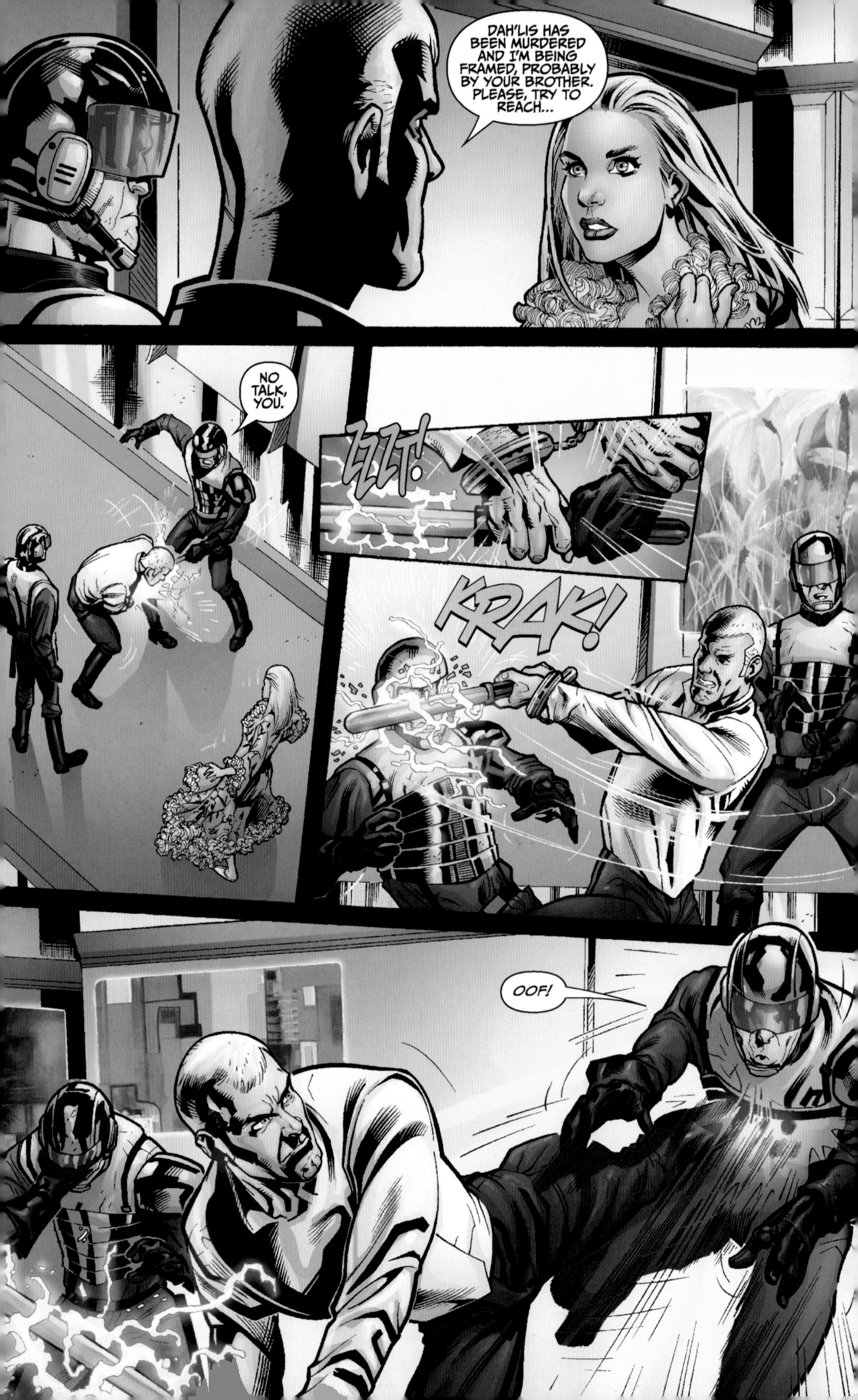
DAH'LIS HAS BEEN MURDERED AND I'M BEING FRAMED, PROBABLY BY YOUR BROTHER. PLEASE, TRY TO REACH...
NO TALK, YOU.
ZZZT!
KRAK!
OOF!

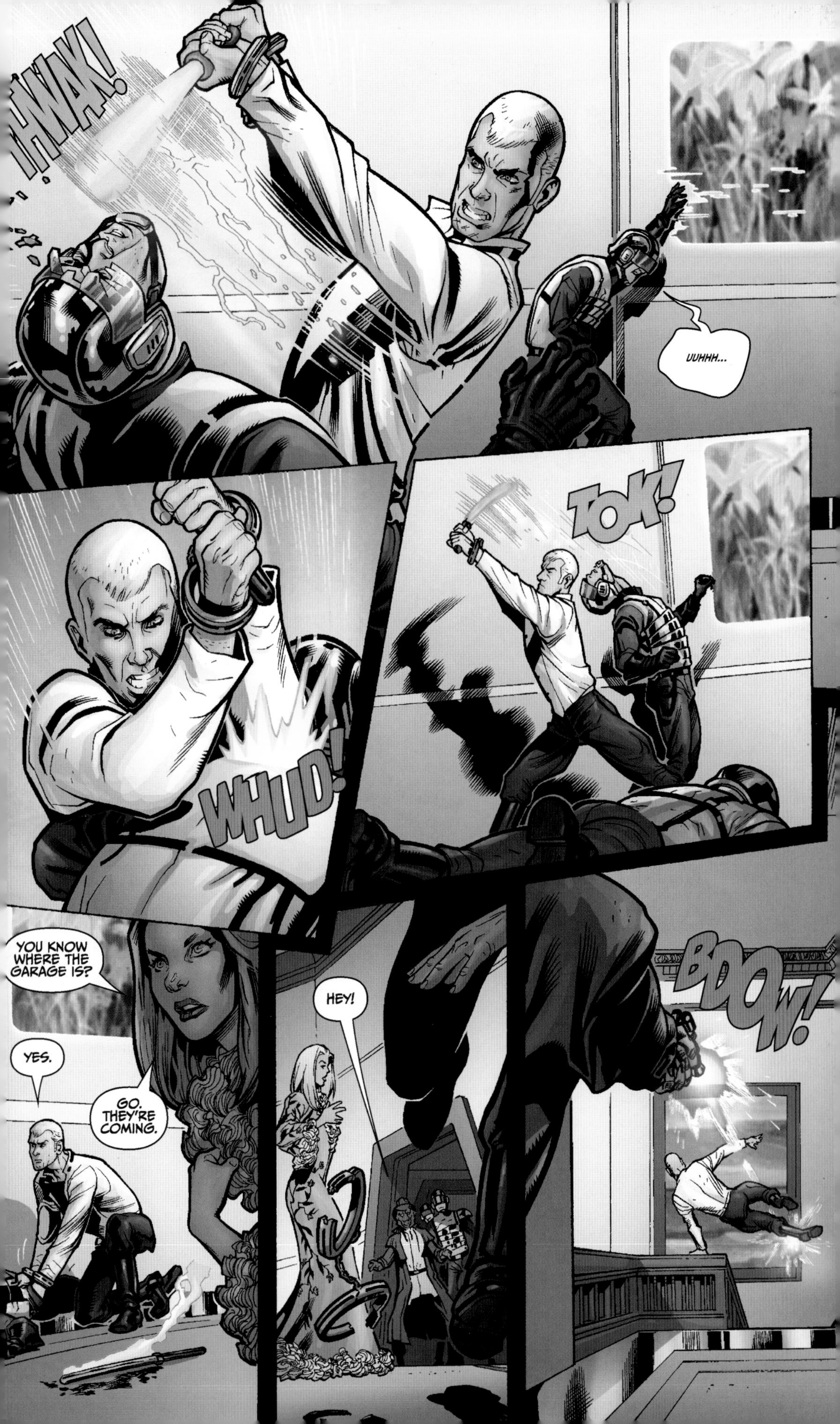
THWAK!
UUHHH...
WHUD!
TOK!
YOU KNOW WHERE THE GARAGE IS?
YES.
GO. THEY'RE COMING.
HEY!
BOOOM!

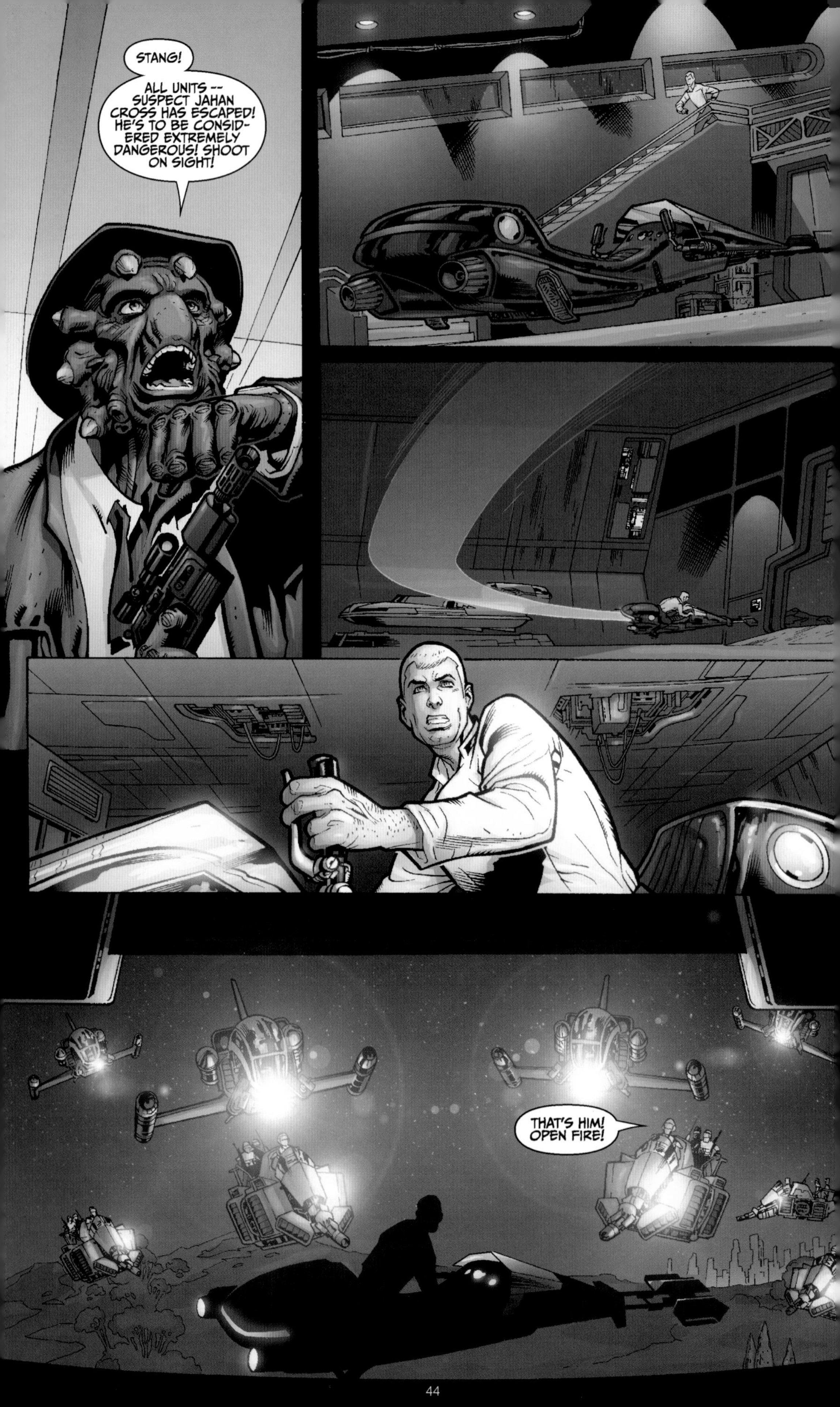
STANG!
ALL UNITS -- SUSPECT JAHAN CROSS HAS ESCAPED! HE'S TO BE CONSID-ERED EXTREMELY DANGEROUS! SHOOT ON SIGHT!
THAT'S HIM! OPEN FIRE!

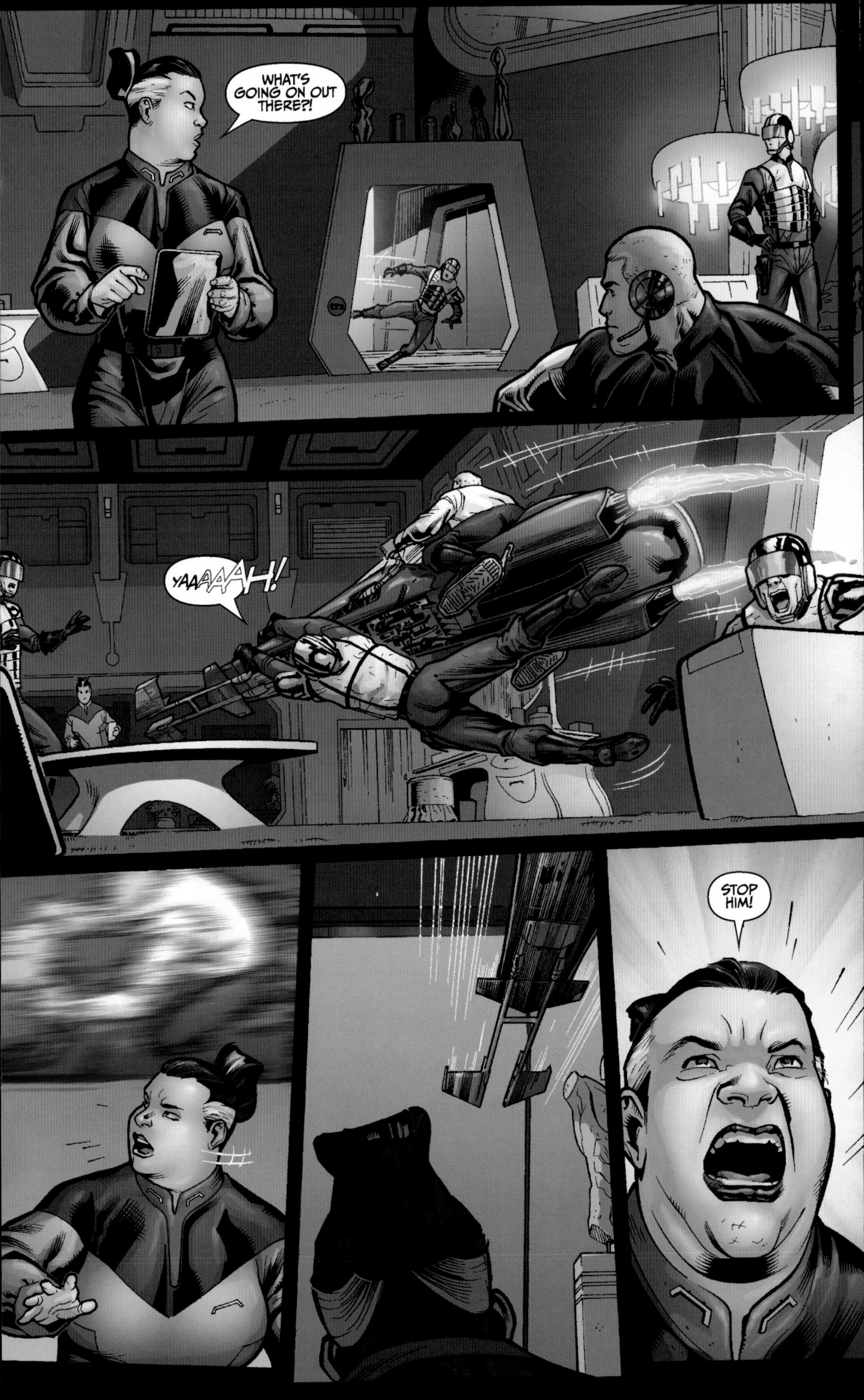
WHAT'S GOING ON OUT THERE?!
YAAAAAH!
STOP HIM!

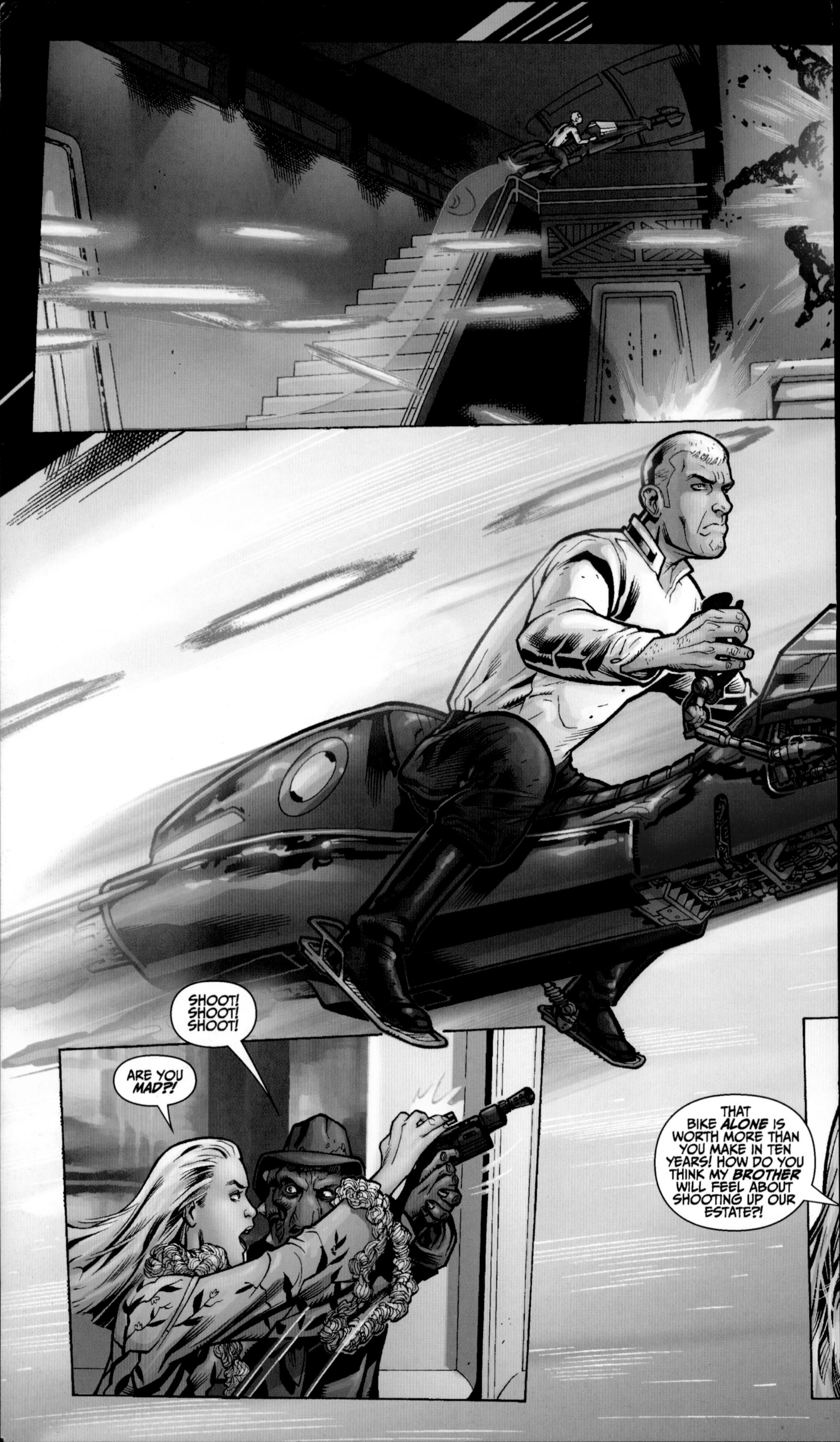
SHOOT! SHOOT! SHOOT!
ARE YOU MAD?!
THAT BIKE ALONE IS WORTH MORE THAN YOU MAKE IN TEN YEARS! HOW DO YOU THINK MY BROTHER WILL FEEL ABOUT SHOOTING UP OUR ESTATE?!

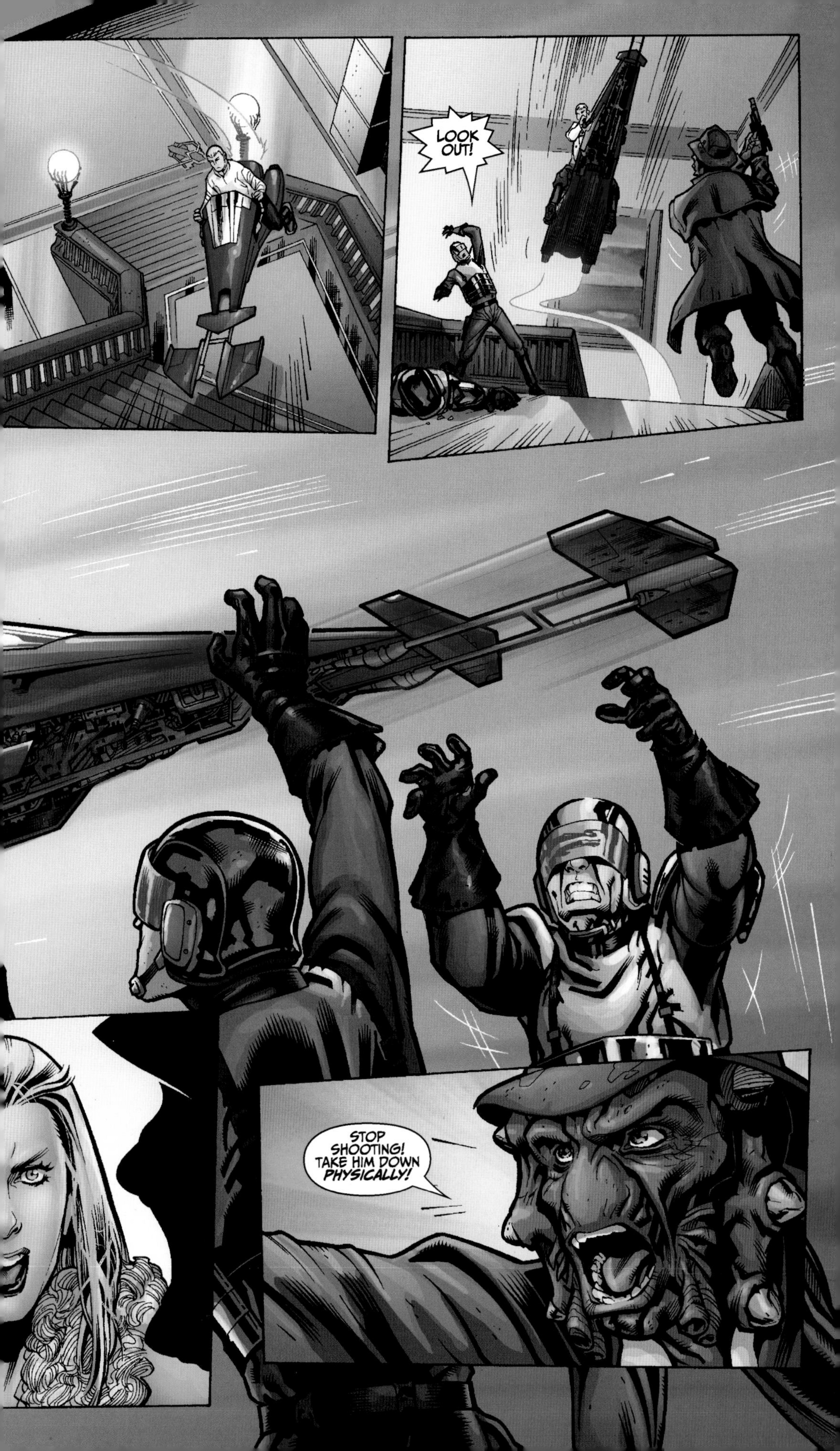
LOOK OUT!
STOP SHOOTING! TAKE HIM DOWN *PHYSICALLY!*

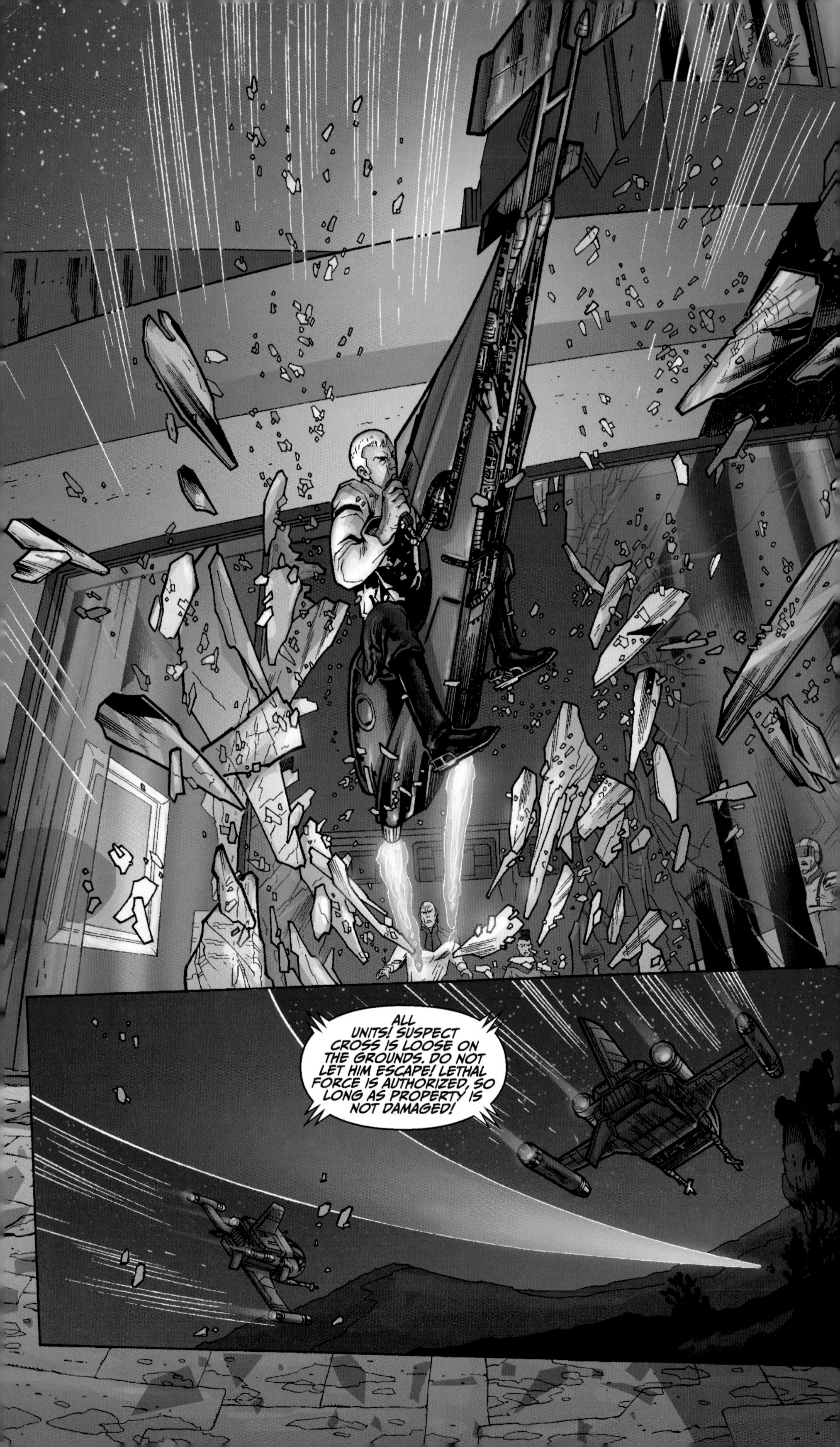
ALL UNITS! SUSPECT CROSS IS LOOSE ON THE GROUNDS. DO NOT LET HIM ESCAPE! LETHAL FORCE IS AUTHORIZED, SO LONG AS PROPERTY IS NOT DAMAGED!

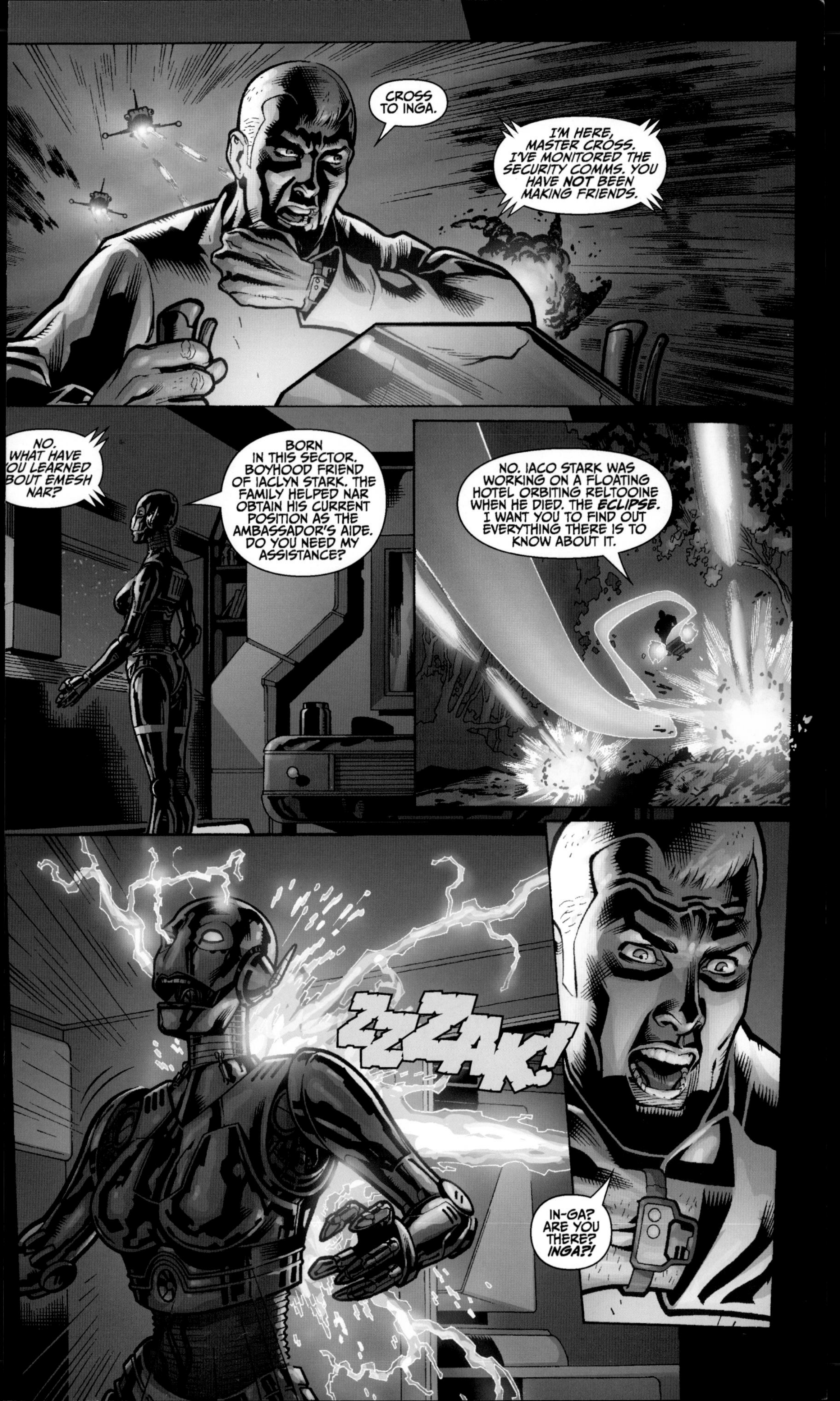
CROSS TO INGA.
I'M HERE, MASTER CROSS. I'VE MONITORED THE SECURITY COMMS. YOU HAVE NOT BEEN MAKING FRIENDS.
NO. WHAT HAVE YOU LEARNED ABOUT EMESH NAR?
BORN IN THIS SECTOR. BOYHOOD FRIEND OF IACLYN STARK. THE FAMILY HELPED NAR OBTAIN HIS CURRENT POSITION AS THE AMBASSADOR'S AIDE. DO YOU NEED MY ASSISTANCE?
NO. IACO STARK WAS WORKING ON A FLOATING HOTEL ORBITING RELTOOINE WHEN HE DIED. THE ECLIPSE. I WANT YOU TO FIND OUT EVERYTHING THERE IS TO KNOW ABOUT IT.
ZZZAK!
IN-GA? ARE YOU THERE? INGA?!

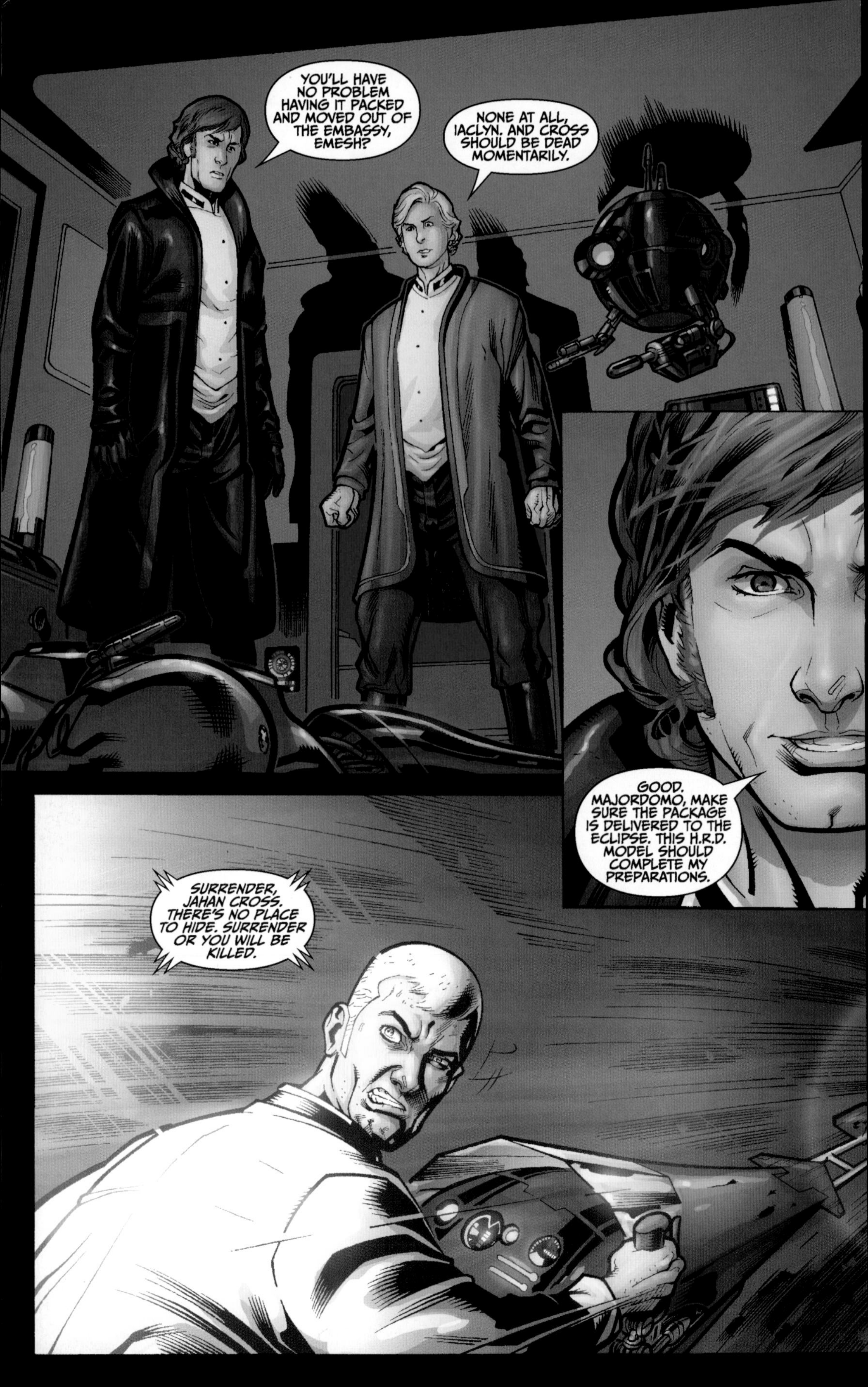
YOU'LL HAVE NO PROBLEM HAVING IT PACKED AND MOVED OUT OF THE EMBASSY, EMESH?
NONE AT ALL, IACLYN. AND CROSS SHOULD BE DEAD MOMENTARILY.
GOOD. MAJORDOMO, MAKE SURE THE PACKAGE IS DELIVERED TO THE ECLIPSE. THIS H.R.D. MODEL SHOULD COMPLETE MY PREPARATIONS.
SURRENDER, JAHAN CROSS. THERE'S NO PLACE TO HIDE. SURRENDER OR YOU WILL BE KILLED.

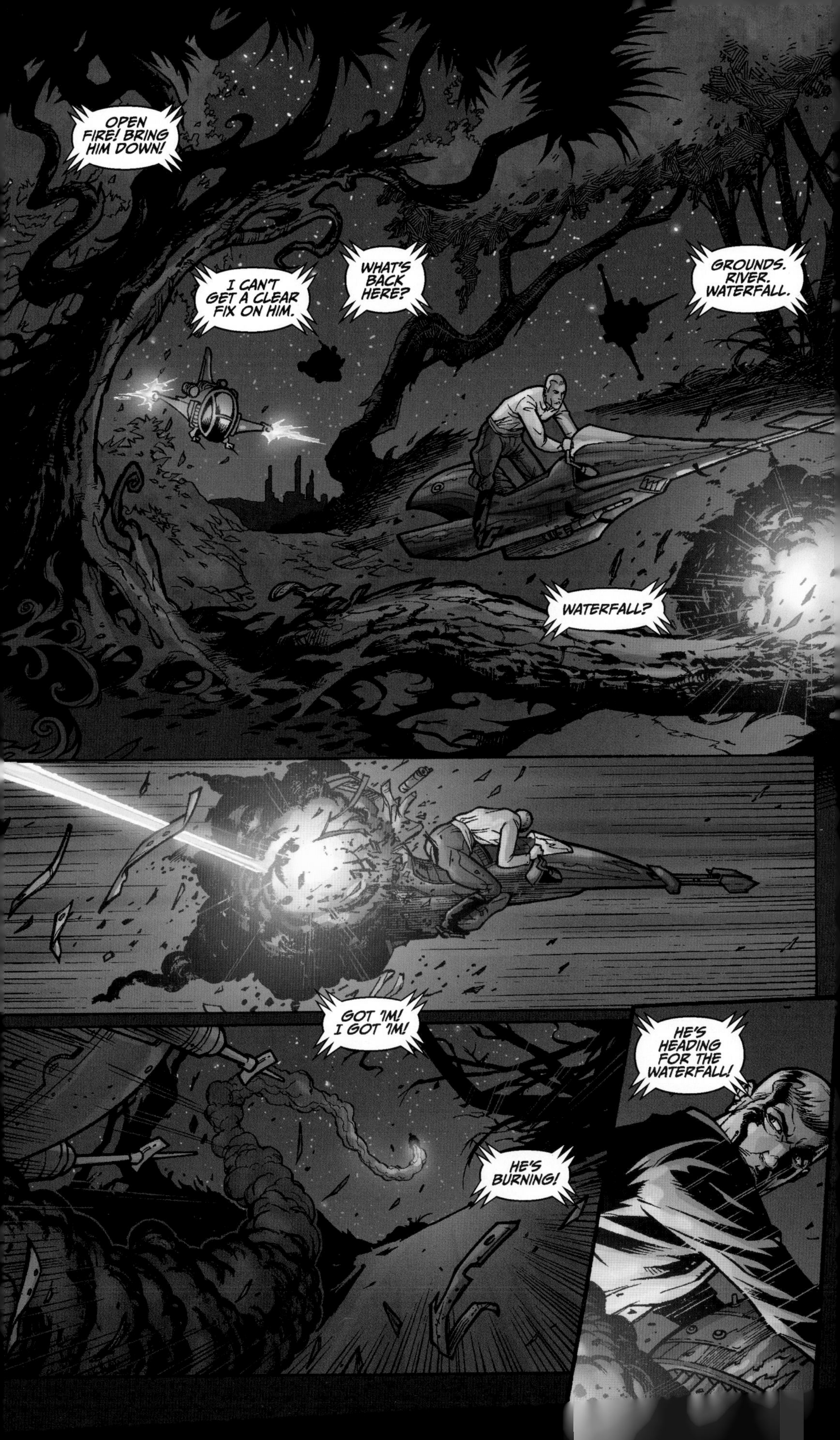
OPEN FIRE! BRING HIM DOWN!
I CAN'T GET A CLEAR FIX ON HIM.
WHAT'S BACK HERE?
GROUNDS. RIVER. WATERFALL.
WATERFALL?
GOT 'IM! I GOT 'IM!
HE'S BURNING!
HE'S HEADING FOR THE WATERFALL!

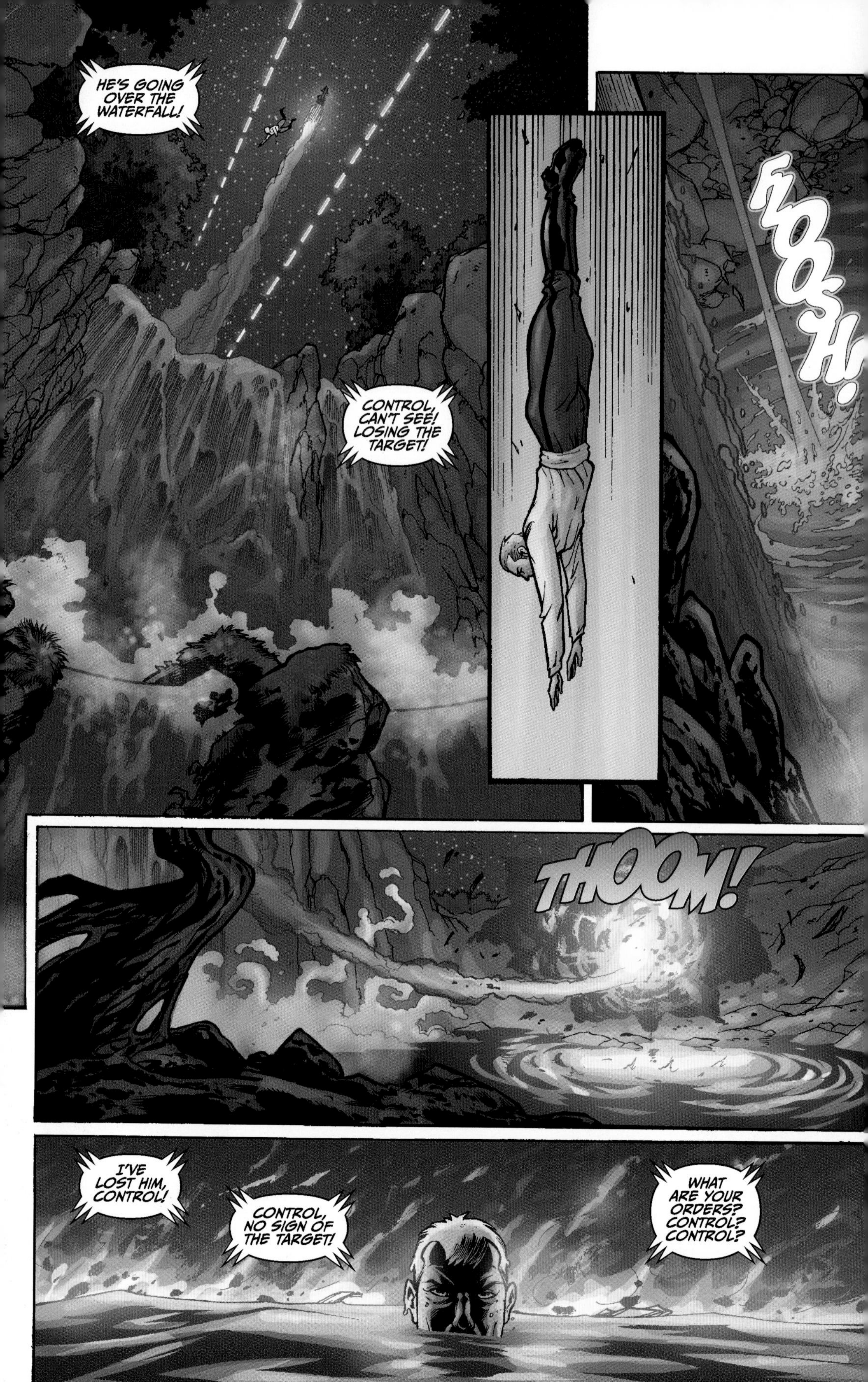
HE'S GOING OVER THE WATERFALL!
CONTROL, CAN'T SEE! LOSING THE TARGET!
FLOOSH!
THOOM!
I'VE LOST HIM, CONTROL!
CONTROL, NO SIGN OF THE TARGET!
WHAT ARE YOUR ORDERS? CONTROL? CONTROL?

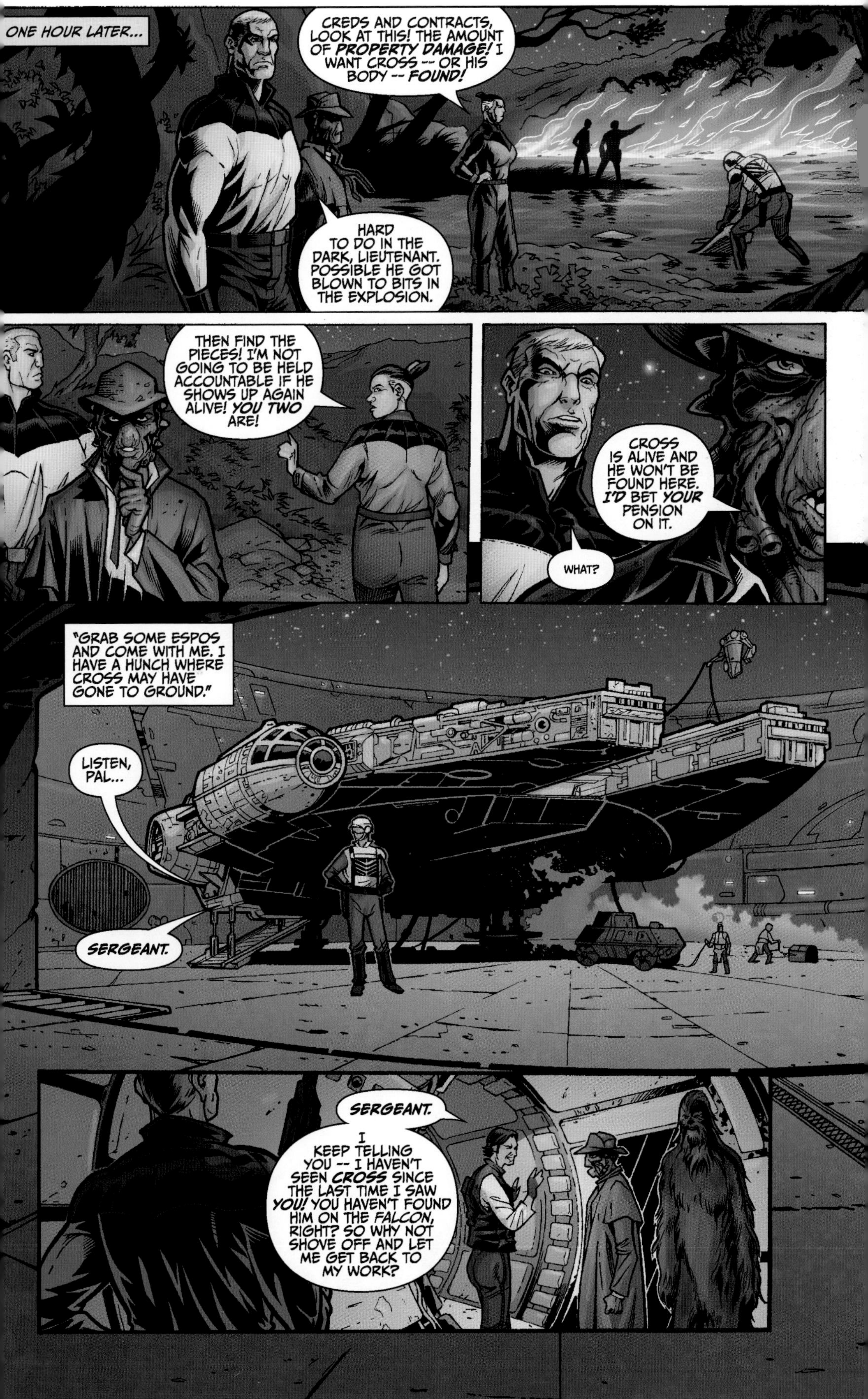

ONE HOUR LATER...
CREDS AND CONTRACTS, LOOK AT THIS! THE AMOUNT OF PROPERTY DAMAGE! I WANT CROSS -- OR HIS BODY -- FOUND!
HARD TO DO IN THE DARK, LIEUTENANT. POSSIBLE HE GOT BLOWN TO BITS IN THE EXPLOSION.
THEN FIND THE PIECES! I'M NOT GOING TO BE HELD ACCOUNTABLE IF HE SHOWS UP AGAIN ALIVE! YOU TWO ARE!
CROSS IS ALIVE AND HE WON'T BE FOUND HERE. I'D BET YOUR PENSION ON IT.
WHAT?
"GRAB SOME ESPOS AND COME WITH ME. I HAVE A HUNCH WHERE CROSS MAY HAVE GONE TO GROUND."
LISTEN, PAL...
SERGEANT.
SERGEANT.
I KEEP TELLING YOU -- I HAVEN'T SEEN CROSS SINCE THE LAST TIME I SAW YOU! YOU HAVEN'T FOUND HIM ON THE FALCON, RIGHT? SO WHY NOT SHOVE OFF AND LET ME GET BACK TO MY WORK?

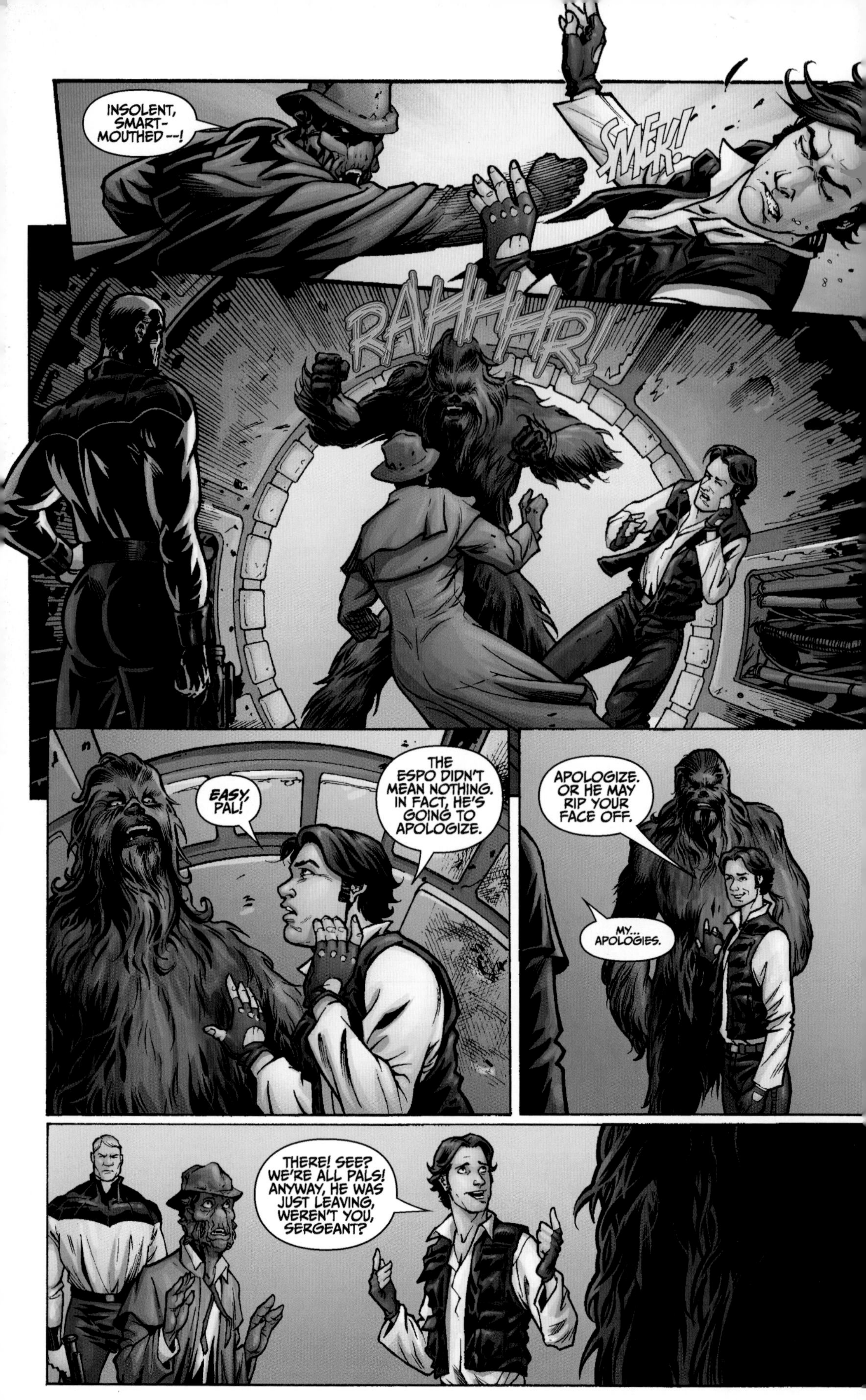
INSOLENT, SMART-MOUTHED --!
SMEK!
RAHHHR!
EASY, PAL!
THE ESPO DIDN'T MEAN NOTHING. IN FACT, HE'S GOING TO APOLOGIZE.
APOLOGIZE. OR HE MAY RIP YOUR FACE OFF.
MY... APOLOGIES.
THERE! SEE? WE'RE ALL PALS! ANYWAY, HE WAS JUST LEAVING, WEREN'T YOU, SERGEANT?

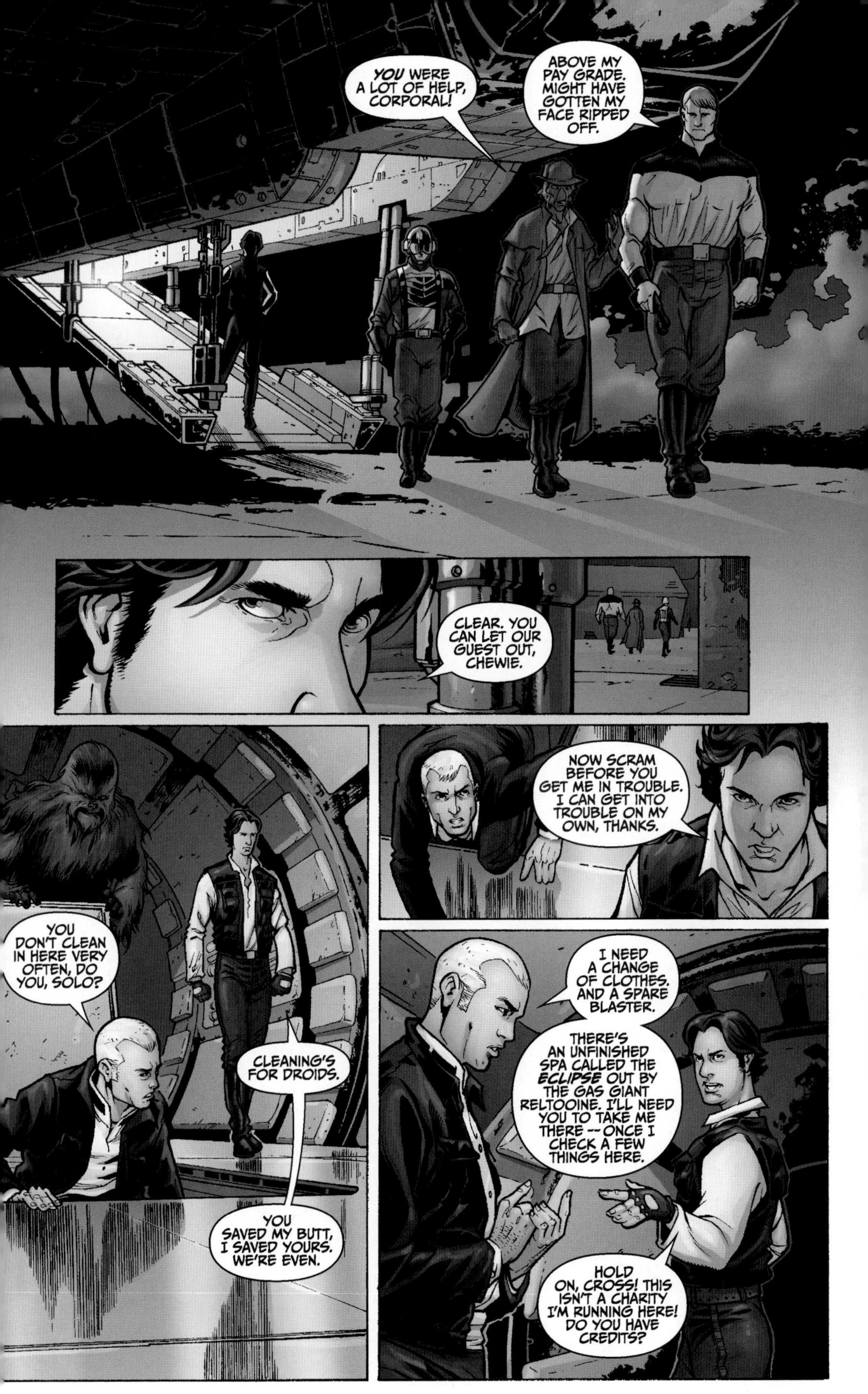
YOU WERE A LOT OF HELP, CORPORAL!
ABOVE MY PAY GRADE. MIGHT HAVE GOTTEN MY FACE RIPPED OFF.
CLEAR. YOU CAN LET OUR GUEST OUT, CHEWIE.
YOU DON'T CLEAN IN HERE VERY OFTEN, DO YOU, SOLO?
CLEANING'S FOR DROIDS.
YOU SAVED MY BUTT, I SAVED YOURS. WE'RE EVEN.
NOW SCRAM BEFORE YOU GET ME IN TROUBLE. I CAN GET INTO TROUBLE ON MY OWN, THANKS.
I NEED A CHANGE OF CLOTHES. AND A SPARE BLASTER.
THERE'S AN UNFINISHED SPA CALLED THE ECLIPSE OUT BY THE GAS GIANT RELTOOINE. I'LL NEED YOU TO TAKE ME THERE -- ONCE I CHECK A FEW THINGS HERE.
HOLD ON, CROSS! THIS ISN'T A CHARITY I'M RUNNING HERE! DO YOU HAVE CREDITS?

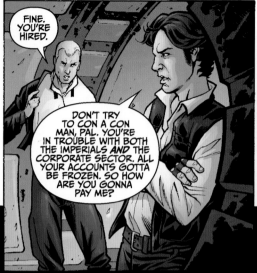

FINE. YOU'RE HIRED.

DON'T TRY TO CON A CON MAN, PAL. YOU'RE IN TROUBLE WITH BOTH THE IMPERIALS *AND* THE CORPORATE SECTOR. ALL YOUR ACCOUNTS GOTTA BE FROZEN. SO HOW ARE YOU GONNA PAY ME?

I'LL GET THE CREDITS FOR YOU -- UPFRONT.

HOW?

LEAVE THAT TO ME. JUST GIVE ME UNTIL MORNING. NOW -- DO YOU HAVE A SPARE SHIRT OR NOT? PREFERABLY *CLEAN.*

WUHR?

NO, I THINK CROSS WILL PLAY FAIR BY US, CHEWIE.

I MEAN, I KNOW HE'S AN IMPERIAL BUT, BACK AT THE ACADEMY, IF HE *SAID* HE WOULD DO SOMETHING, HE *DID* IT.

RAHR RUHHR!

YOU'RE RIGHT. PEOPLE CHANGE. WE'LL GIVE HIM UNTIL MORNING. KEEP OUR EYES OPEN.

I HAVE A GOOD FEELING ABOUT THIS, THOUGH. I SMELL CREDS.

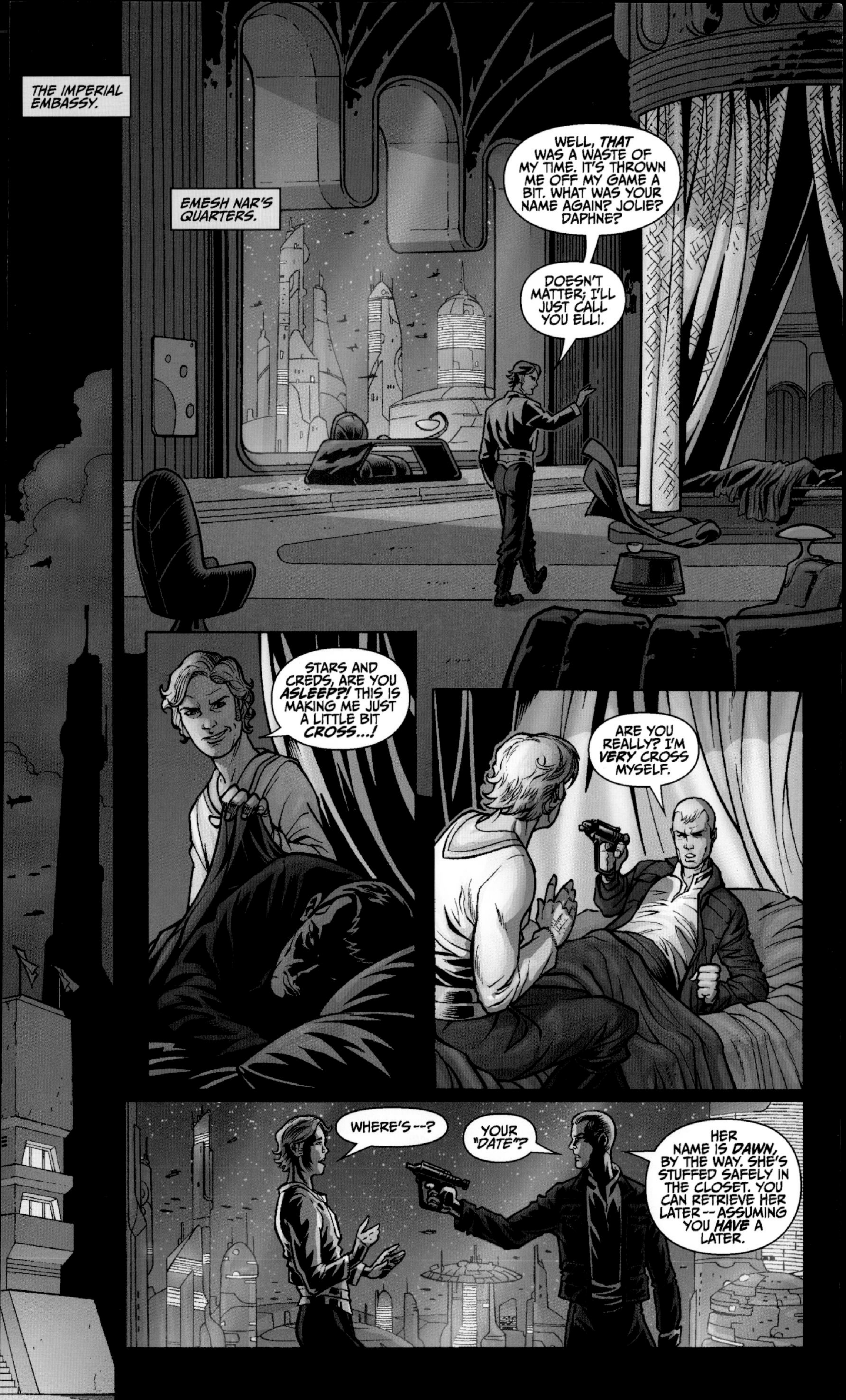
THE IMPERIAL EMBASSY.
EMESH NAR'S QUARTERS.
WELL, THAT WAS A WASTE OF MY TIME. IT'S THROWN ME OFF MY GAME A BIT. WHAT WAS YOUR NAME AGAIN? JOLIE? DAPHNE?
DOESN'T MATTER; I'LL JUST CALL YOU ELLI.
STARS AND CREDS, ARE YOU ASLEEP?! THIS IS MAKING ME JUST A LITTLE BIT CROSS...!
ARE YOU REALLY? I'M VERY CROSS MYSELF.
WHERE'S--?
YOUR "DATE"?
HER NAME IS DAWN, BY THE WAY. SHE'S STUFFED SAFELY IN THE CLOSET. YOU CAN RETRIEVE HER LATER--ASSUMING YOU HAVE A LATER.

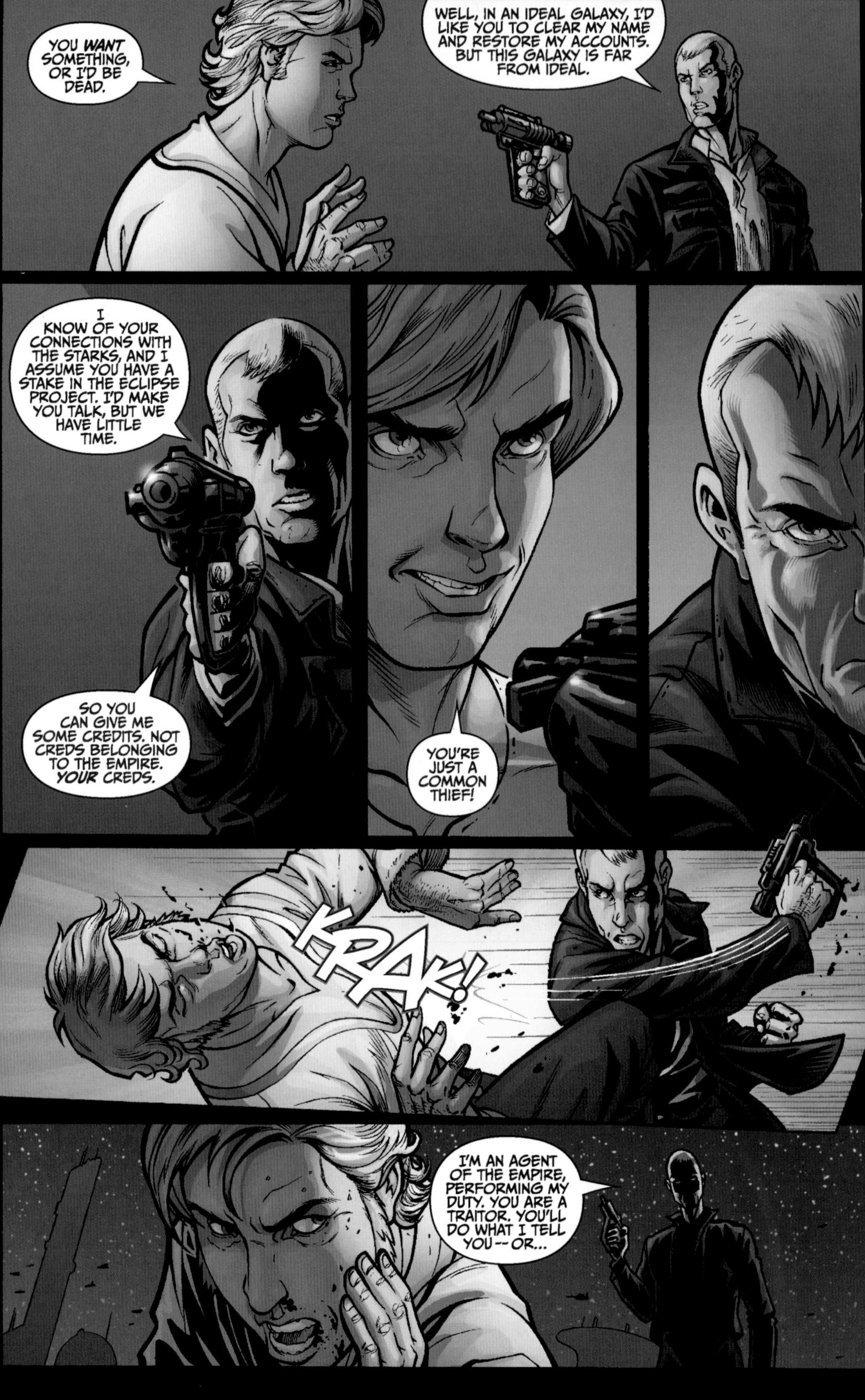
YOU *WANT* SOMETHING, OR I'D BE DEAD.
WELL, IN AN IDEAL GALAXY, I'D LIKE YOU TO CLEAR MY NAME AND RESTORE MY ACCOUNTS. BUT THIS GALAXY IS FAR FROM IDEAL.
I KNOW OF YOUR CONNECTIONS WITH THE STARKS, AND I ASSUME YOU HAVE A STAKE IN THE ECLIPSE PROJECT. I'D MAKE YOU TALK, BUT WE HAVE LITTLE TIME.
SO YOU CAN GIVE ME SOME CREDITS. NOT CREDS BELONGING TO THE EMPIRE. *YOUR* CREDS.
YOU'RE JUST A COMMON THIEF!
KRAK!
I'M AN AGENT OF THE EMPIRE, PERFORMING MY DUTY. YOU ARE A TRAITOR. YOU'LL DO WHAT I TELL YOU--OR...

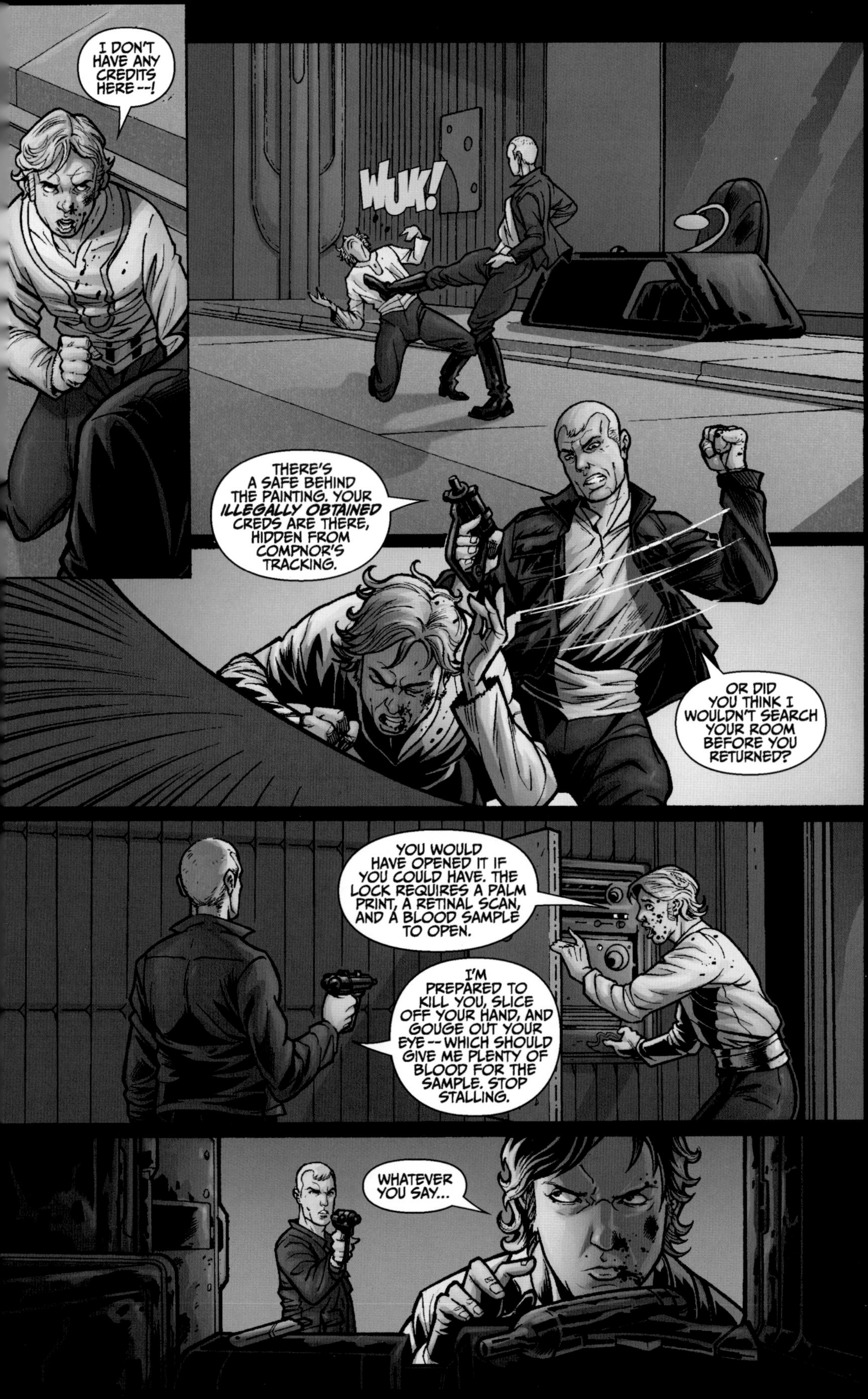
I DON'T HAVE ANY CREDITS HERE--!
WUK!
THERE'S A SAFE BEHIND THE PAINTING. YOUR ILLEGALLY OBTAINED CREDS ARE THERE, HIDDEN FROM COMPNOR'S TRACKING.
OR DID YOU THINK I WOULDN'T SEARCH YOUR ROOM BEFORE YOU RETURNED?
YOU WOULD HAVE OPENED IT IF YOU COULD HAVE. THE LOCK REQUIRES A PALM PRINT, A RETINAL SCAN, AND A BLOOD SAMPLE TO OPEN.
I'M PREPARED TO KILL YOU, SLICE OFF YOUR HAND, AND GOUGE OUT YOUR EYE--WHICH SHOULD GIVE ME PLENTY OF BLOOD FOR THE SAMPLE. STOP STALLING.
WHATEVER YOU SAY...

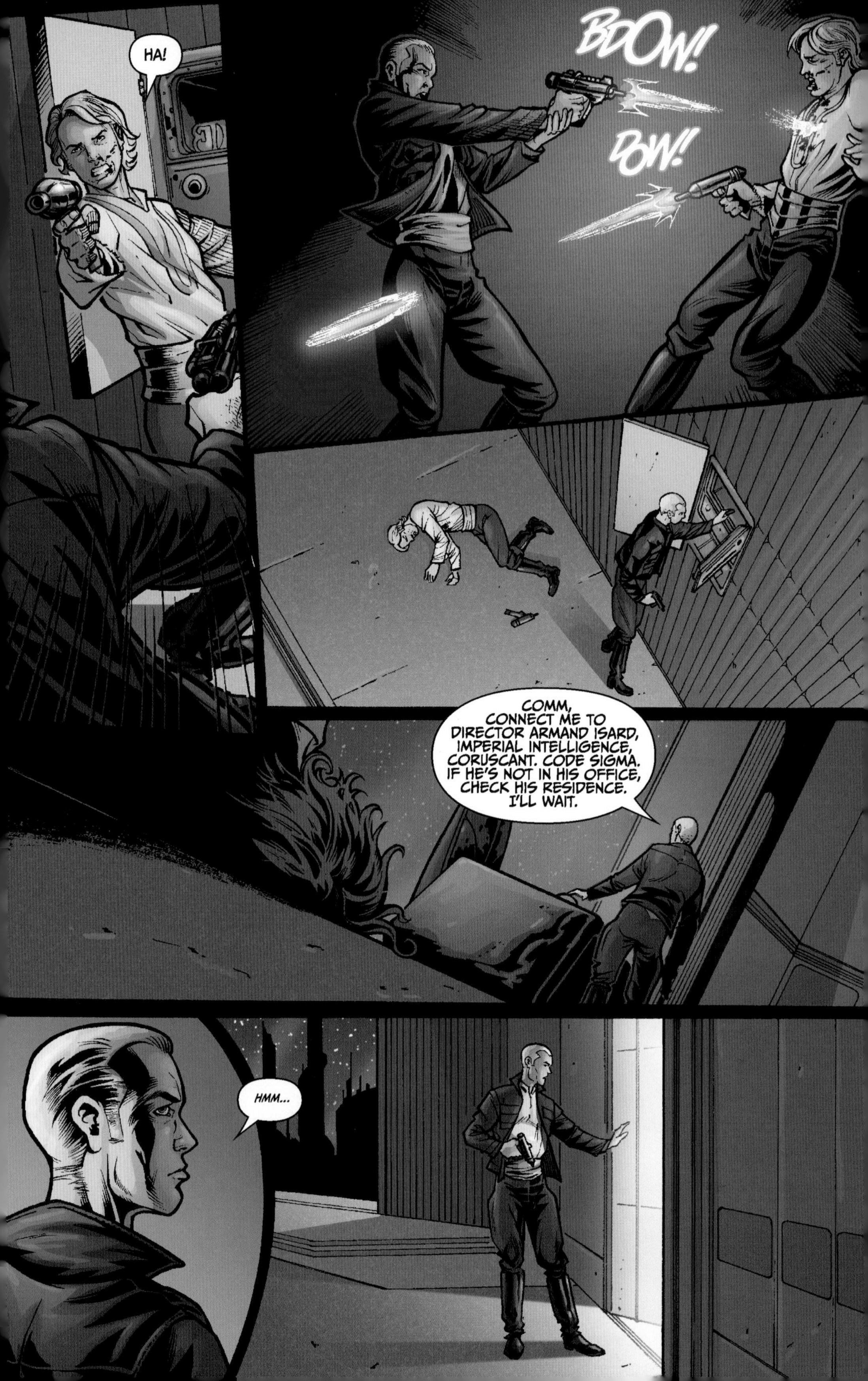
HA!
BDOW!
DOW!
COMM, CONNECT ME TO DIRECTOR ARMAND ISARD, IMPERIAL INTELLIGENCE, CORUSCANT. CODE SIGMA. IF HE'S NOT IN HIS OFFICE, CHECK HIS RESIDENCE. I'LL WAIT.
HMM...

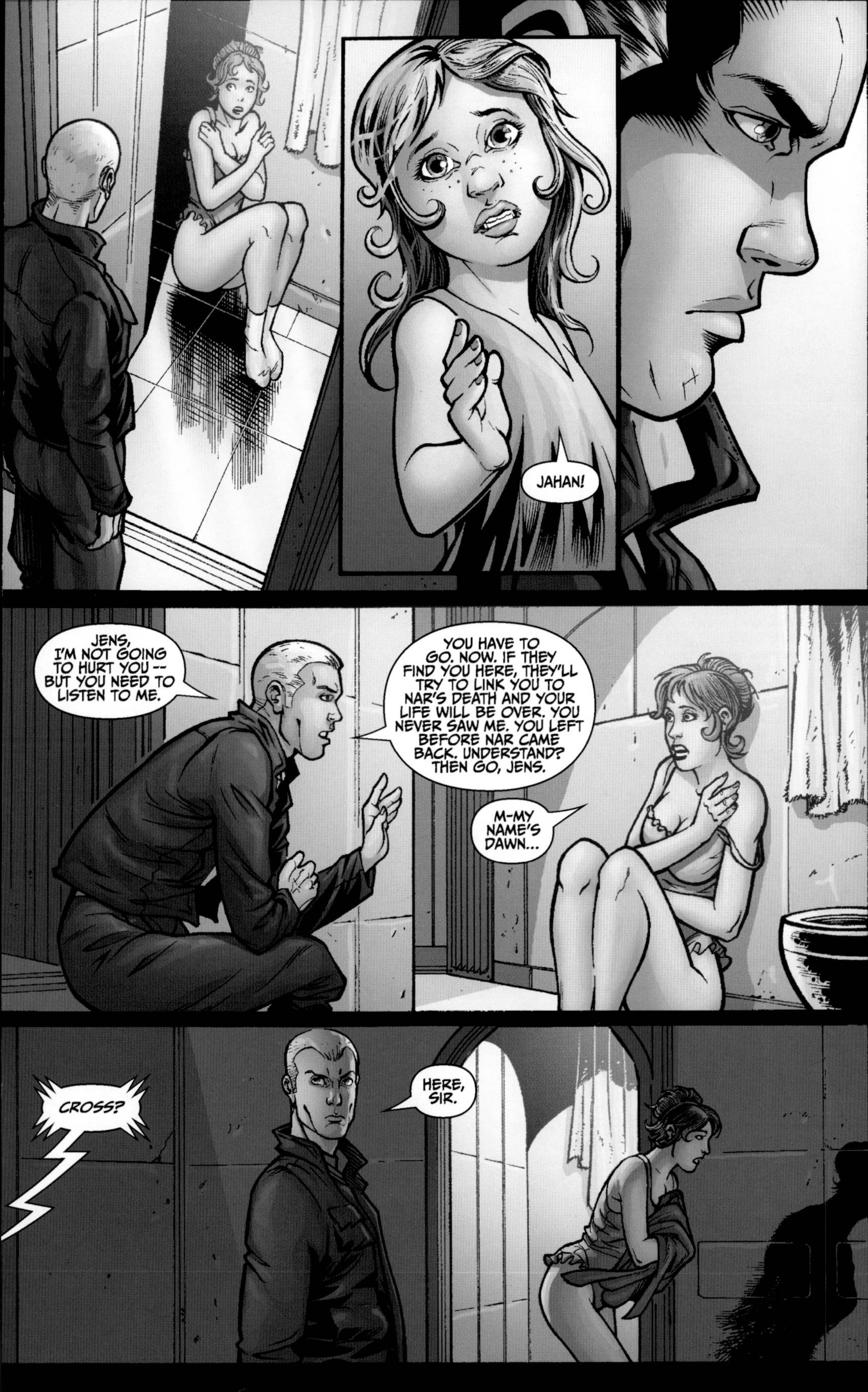
JAHAN!
JENS, I'M NOT GOING TO HURT YOU -- BUT YOU NEED TO LISTEN TO ME.
YOU HAVE TO GO. NOW. IF THEY FIND YOU HERE, THEY'LL TRY TO LINK YOU TO NAR'S DEATH AND YOUR LIFE WILL BE OVER. YOU NEVER SAW ME. YOU LEFT BEFORE NAR CAME BACK. UNDERSTAND? THEN GO, JENS.
M-MY NAME'S DAWN...
CROSS?
HERE, SIR.

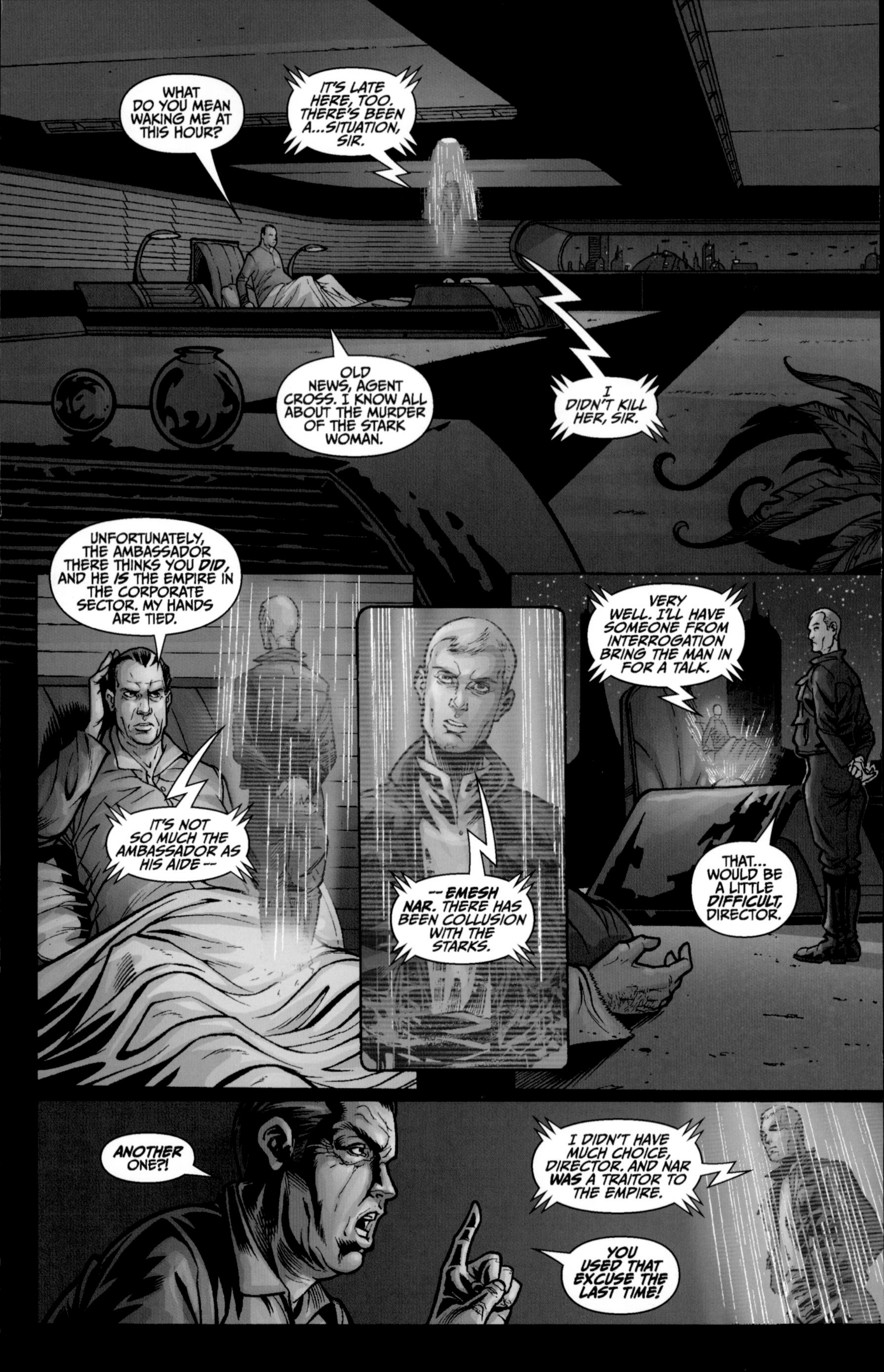
WHAT DO YOU MEAN WAKING ME AT THIS HOUR?
IT'S LATE HERE, TOO. THERE'S BEEN A...SITUATION, SIR.
OLD NEWS, AGENT CROSS. I KNOW ALL ABOUT THE MURDER OF THE STARK WOMAN.
I DIDN'T KILL HER, SIR.
UNFORTUNATELY, THE AMBASSADOR THERE THINKS YOU DID, AND HE IS THE EMPIRE IN THE CORPORATE SECTOR. MY HANDS ARE TIED.
IT'S NOT SO MUCH THE AMBASSADOR AS HIS AIDE --
-- EMESH NAR. THERE HAS BEEN COLLUSION WITH THE STARKS.
VERY WELL. I'LL HAVE SOMEONE FROM INTERROGATION BRING THE MAN IN FOR A TALK.
THAT... WOULD BE A LITTLE DIFFICULT, DIRECTOR.
ANOTHER ONE?!
I DIDN'T HAVE MUCH CHOICE, DIRECTOR. AND NAR WAS A TRAITOR TO THE EMPIRE.
YOU USED THAT EXCUSE THE LAST TIME!

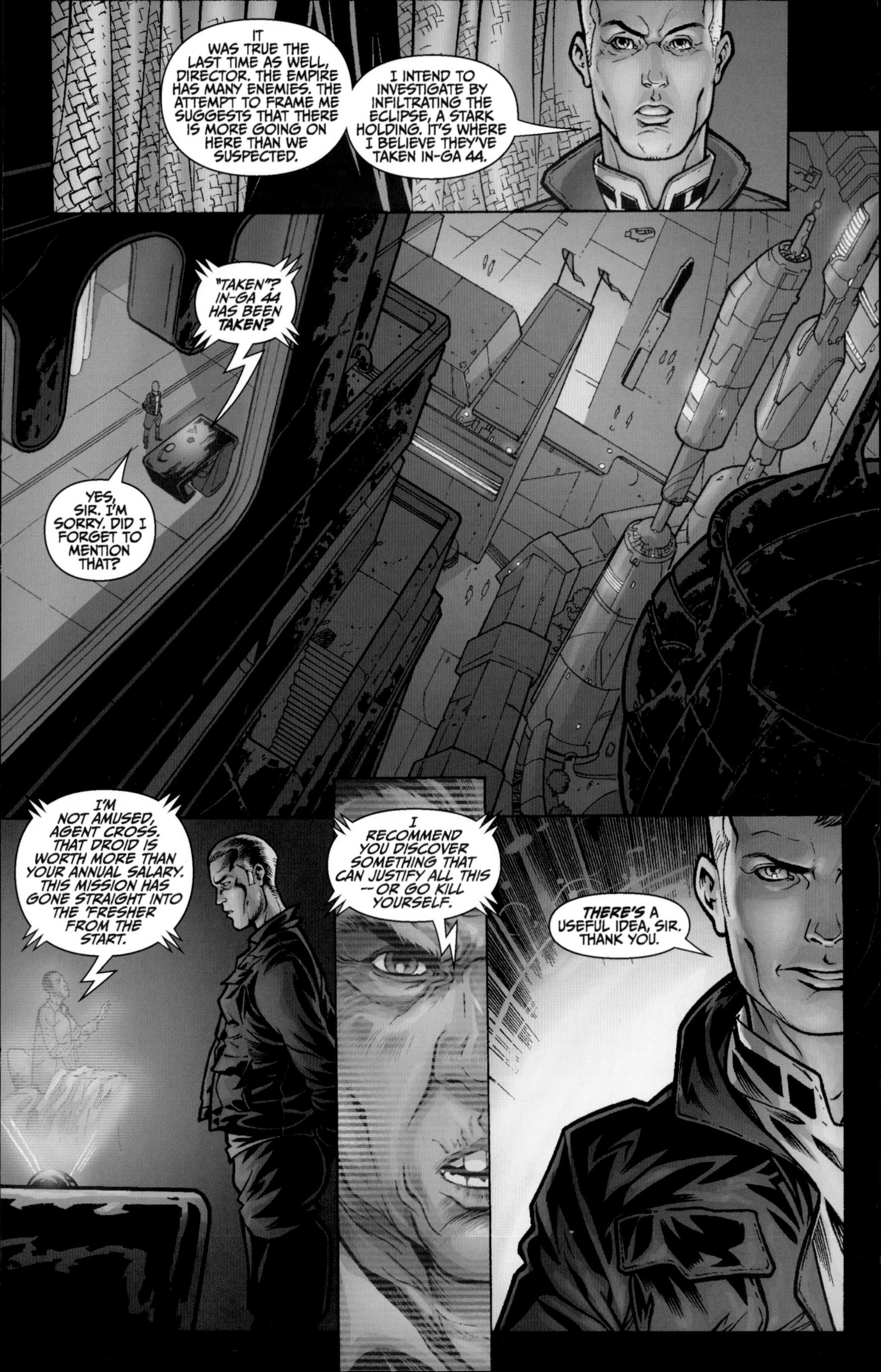
IT WAS TRUE THE LAST TIME AS WELL, DIRECTOR. THE EMPIRE HAS MANY ENEMIES. THE ATTEMPT TO FRAME ME SUGGESTS THAT THERE IS MORE GOING ON HERE THAN WE SUSPECTED.
I INTEND TO INVESTIGATE BY INFILTRATING THE ECLIPSE, A STARK HOLDING. IT'S WHERE I BELIEVE THEY'VE TAKEN IN-GA 44.
"TAKEN"? IN-GA 44 HAS BEEN *TAKEN?*
YES, SIR. I'M SORRY. DID I FORGET TO MENTION THAT?
I'M NOT AMUSED, AGENT CROSS. THAT DROID IS WORTH MORE THAN YOUR ANNUAL SALARY. THIS MISSION HAS GONE STRAIGHT INTO THE 'FRESHER FROM THE START.
I RECOMMEND YOU DISCOVER SOMETHING THAT CAN JUSTIFY ALL THIS --OR GO KILL YOURSELF.
THERE'S A USEFUL IDEA, SIR. THANK YOU.

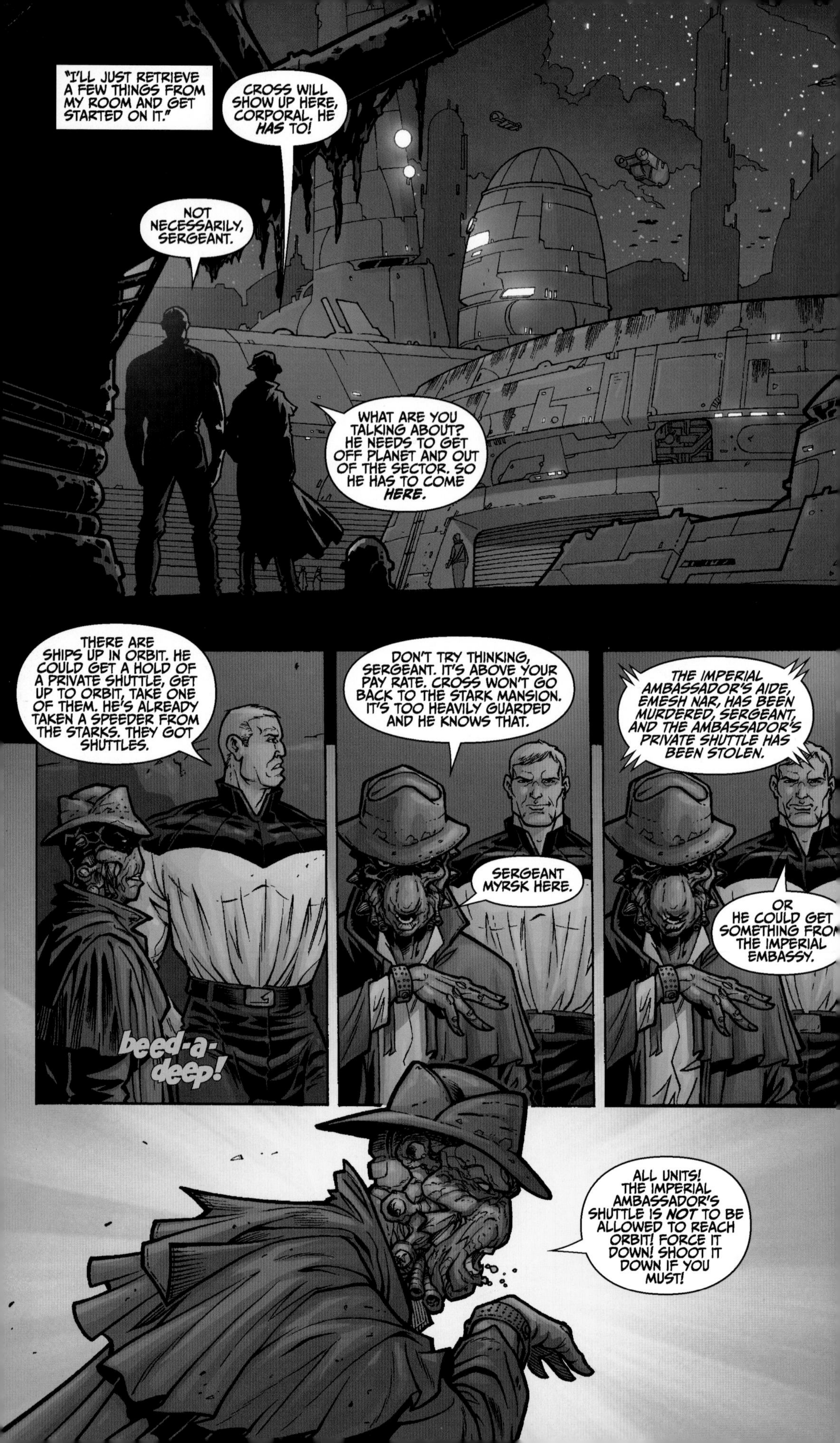
"I'LL JUST RETRIEVE A FEW THINGS FROM MY ROOM AND GET STARTED ON IT."
CROSS WILL SHOW UP HERE, CORPORAL. HE *HAS* TO!
NOT NECESSARILY, SERGEANT.
WHAT ARE YOU TALKING ABOUT? HE NEEDS TO GET OFF PLANET AND OUT OF THE SECTOR. SO HE HAS TO COME *HERE*.
THERE ARE SHIPS UP IN ORBIT. HE COULD GET A HOLD OF A PRIVATE SHUTTLE, GET UP TO ORBIT, TAKE ONE OF THEM. HE'S ALREADY TAKEN A SPEEDER FROM THE STARKS. THEY GOT SHUTTLES.
beed-a-deep!
DON'T TRY THINKING, SERGEANT. IT'S ABOVE YOUR PAY RATE. CROSS WON'T GO BACK TO THE STARK MANSION. IT'S TOO HEAVILY GUARDED AND HE KNOWS THAT.
SERGEANT MYRSK HERE.
THE IMPERIAL AMBASSADOR'S AIDE, EMESH NAR, HAS BEEN MURDERED, SERGEANT, AND THE AMBASSADOR'S PRIVATE SHUTTLE HAS BEEN STOLEN.
OR HE COULD GET SOMETHING FROM THE IMPERIAL EMBASSY.
ALL UNITS! THE IMPERIAL AMBASSADOR'S SHUTTLE IS *NOT* TO BE ALLOWED TO REACH ORBIT! FORCE IT DOWN! SHOOT IT DOWN IF YOU MUST!

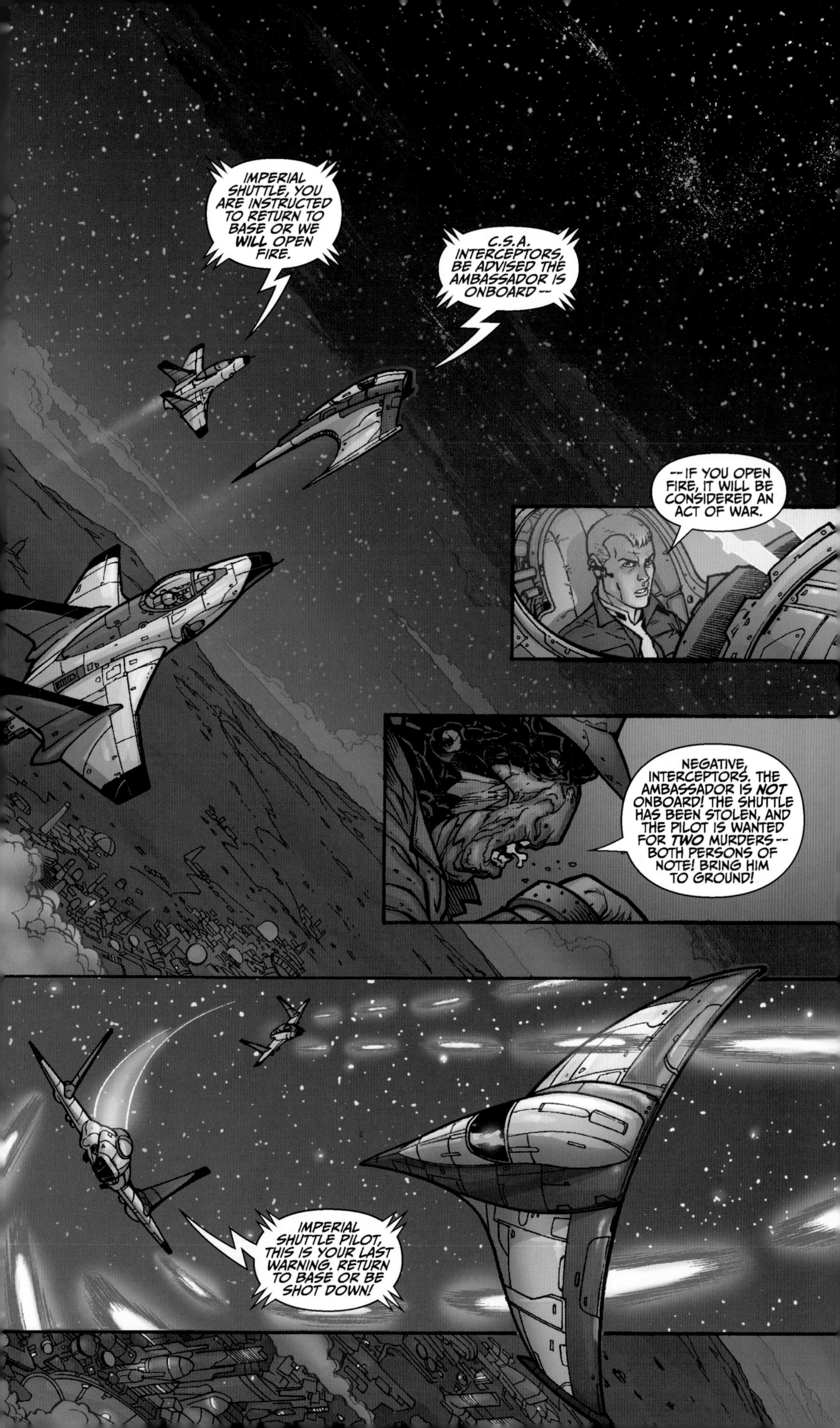
IMPERIAL SHUTTLE, YOU ARE INSTRUCTED TO RETURN TO BASE OR WE WILL OPEN FIRE.
C.S.A. INTERCEPTORS, BE ADVISED THE AMBASSADOR IS ONBOARD--
--IF YOU OPEN FIRE, IT WILL BE CONSIDERED AN ACT OF WAR.
NEGATIVE, INTERCEPTORS. THE AMBASSADOR IS NOT ONBOARD! THE SHUTTLE HAS BEEN STOLEN, AND THE PILOT IS WANTED FOR TWO MURDERS--BOTH PERSONS OF NOTE! BRING HIM TO GROUND!
IMPERIAL SHUTTLE PILOT, THIS IS YOUR LAST WARNING. RETURN TO BASE OR BE SHOT DOWN!

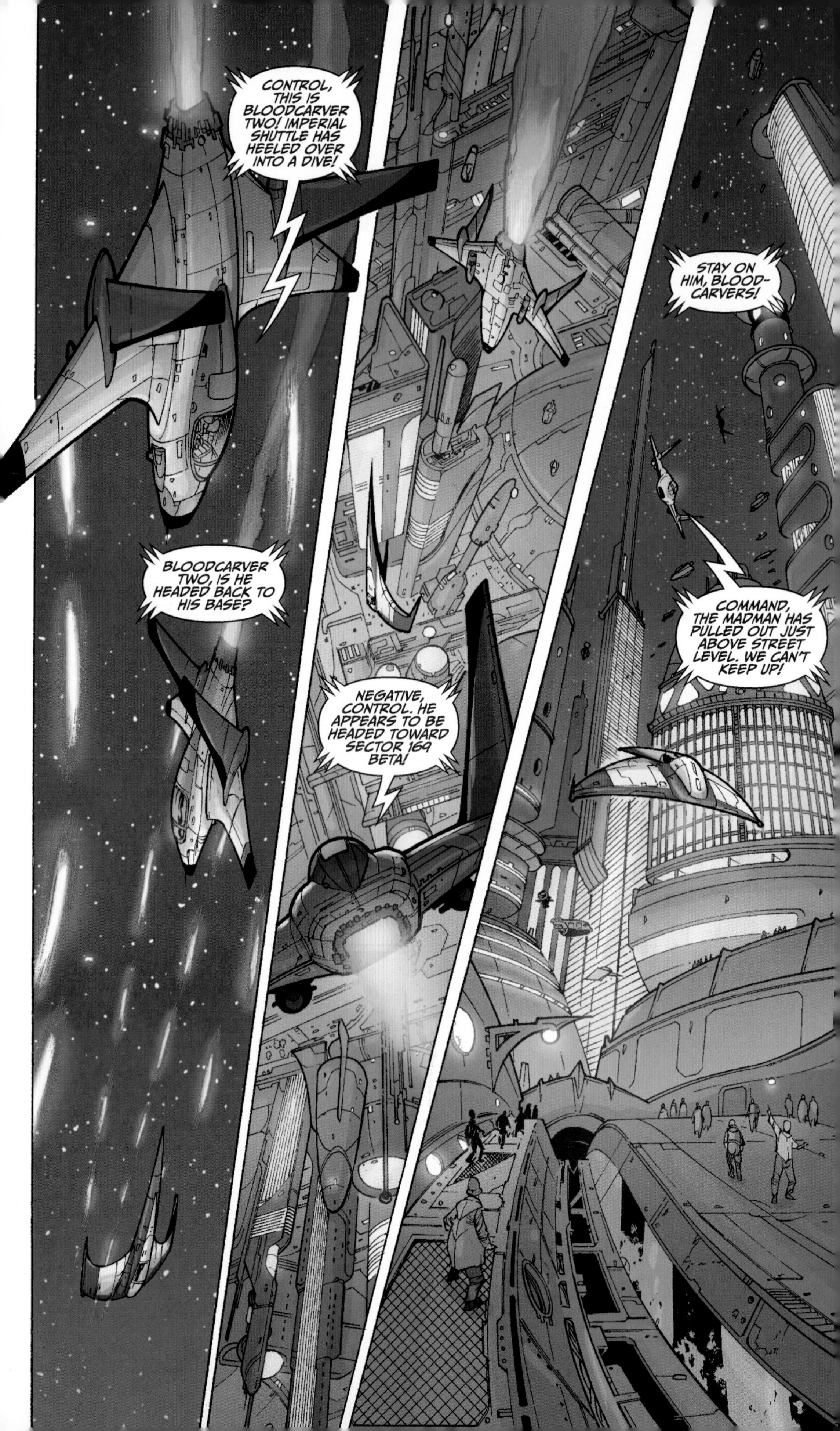
CONTROL, THIS IS BLOODCARVER TWO! IMPERIAL SHUTTLE HAS HEELED OVER INTO A DIVE!
BLOODCARVER TWO, IS HE HEADED BACK TO HIS BASE?
NEGATIVE, CONTROL. HE APPEARS TO BE HEADED TOWARD SECTOR 169 BETA!
STAY ON HIM, BLOOD-CARVERS!
COMMAND, THE MADMAN HAS PULLED OUT JUST ABOVE STREET LEVEL. WE CAN'T KEEP UP!

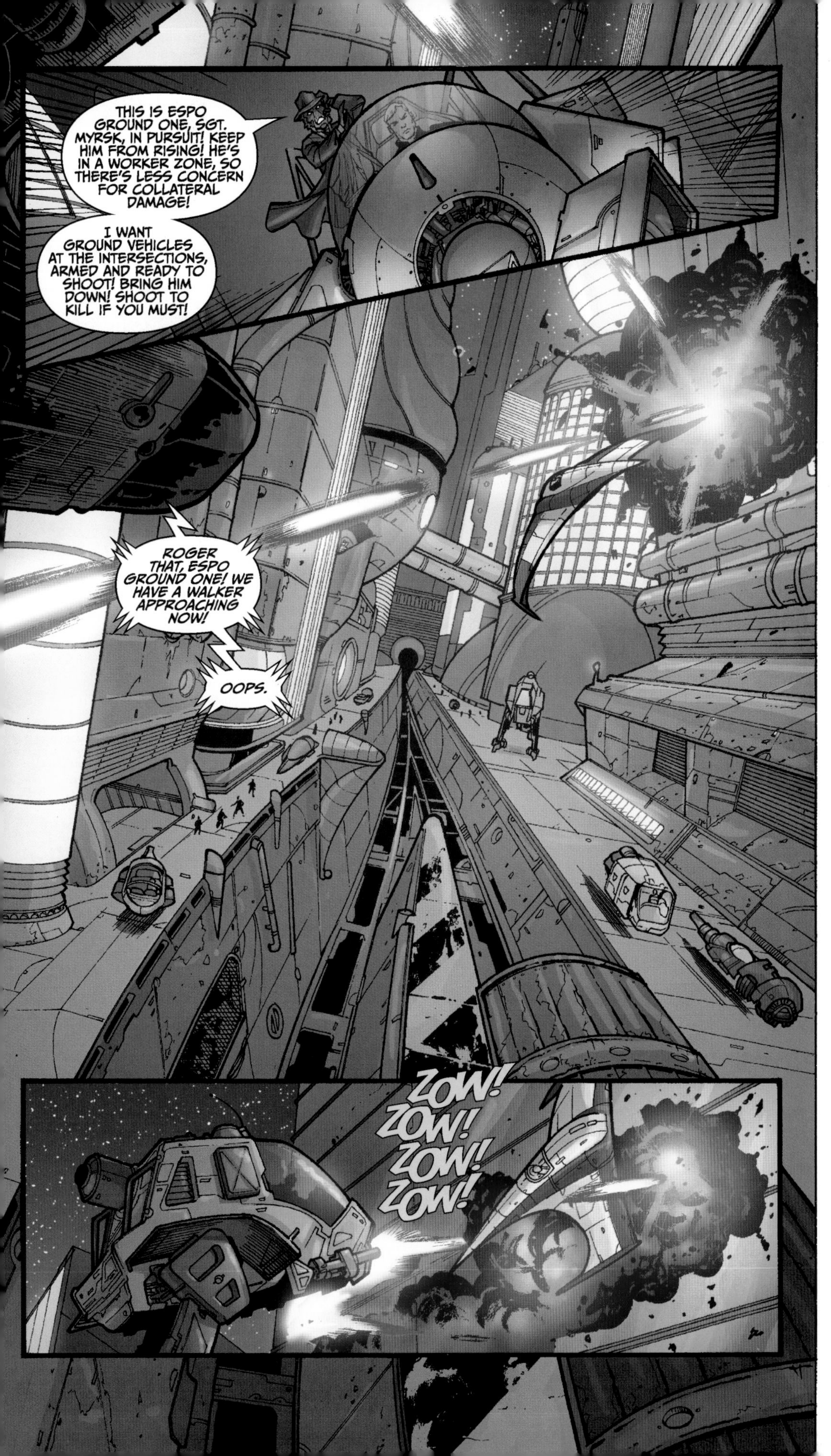
THIS IS ESPO GROUND ONE, SGT. MYRSK, IN PURSUIT! KEEP HIM FROM RISING! HE'S IN A WORKER ZONE, SO THERE'S LESS CONCERN FOR COLLATERAL DAMAGE!
I WANT GROUND VEHICLES AT THE INTERSECTIONS, ARMED AND READY TO SHOOT! BRING HIM DOWN! SHOOT TO KILL IF YOU MUST!
ROGER THAT, ESPO GROUND ONE! WE HAVE A WALKER APPROACHING NOW!
OOPS.
ZOW! ZOW! ZOW! ZOW!

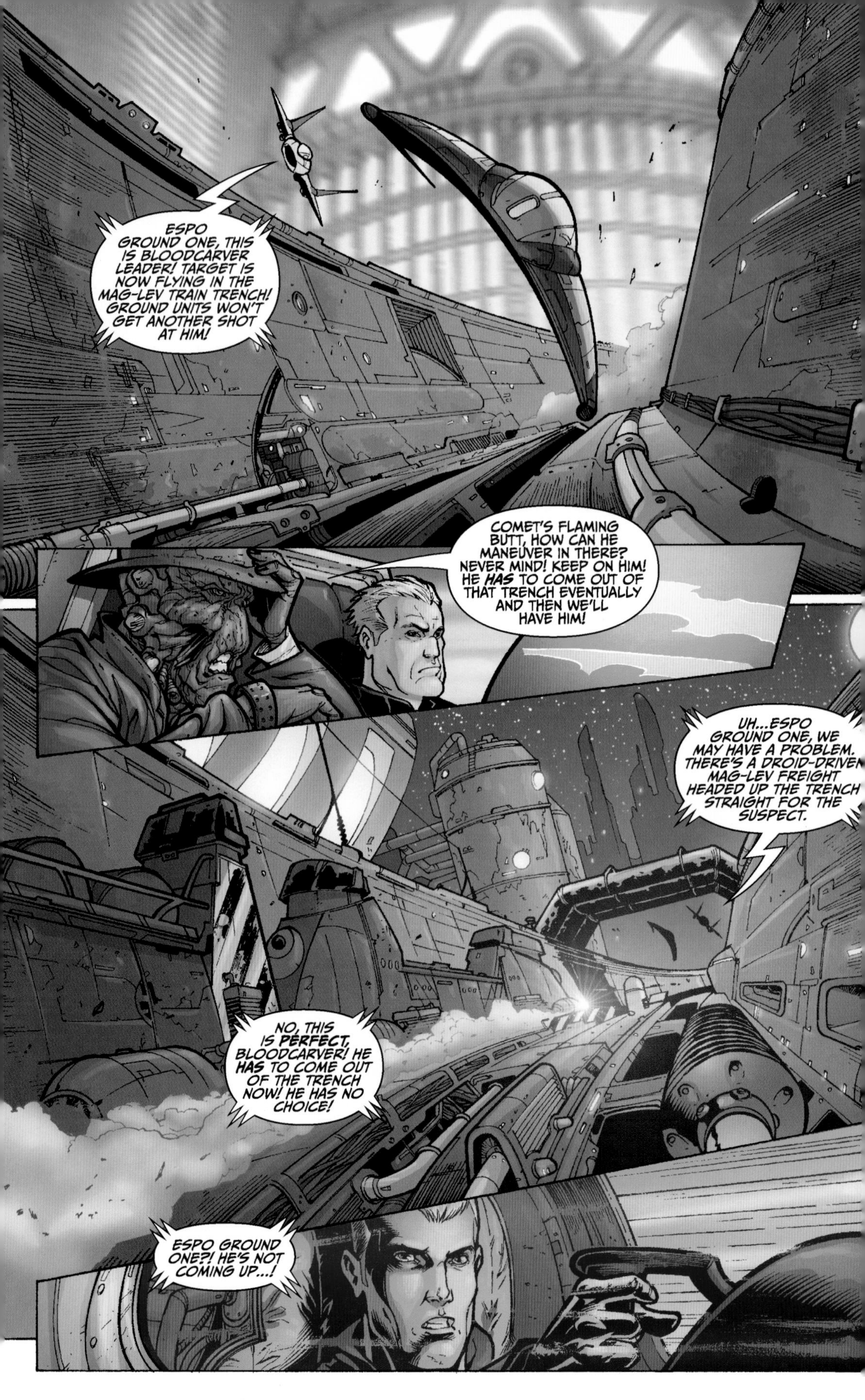
ESPO GROUND ONE, THIS IS BLOODCARVER LEADER! TARGET IS NOW FLYING IN THE MAG-LEV TRAIN TRENCH! GROUND UNITS WON'T GET ANOTHER SHOT AT HIM!
COMET'S FLAMING BUTT, HOW CAN HE MANEUVER IN THERE? NEVER MIND! KEEP ON HIM! HE HAS TO COME OUT OF THAT TRENCH EVENTUALLY AND THEN WE'LL HAVE HIM!
UH...ESPO GROUND ONE, WE MAY HAVE A PROBLEM. THERE'S A DROID-DRIVEN MAG-LEV FREIGHT HEADED UP THE TRENCH STRAIGHT FOR THE SUSPECT.
NO, THIS IS PERFECT, BLOODCARVER! HE HAS TO COME OUT OF THE TRENCH NOW! HE HAS NO CHOICE!
ESPO GROUND ONE?! HE'S NOT COMING UP...!

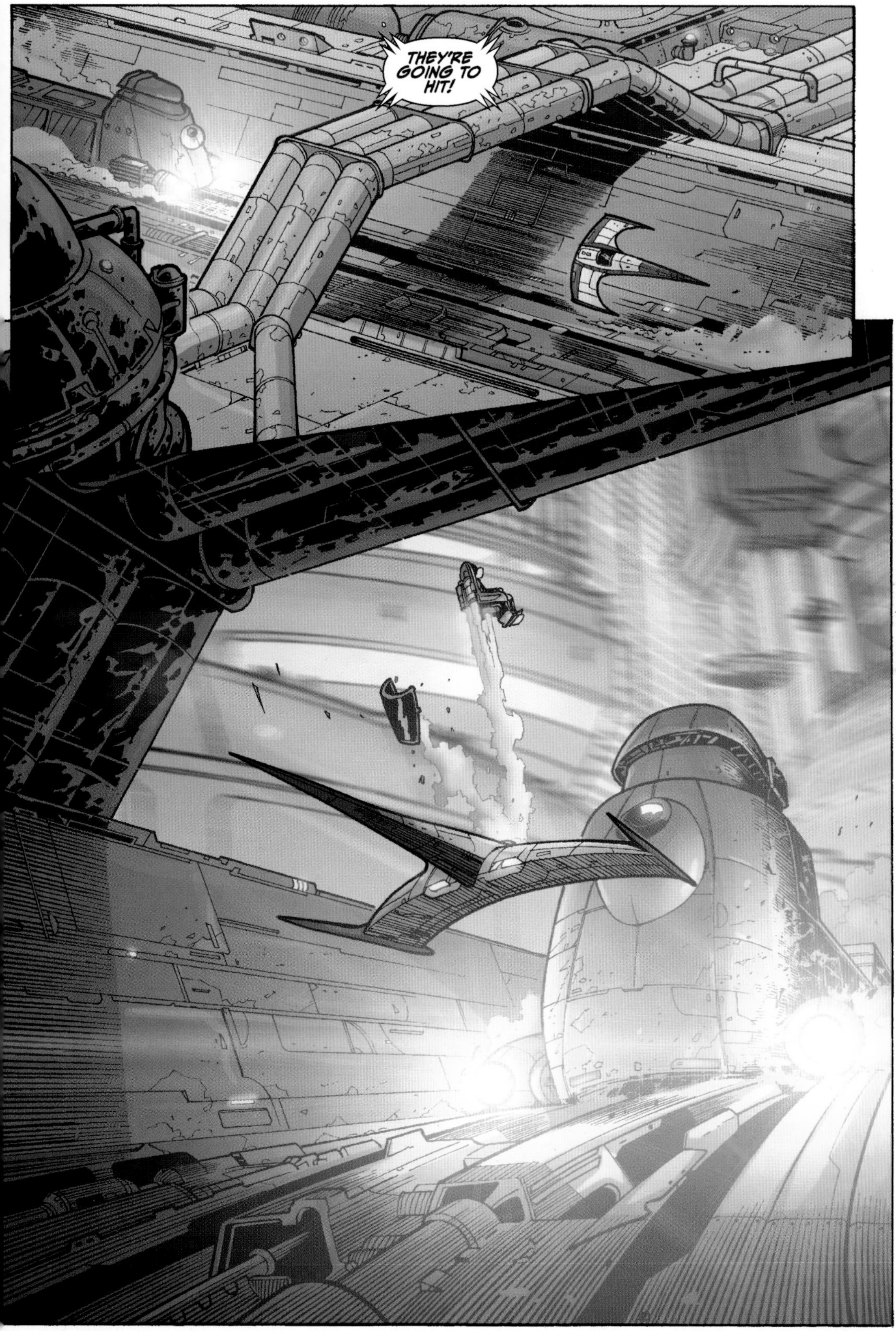
THEY'RE GOING TO HIT!

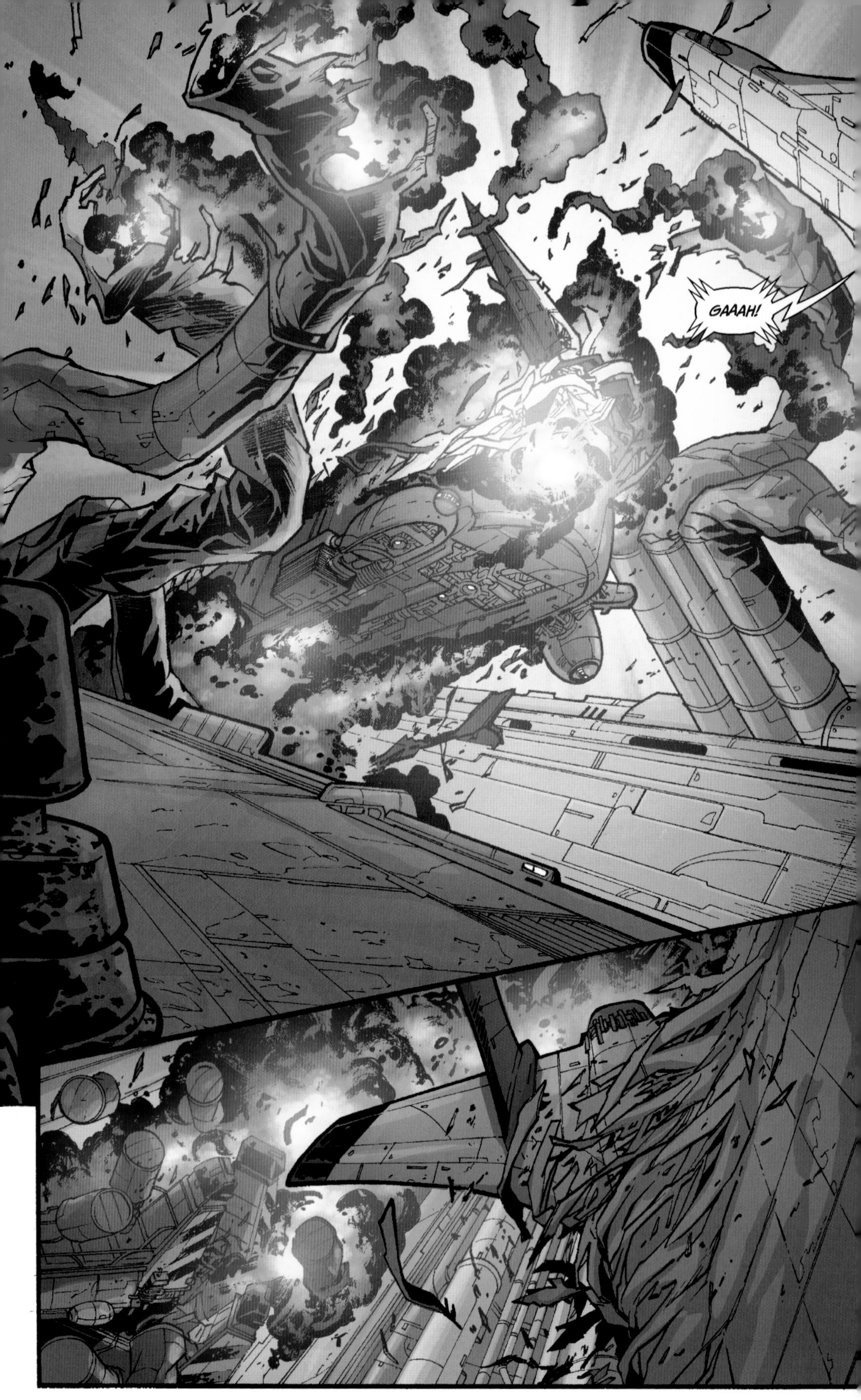
GAAAH!

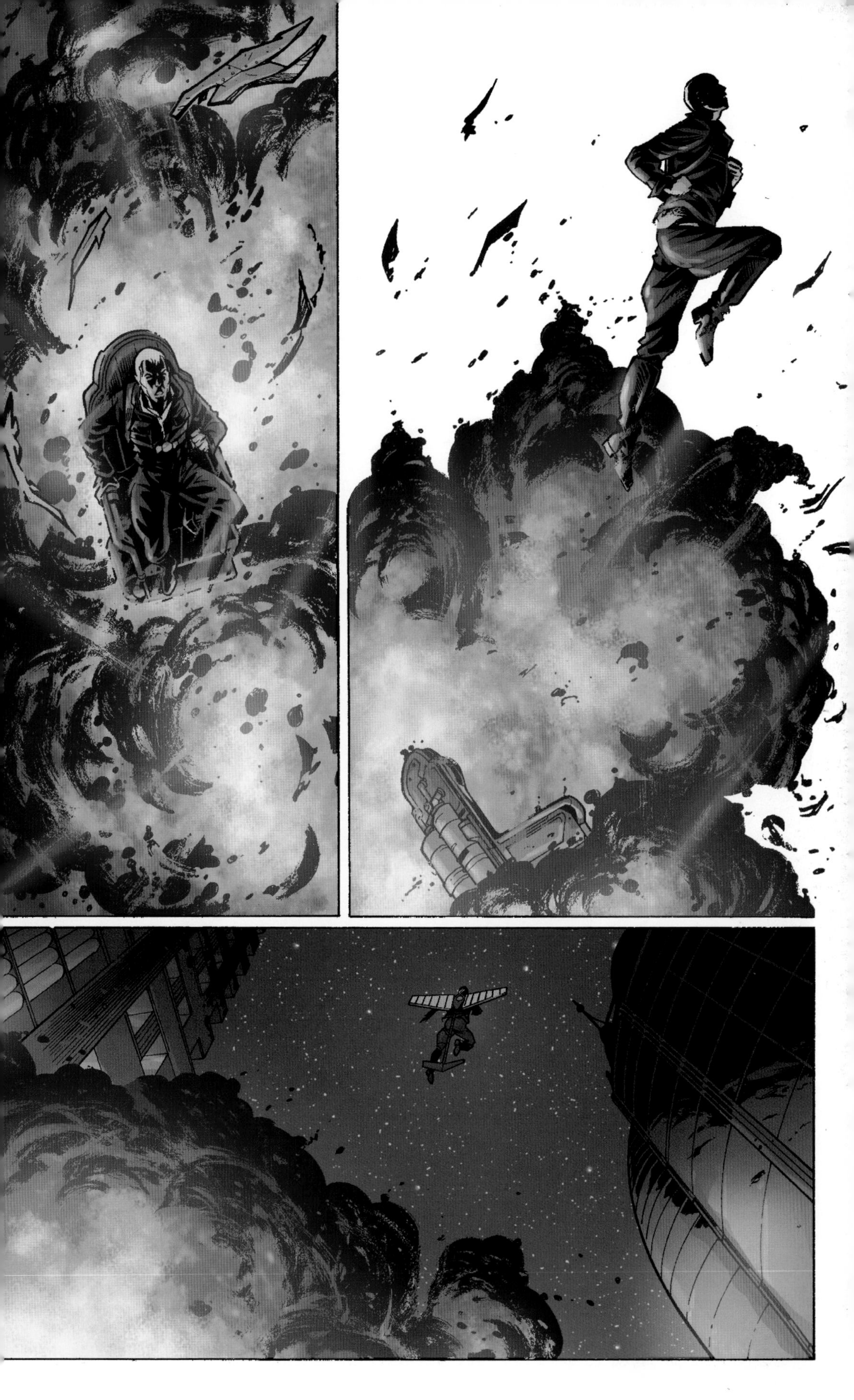

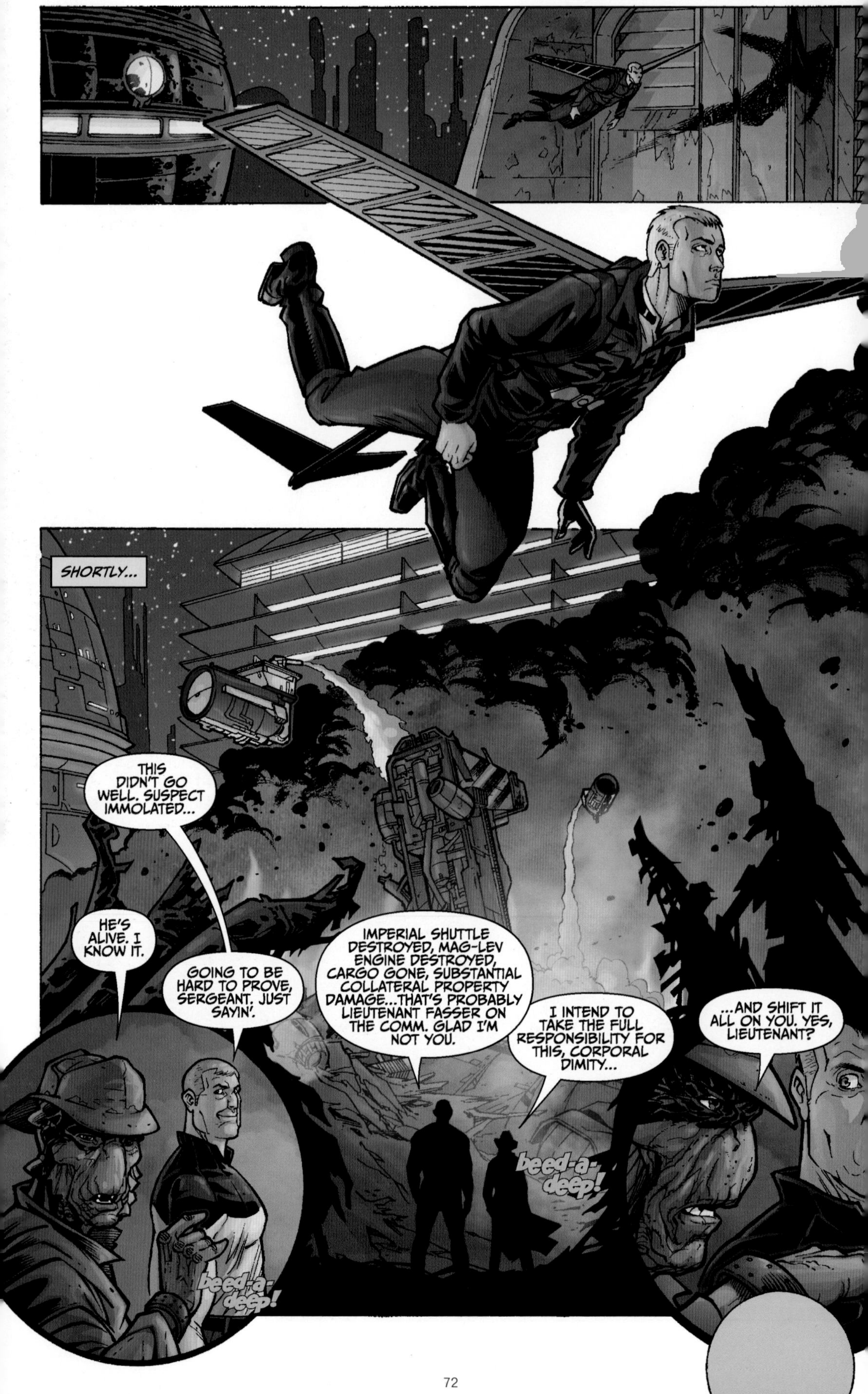
SHORTLY...
THIS DIDN'T GO WELL. SUSPECT IMMOLATED...
HE'S ALIVE. I KNOW IT.
GOING TO BE HARD TO PROVE, SERGEANT. JUST SAYIN'.
IMPERIAL SHUTTLE DESTROYED, MAG-LEV ENGINE DESTROYED, CARGO GONE, SUBSTANTIAL COLLATERAL PROPERTY DAMAGE...THAT'S PROBABLY LIEUTENANT FASSER ON THE COMM. GLAD I'M NOT YOU.
beed-a-deep!
beed-a-deep!
I INTEND TO TAKE THE FULL RESPONSIBILITY FOR THIS, CORPORAL DIMITY...
...AND SHIFT IT ALL ON YOU. YES, LIEUTENANT?

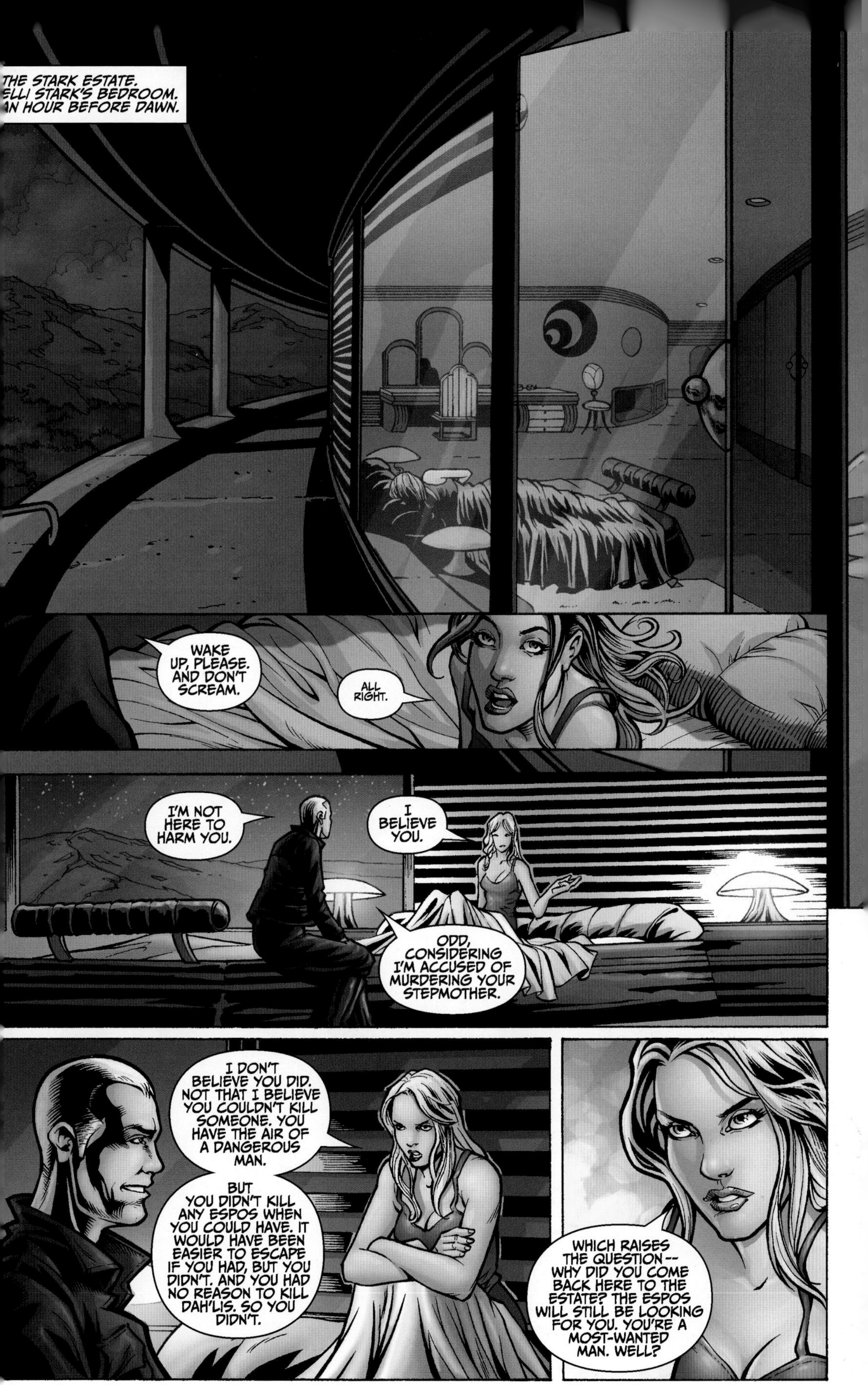

THE STARK ESTATE. ELLI STARK'S BEDROOM. AN HOUR BEFORE DAWN.
WAKE UP, PLEASE. AND DON'T SCREAM.
ALL RIGHT.
I'M NOT HERE TO HARM YOU.
I BELIEVE YOU.
ODD, CONSIDERING I'M ACCUSED OF MURDERING YOUR STEPMOTHER.
I DON'T BELIEVE YOU DID. NOT THAT I BELIEVE YOU COULDN'T KILL SOMEONE. YOU HAVE THE AIR OF A DANGEROUS MAN.
BUT YOU DIDN'T KILL ANY ESPOS WHEN YOU COULD HAVE. IT WOULD HAVE BEEN EASIER TO ESCAPE IF YOU HAD, BUT YOU DIDN'T. AND YOU HAD NO REASON TO KILL DAH'LIS. SO YOU DIDN'T.
WHICH RAISES THE QUESTION -- WHY DID YOU COME BACK HERE TO THE ESTATE? THE ESPOS WILL STILL BE LOOKING FOR YOU. YOU'RE A MOST-WANTED MAN. WELL?

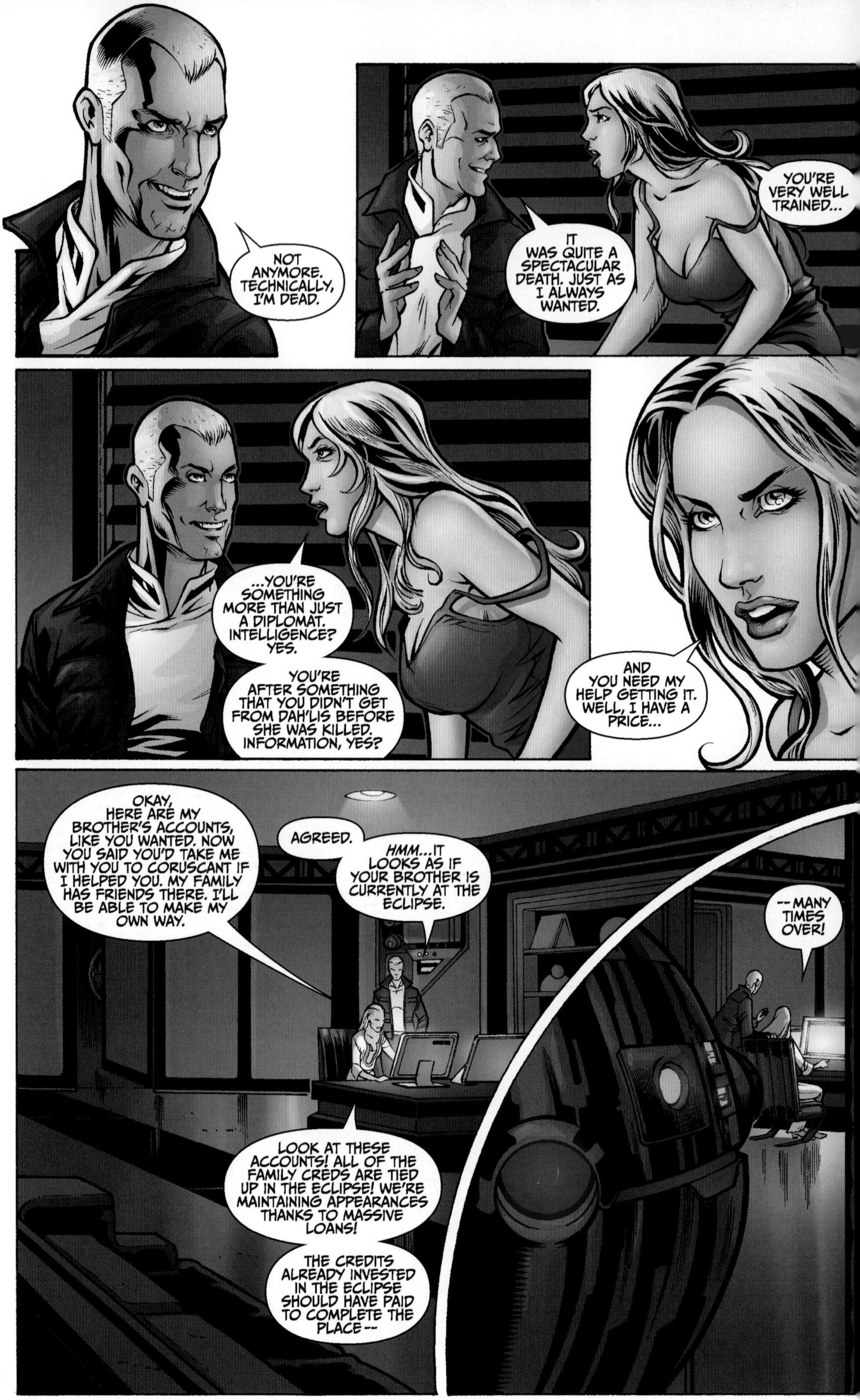
NOT ANYMORE. TECHNICALLY, I'M DEAD.
IT WAS QUITE A SPECTACULAR DEATH. JUST AS I ALWAYS WANTED.
YOU'RE VERY WELL TRAINED...
...YOU'RE SOMETHING MORE THAN JUST A DIPLOMAT. INTELLIGENCE? YES.
YOU'RE AFTER SOMETHING THAT YOU DIDN'T GET FROM DAH'LIS BEFORE SHE WAS KILLED. INFORMATION, YES?
AND YOU NEED MY HELP GETTING IT. WELL, I HAVE A PRICE...
OKAY, HERE ARE MY BROTHER'S ACCOUNTS, LIKE YOU WANTED. NOW YOU SAID YOU'D TAKE ME WITH YOU TO CORUSCANT IF I HELPED YOU. MY FAMILY HAS FRIENDS THERE. I'LL BE ABLE TO MAKE MY OWN WAY.
AGREED.
HMM...IT LOOKS AS IF YOUR BROTHER IS CURRENTLY AT THE ECLIPSE.
LOOK AT THESE ACCOUNTS! ALL OF THE FAMILY CREDS ARE TIED UP IN THE ECLIPSE! WE'RE MAINTAINING APPEARANCES THANKS TO MASSIVE LOANS!
THE CREDITS ALREADY INVESTED IN THE ECLIPSE SHOULD HAVE PAID TO COMPLETE THE PLACE --
-- MANY TIMES OVER!

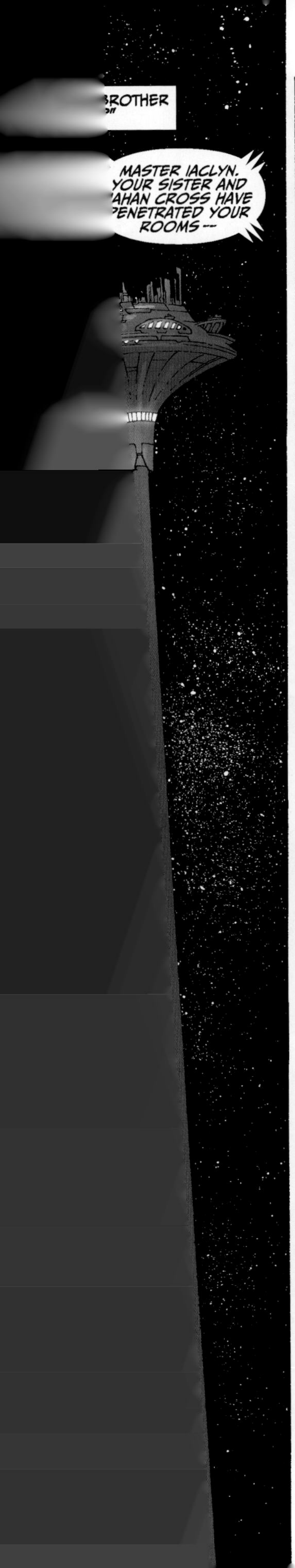

BROTHER
MASTER IACLYN. YOUR SISTER AND AHAN CROSS HAVE PENETRATED YOUR ROOMS --

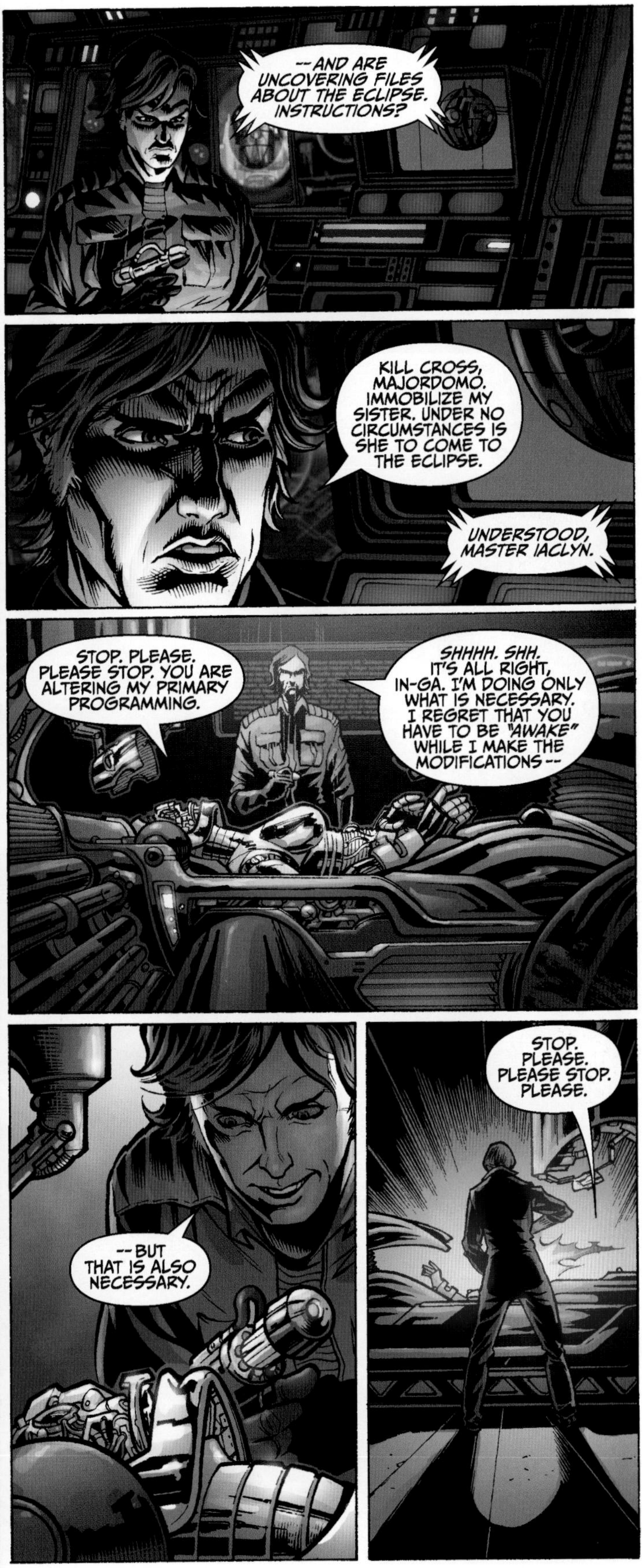

--AND ARE UNCOVERING FILES ABOUT THE ECLIPSE. INSTRUCTIONS?
KILL CROSS, MAJORDOMO. IMMOBILIZE MY SISTER. UNDER NO CIRCUMSTANCES IS SHE TO COME TO THE ECLIPSE.
UNDERSTOOD, MASTER IACLYN.
STOP. PLEASE. PLEASE STOP. YOU ARE ALTERING MY PRIMARY PROGRAMMING.
SHHHH. SHH. IT'S ALL RIGHT, IN-GA. I'M DOING ONLY WHAT IS NECESSARY. I REGRET THAT YOU HAVE TO BE "AWAKE" WHILE I MAKE THE MODIFICATIONS--
--BUT THAT IS ALSO NECESSARY.
STOP. PLEASE. PLEASE STOP. PLEASE.

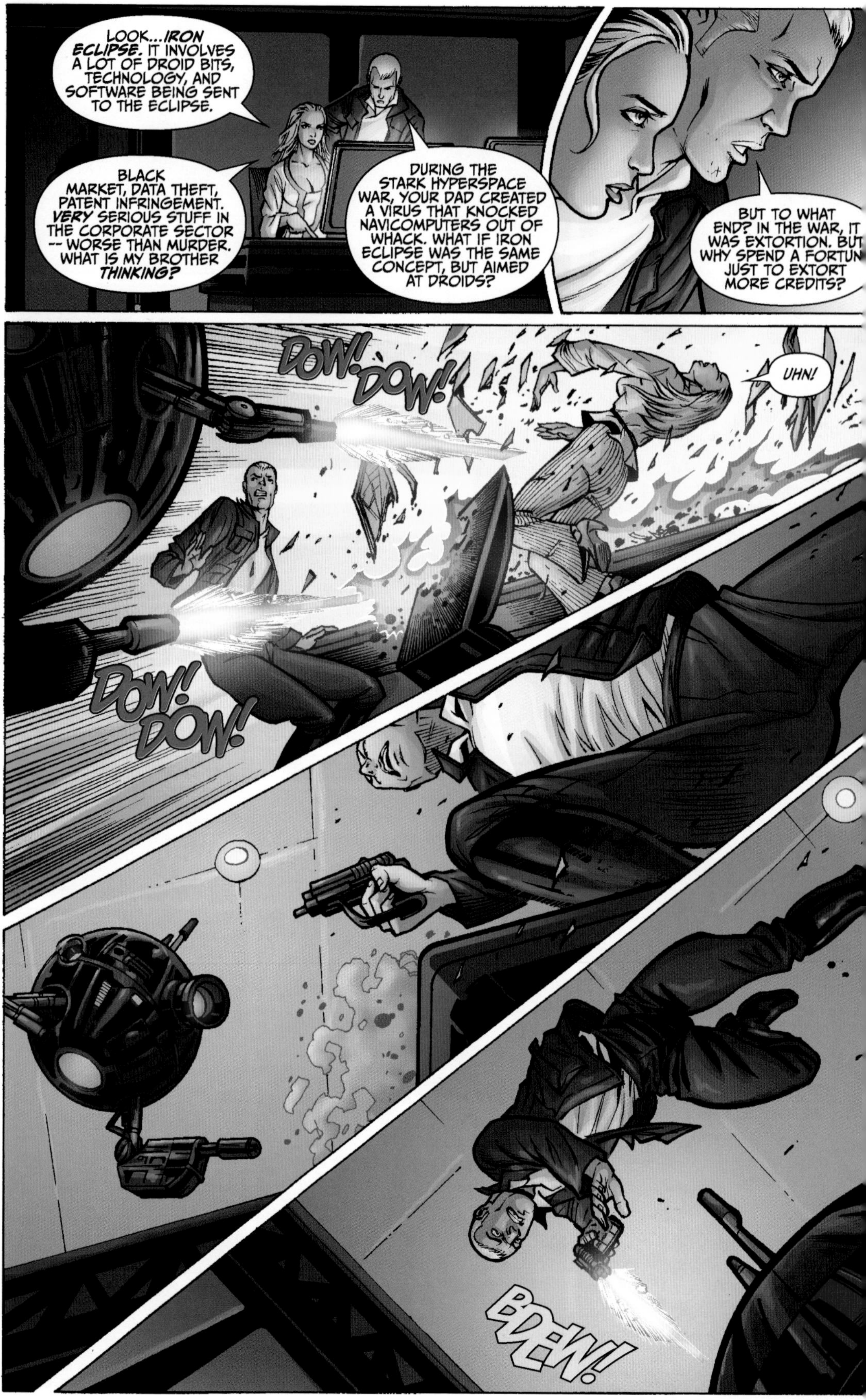
LOOK... IRON ECLIPSE. IT INVOLVES A LOT OF DROID BITS, TECHNOLOGY, AND SOFTWARE BEING SENT TO THE ECLIPSE.
BLACK MARKET, DATA THEFT, PATENT INFRINGEMENT. VERY SERIOUS STUFF IN THE CORPORATE SECTOR -- WORSE THAN MURDER. WHAT IS MY BROTHER THINKING?
DURING THE STARK HYPERSPACE WAR, YOUR DAD CREATED A VIRUS THAT KNOCKED NAVICOMPUTERS OUT OF WHACK. WHAT IF IRON ECLIPSE WAS THE SAME CONCEPT, BUT AIMED AT DROIDS?
BUT TO WHAT END? IN THE WAR, IT WAS EXTORTION. BUT WHY SPEND A FORTUN JUST TO EXTORT MORE CREDITS?
DOW! DOW!
UHN!
DOW! DOW!
BDEW!

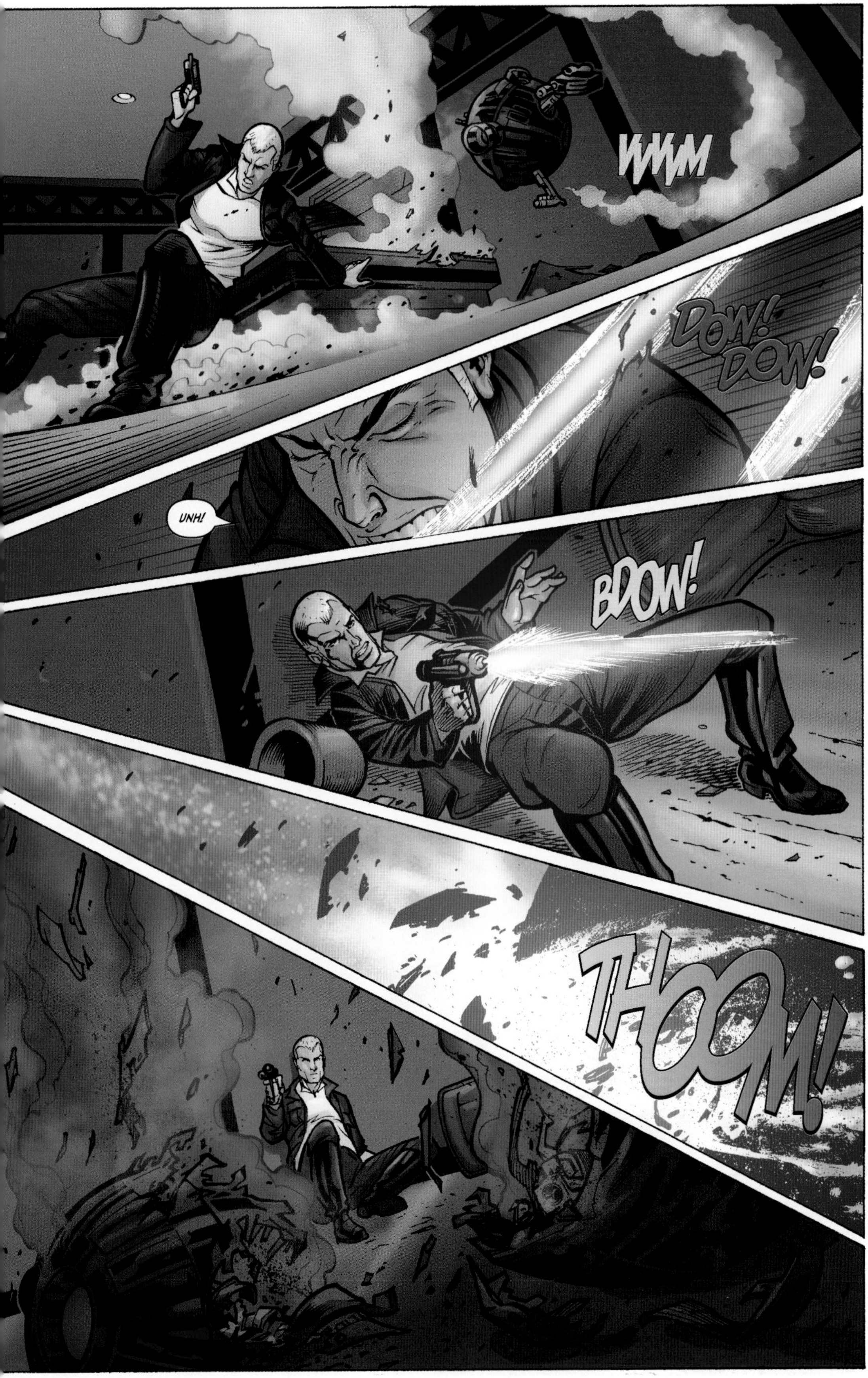
VWVM
DOW! DOW!
UNH!
BDOW!
THOOM!

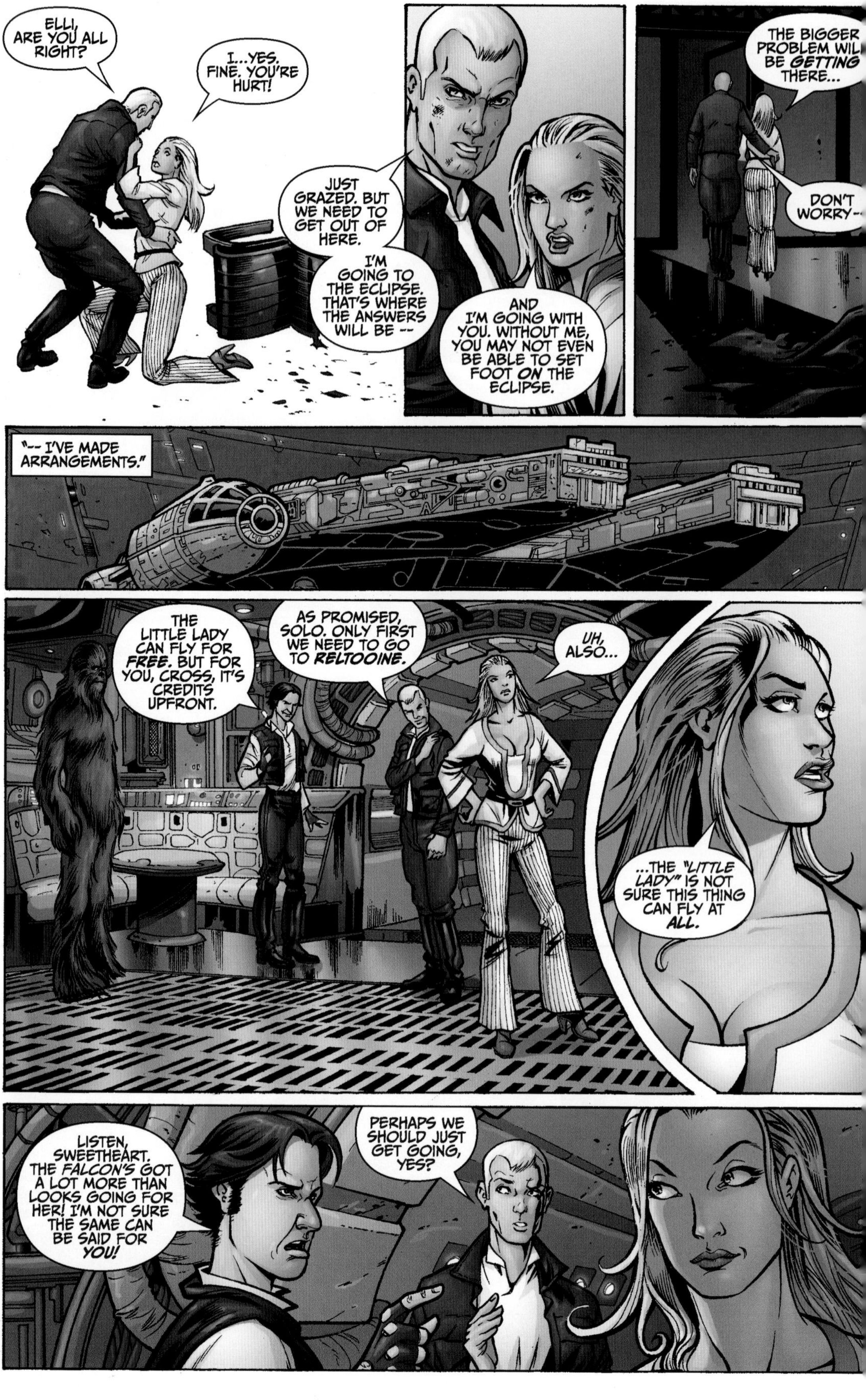
ELLI, ARE YOU ALL RIGHT?
I...YES. FINE. YOU'RE HURT!
JUST GRAZED. BUT WE NEED TO GET OUT OF HERE.
I'M GOING TO THE ECLIPSE. THAT'S WHERE THE ANSWERS WILL BE --
AND I'M GOING WITH YOU. WITHOUT ME, YOU MAY NOT EVEN BE ABLE TO SET FOOT ON THE ECLIPSE.
THE BIGGER PROBLEM WILL BE GETTING THERE...
DON'T WORRY--
"-- I'VE MADE ARRANGEMENTS."
THE LITTLE LADY CAN FLY FOR FREE. BUT FOR YOU, CROSS, IT'S CREDITS UPFRONT.
AS PROMISED, SOLO. ONLY FIRST WE NEED TO GO TO RELTOOINE.
UH, ALSO...
...THE "LITTLE LADY" IS NOT SURE THIS THING CAN FLY AT ALL.
LISTEN, SWEETHEART. THE FALCON'S GOT A LOT MORE THAN LOOKS GOING FOR HER! I'M NOT SURE THE SAME CAN BE SAID FOR YOU!
PERHAPS WE SHOULD JUST GET GOING, YES?

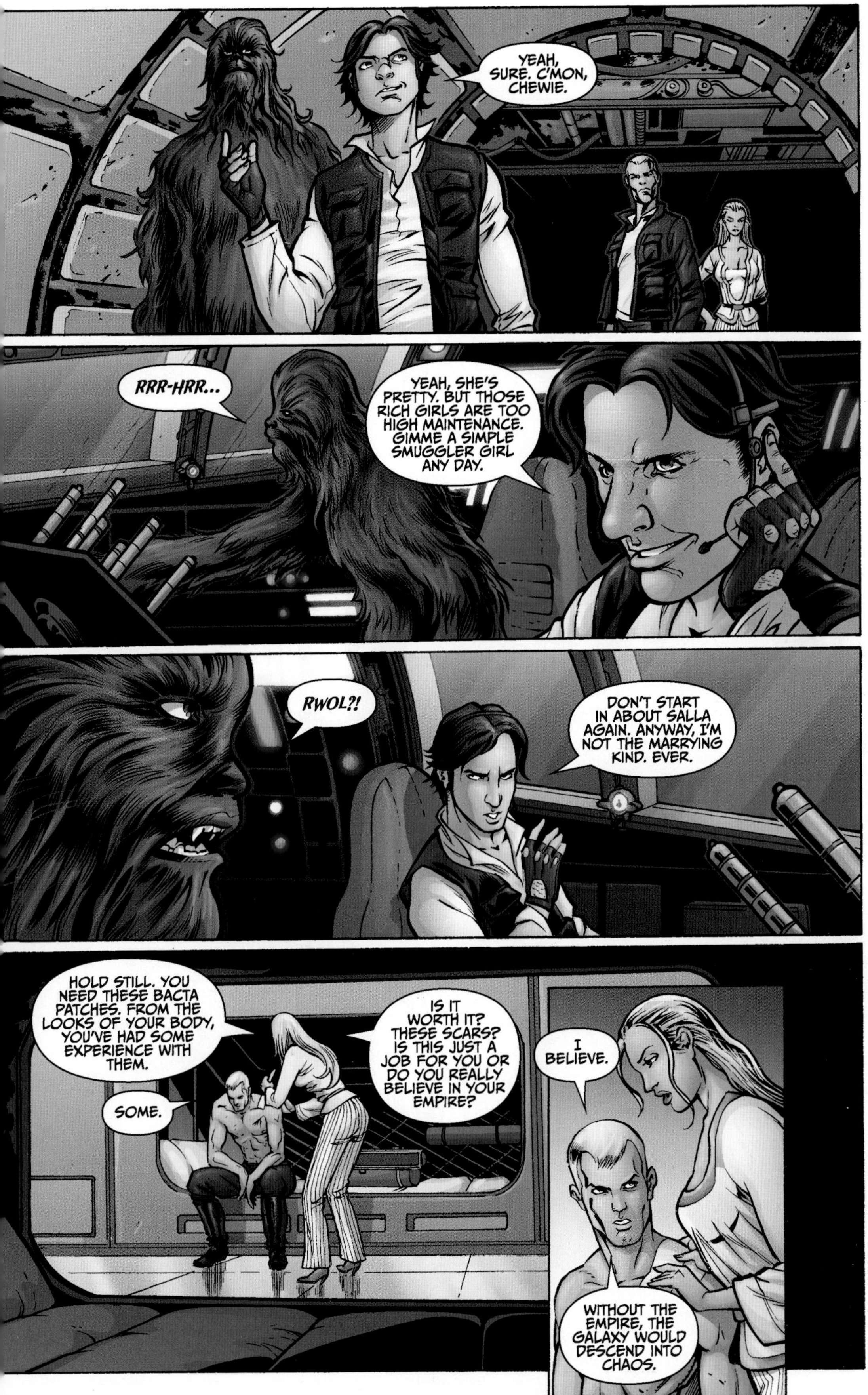

YEAH, SURE. C'MON, CHEWIE.
RRR-HRR...
YEAH, SHE'S PRETTY. BUT THOSE RICH GIRLS ARE TOO HIGH MAINTENANCE. GIMME A SIMPLE SMUGGLER GIRL ANY DAY.
RWOL?!
DON'T START IN ABOUT SALLA AGAIN. ANYWAY, I'M NOT THE MARRYING KIND. EVER.
HOLD STILL. YOU NEED THESE BACTA PATCHES. FROM THE LOOKS OF YOUR BODY, YOU'VE HAD SOME EXPERIENCE WITH THEM.
SOME.
IS IT WORTH IT? THESE SCARS? IS THIS JUST A JOB FOR YOU OR DO YOU REALLY BELIEVE IN YOUR EMPIRE?
I BELIEVE.
WITHOUT THE EMPIRE, THE GALAXY WOULD DESCEND INTO CHAOS.

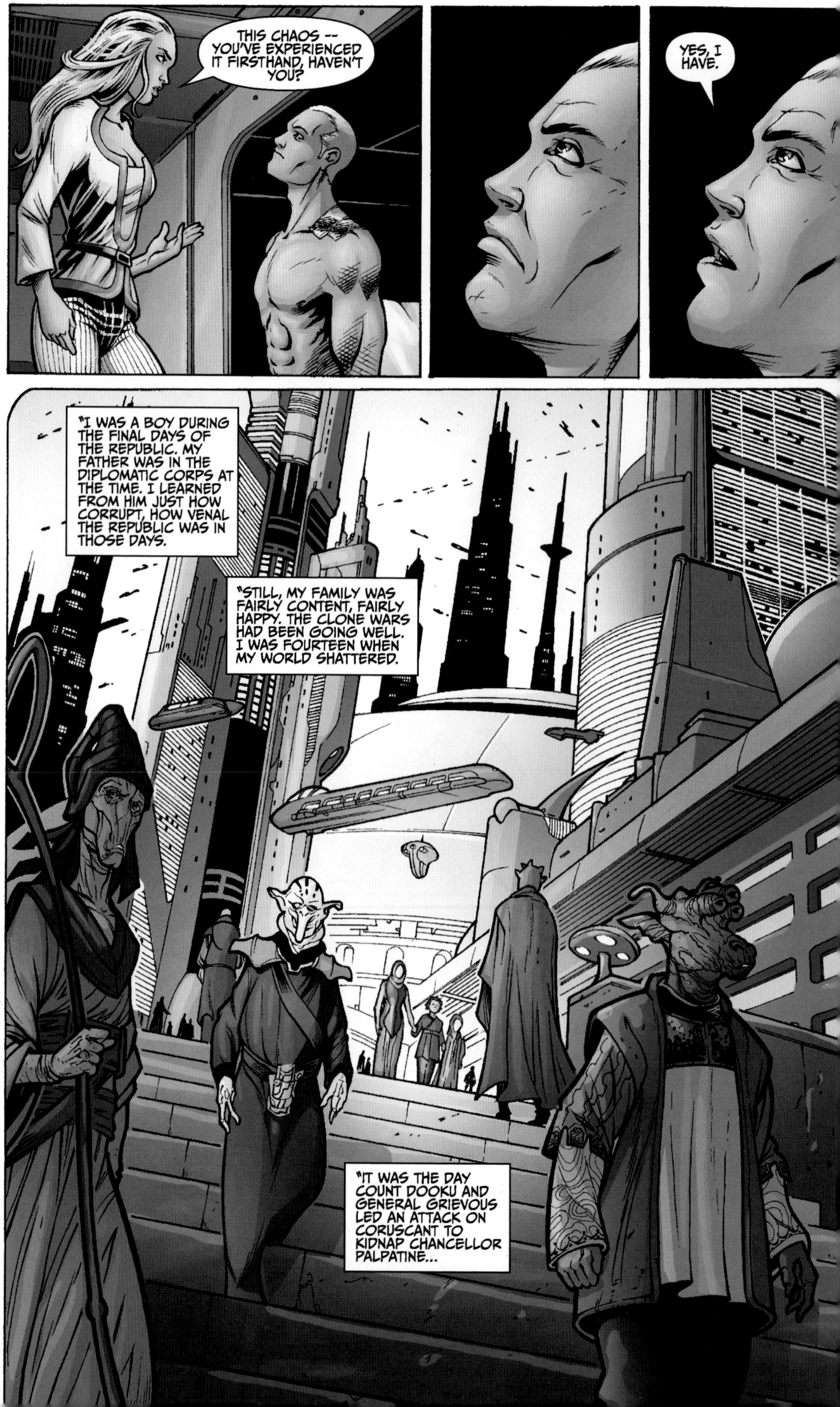

THIS CHAOS -- YOU'VE EXPERIENCED IT FIRSTHAND, HAVEN'T YOU?
YES, I HAVE.
"I WAS A BOY DURING THE FINAL DAYS OF THE REPUBLIC. MY FATHER WAS IN THE DIPLOMATIC CORPS AT THE TIME. I LEARNED FROM HIM JUST HOW CORRUPT, HOW VENAL THE REPUBLIC WAS IN THOSE DAYS.
"STILL, MY FAMILY WAS FAIRLY CONTENT, FAIRLY HAPPY. THE CLONE WARS HAD BEEN GOING WELL. I WAS FOURTEEN WHEN MY WORLD SHATTERED.
"IT WAS THE DAY COUNT DOOKU AND GENERAL GRIEVOUS LED AN ATTACK ON CORUSCANT TO KIDNAP CHANCELLOR PALPATINE...

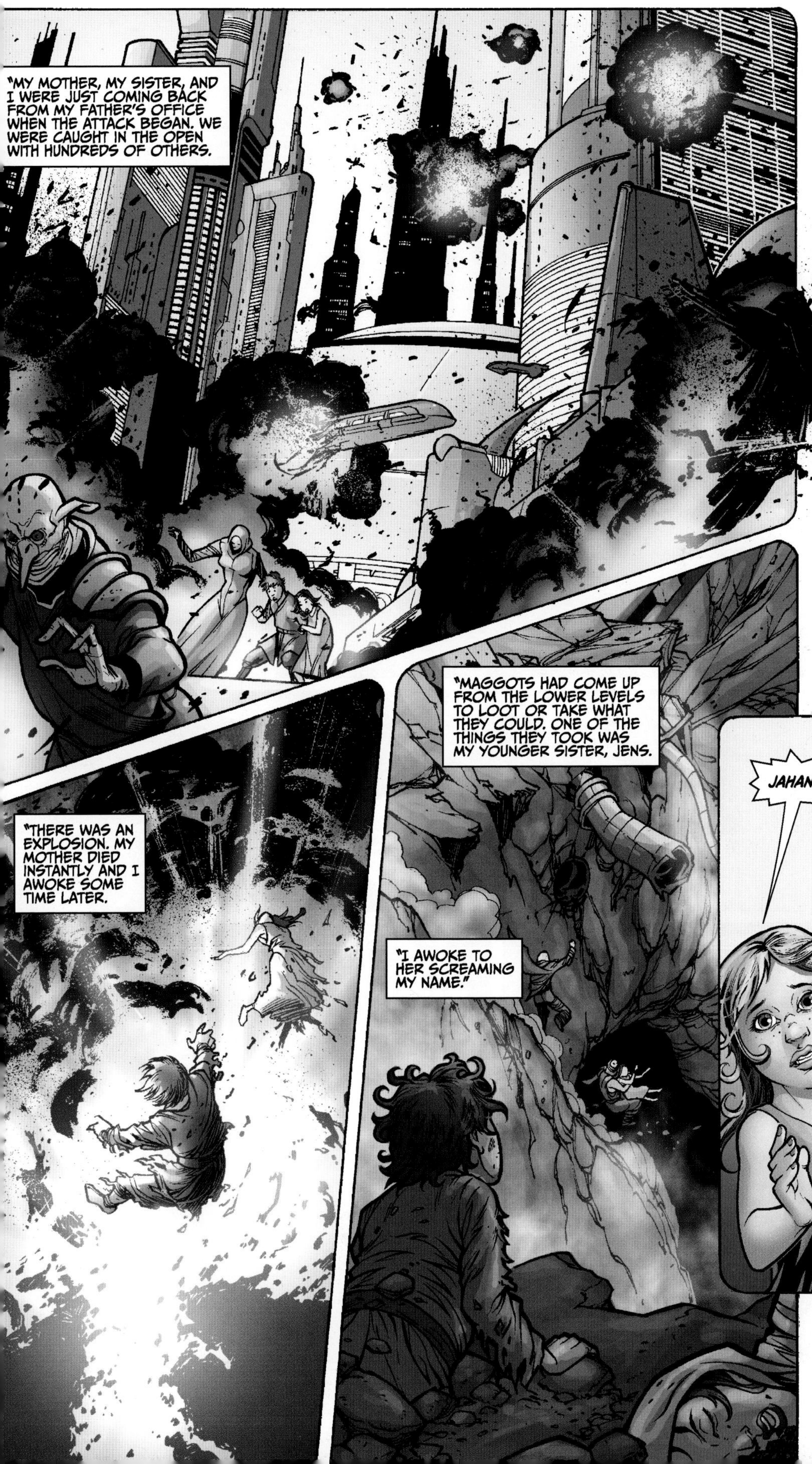
"MY MOTHER, MY SISTER, AND I WERE JUST COMING BACK FROM MY FATHER'S OFFICE WHEN THE ATTACK BEGAN. WE WERE CAUGHT IN THE OPEN WITH HUNDREDS OF OTHERS.
"THERE WAS AN EXPLOSION. MY MOTHER DIED INSTANTLY AND I AWOKE SOME TIME LATER.
"MAGGOTS HAD COME UP FROM THE LOWER LEVELS TO LOOT OR TAKE WHAT THEY COULD. ONE OF THE THINGS THEY TOOK WAS MY YOUNGER SISTER, JENS.
"I AWOKE TO HER SCREAMING MY NAME."
JAHAN!

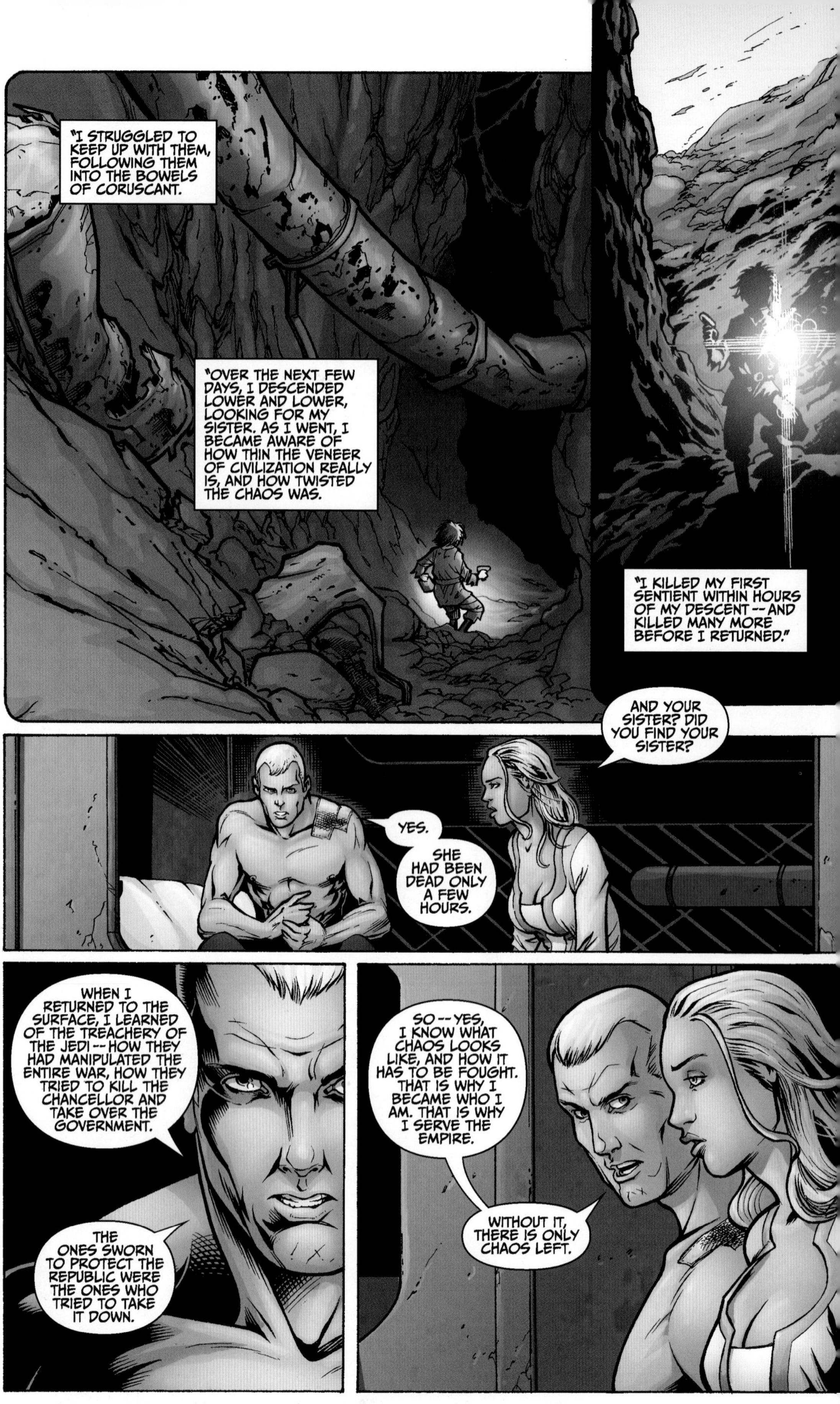

"I STRUGGLED TO KEEP UP WITH THEM, FOLLOWING THEM INTO THE BOWELS OF CORUSCANT.
"OVER THE NEXT FEW DAYS, I DESCENDED LOWER AND LOWER, LOOKING FOR MY SISTER. AS I WENT, I BECAME AWARE OF HOW THIN THE VENEER OF CIVILIZATION REALLY IS, AND HOW TWISTED THE CHAOS WAS.
"I KILLED MY FIRST SENTIENT WITHIN HOURS OF MY DESCENT -- AND KILLED MANY MORE BEFORE I RETURNED."
AND YOUR SISTER? DID YOU FIND YOUR SISTER?
YES.
SHE HAD BEEN DEAD ONLY A FEW HOURS.
WHEN I RETURNED TO THE SURFACE, I LEARNED OF THE TREACHERY OF THE JEDI -- HOW THEY HAD MANIPULATED THE ENTIRE WAR, HOW THEY TRIED TO KILL THE CHANCELLOR AND TAKE OVER THE GOVERNMENT.
THE ONES SWORN TO PROTECT THE REPUBLIC WERE THE ONES WHO TRIED TO TAKE IT DOWN.
SO -- YES, I KNOW WHAT CHAOS LOOKS LIKE, AND HOW IT HAS TO BE FOUGHT. THAT IS WHY I BECAME WHO I AM. THAT IS WHY I SERVE THE EMPIRE.
WITHOUT IT, THERE IS ONLY CHAOS LEFT.

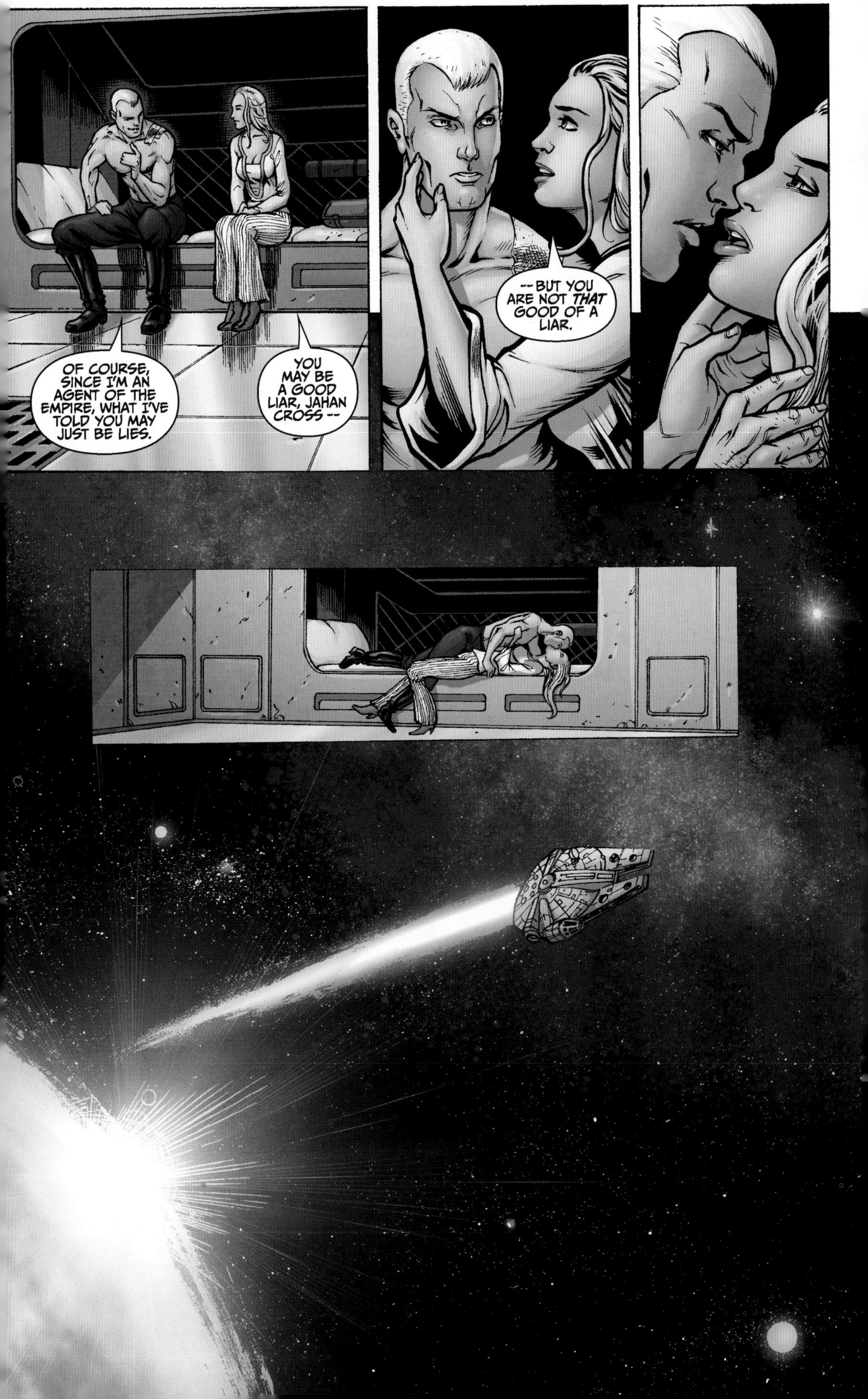
OF COURSE, SINCE I'M AN AGENT OF THE EMPIRE, WHAT I'VE TOLD YOU MAY JUST BE LIES.
YOU MAY BE A GOOD LIAR, JAHAN CROSS --
-- BUT YOU ARE NOT *THAT* GOOD OF A LIAR.

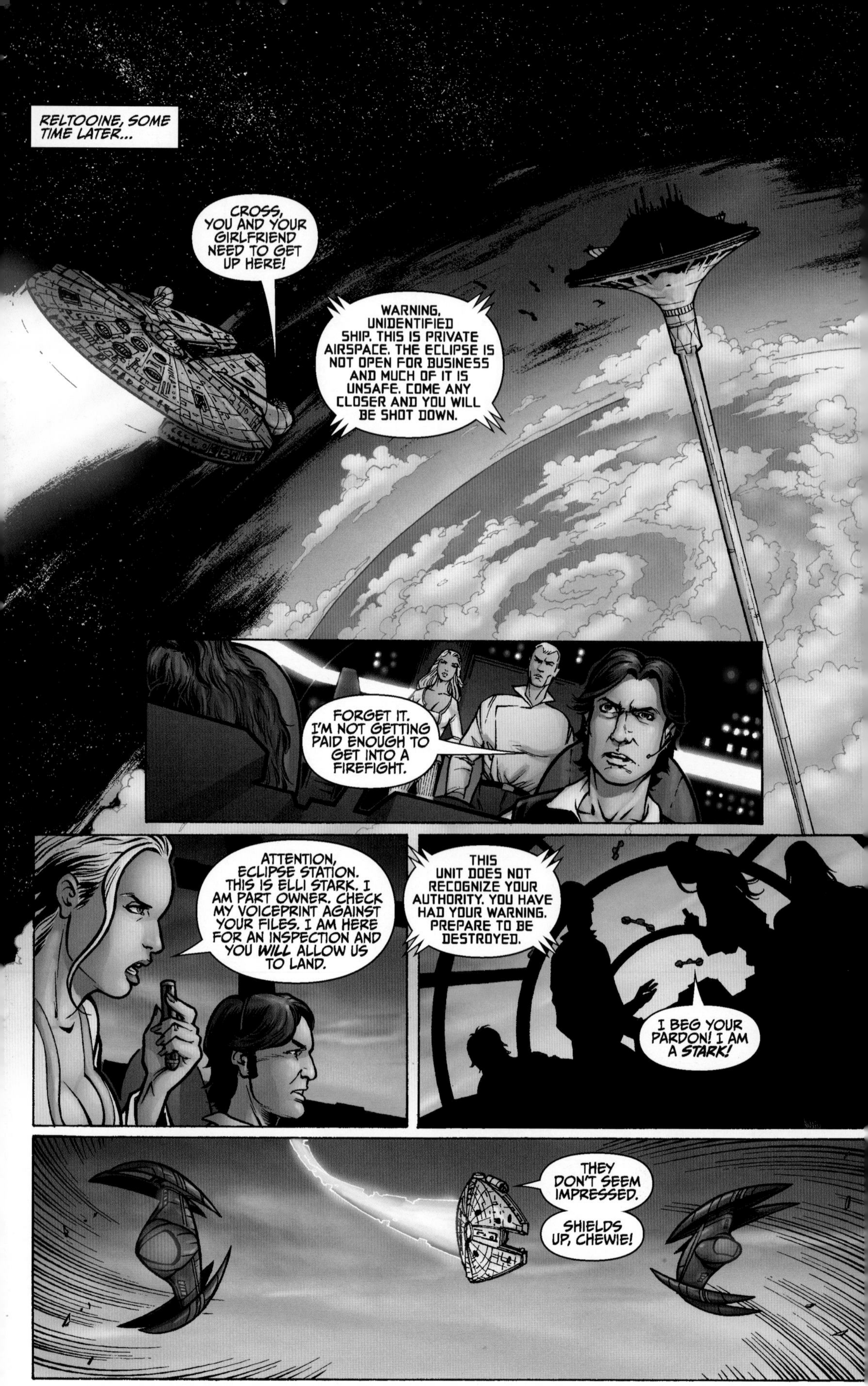
RELTOOINE, SOME TIME LATER...
CROSS, YOU AND YOUR GIRLFRIEND NEED TO GET UP HERE!
WARNING, UNIDENTIFIED SHIP. THIS IS PRIVATE AIRSPACE. THE ECLIPSE IS NOT OPEN FOR BUSINESS AND MUCH OF IT IS UNSAFE. COME ANY CLOSER AND YOU WILL BE SHOT DOWN.
FORGET IT. I'M NOT GETTING PAID ENOUGH TO GET INTO A FIREFIGHT.
ATTENTION, ECLIPSE STATION. THIS IS ELLI STARK. I AM PART OWNER. CHECK MY VOICEPRINT AGAINST YOUR FILES. I AM HERE FOR AN INSPECTION AND YOU WILL ALLOW US TO LAND.
THIS UNIT DOES NOT RECOGNIZE YOUR AUTHORITY. YOU HAVE HAD YOUR WARNING. PREPARE TO BE DESTROYED.
I BEG YOUR PARDON! I AM A STARK!
THEY DON'T SEEM IMPRESSED.
SHIELDS UP, CHEWIE!

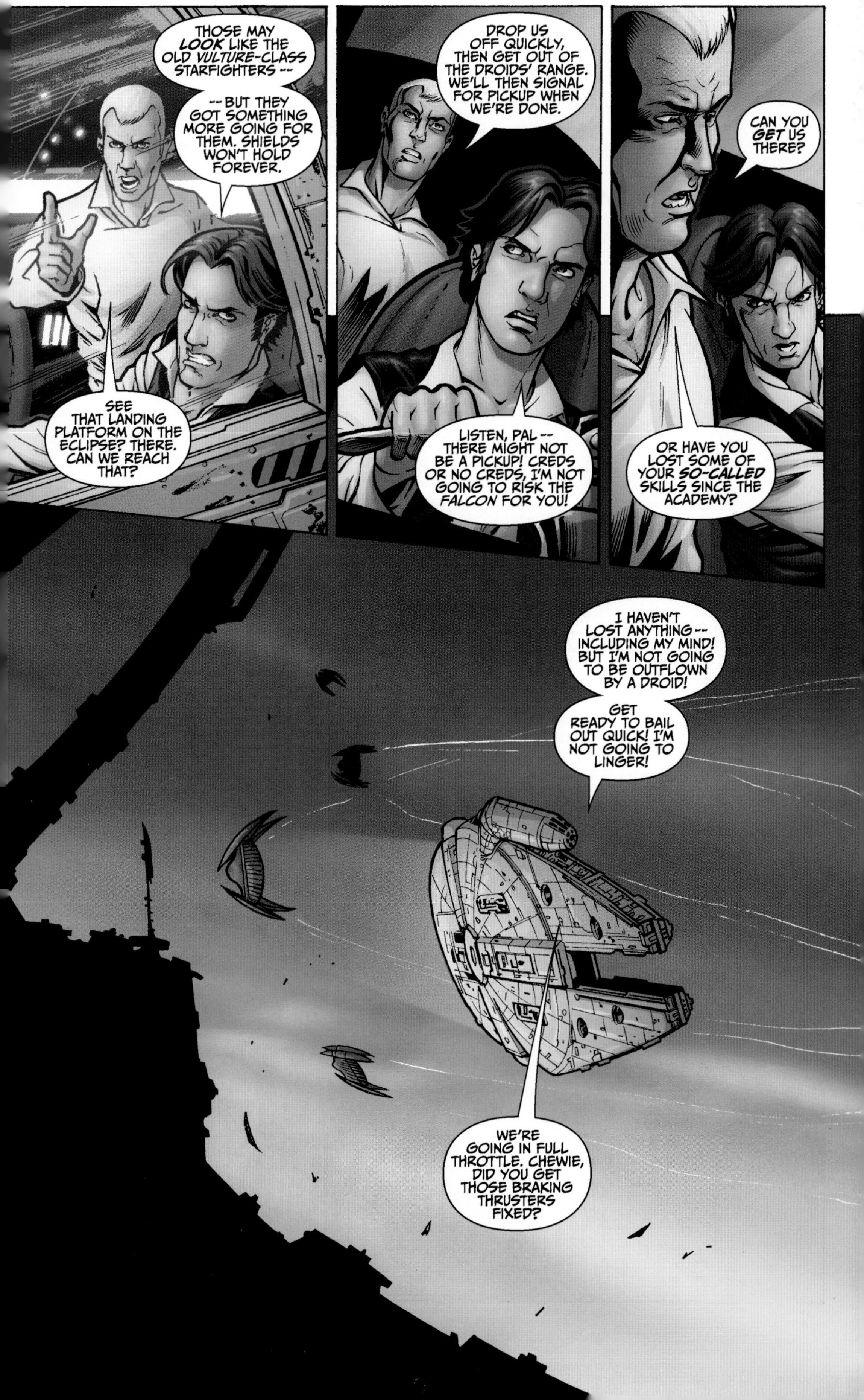
THOSE MAY LOOK LIKE THE OLD VULTURE-CLASS STARFIGHTERS --
-- BUT THEY GOT SOMETHING MORE GOING FOR THEM. SHIELDS WON'T HOLD FOREVER.
SEE THAT LANDING PLATFORM ON THE ECLIPSE? THERE. CAN WE REACH THAT?
DROP US OFF QUICKLY, THEN GET OUT OF THE DROIDS' RANGE. WE'LL THEN SIGNAL FOR PICKUP WHEN WE'RE DONE.
LISTEN, PAL -- THERE MIGHT NOT BE A PICKUP! CREDS OR NO CREDS, I'M NOT GOING TO RISK THE FALCON FOR YOU!
CAN YOU GET US THERE?
OR HAVE YOU LOST SOME OF YOUR SO-CALLED SKILLS SINCE THE ACADEMY?
I HAVEN'T LOST ANYTHING -- INCLUDING MY MIND! BUT I'M NOT GOING TO BE OUTFLOWN BY A DROID!
GET READY TO BAIL OUT QUICK! I'M NOT GOING TO LINGER!
WE'RE GOING IN FULL THROTTLE. CHEWIE, DID YOU GET THOSE BRAKING THRUSTERS FIXED?

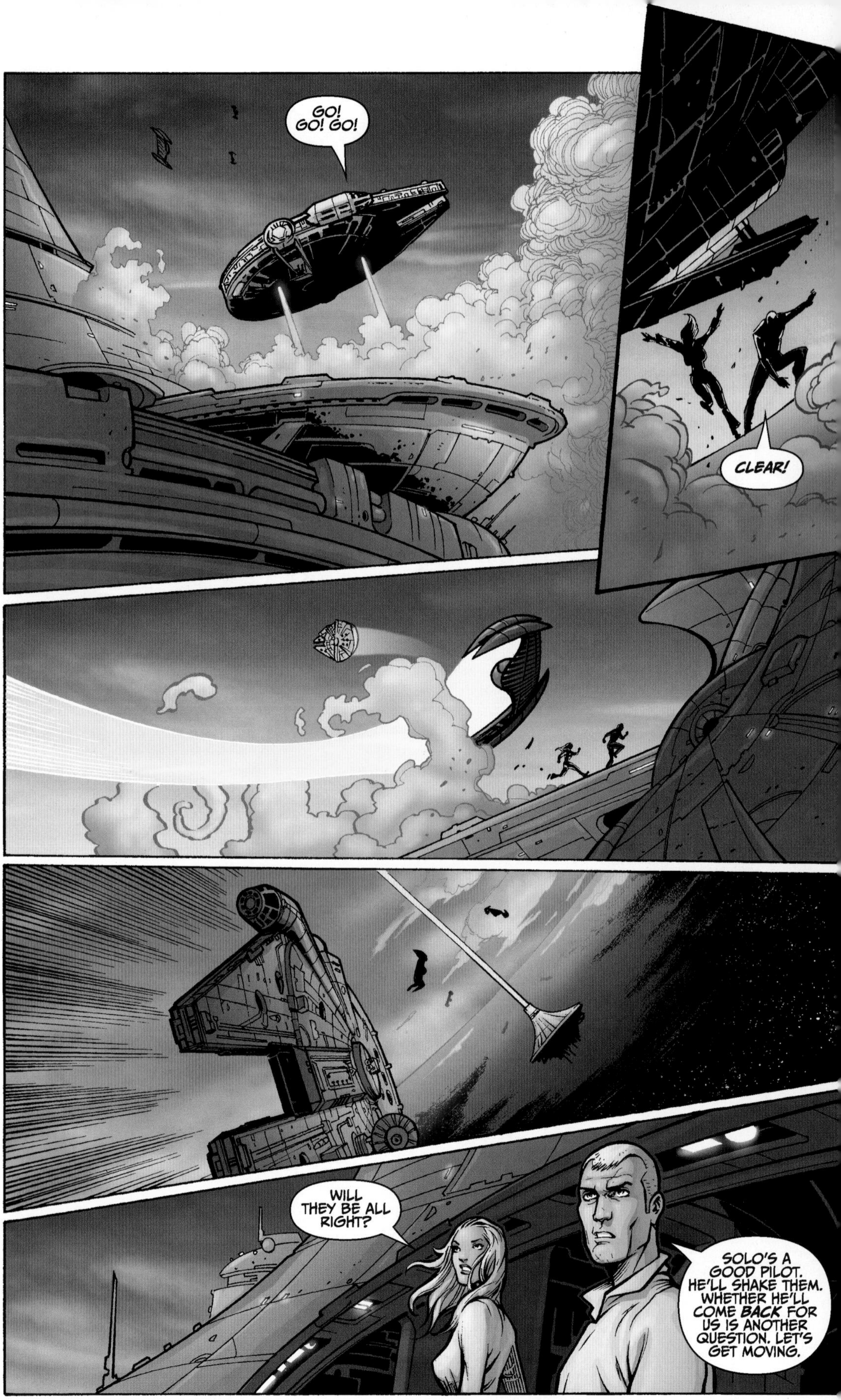
GO! GO! GO!
CLEAR!
WILL THEY BE ALL RIGHT?
SOLO'S A GOOD PILOT. HE'LL SHAKE THEM. WHETHER HE'LL COME BACK FOR US IS ANOTHER QUESTION. LET'S GET MOVING.

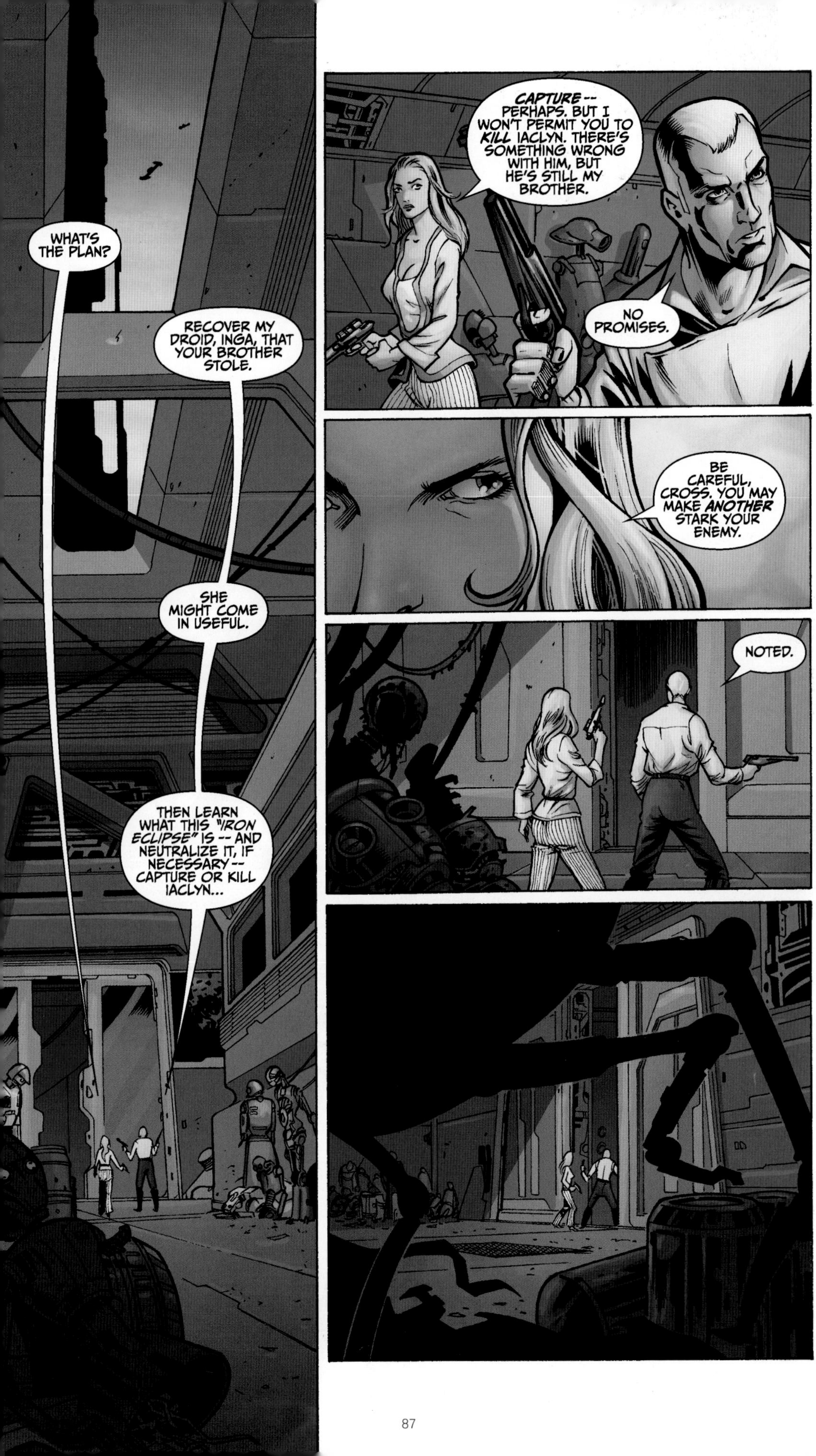
WHAT'S THE PLAN?
RECOVER MY DROID, INGA, THAT YOUR BROTHER STOLE.
SHE MIGHT COME IN USEFUL.
THEN LEARN WHAT THIS "IRON ECLIPSE" IS -- AND NEUTRALIZE IT, IF NECESSARY -- CAPTURE OR KILL IACLYN...
CAPTURE -- PERHAPS. BUT I WON'T PERMIT YOU TO KILL IACLYN. THERE'S SOMETHING WRONG WITH HIM, BUT HE'S STILL MY BROTHER.
NO PROMISES.
BE CAREFUL, CROSS. YOU MAY MAKE ANOTHER STARK YOUR ENEMY.
NOTED.

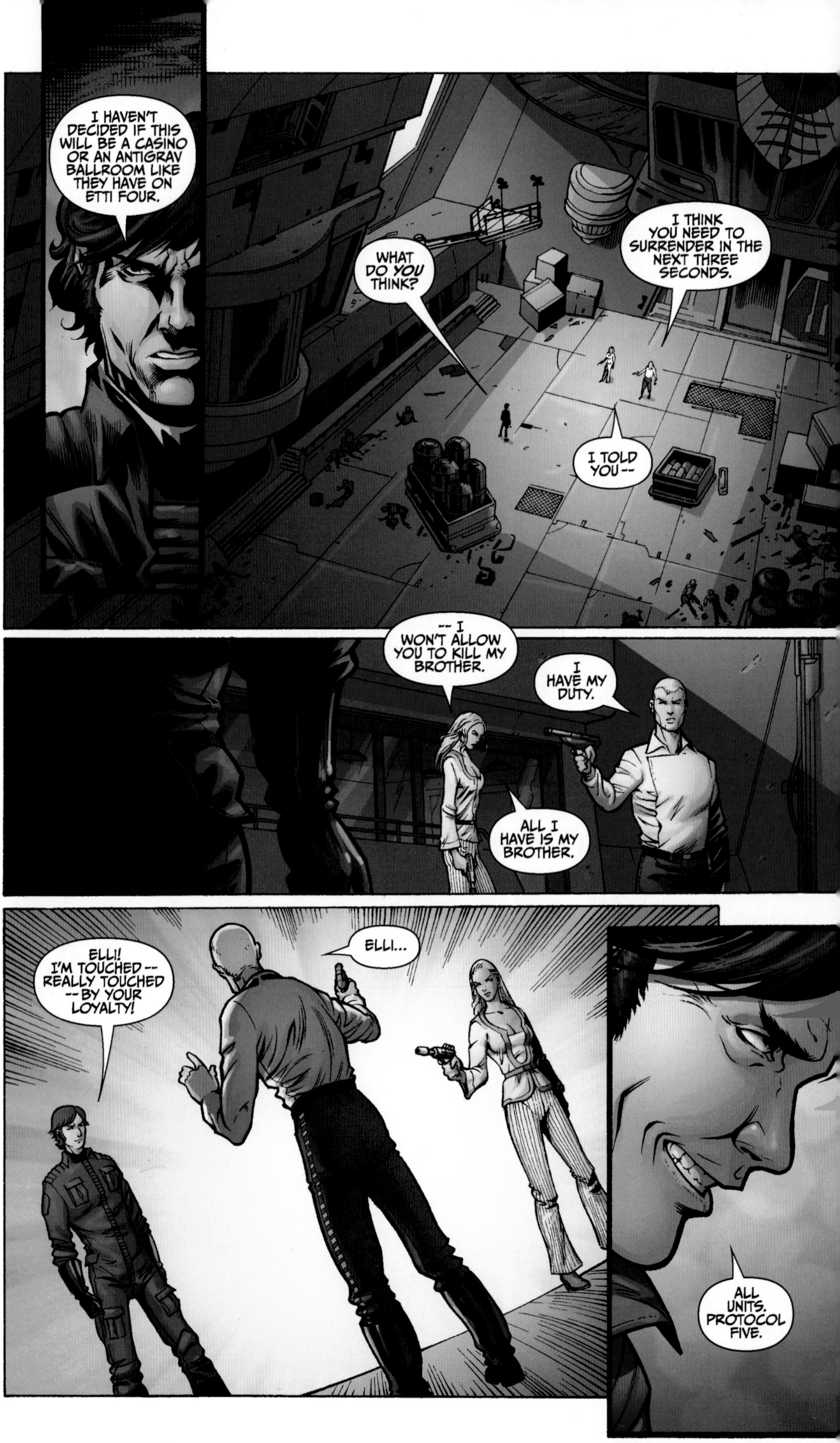
I HAVEN'T DECIDED IF THIS WILL BE A CASINO OR AN ANTIGRAV BALLROOM LIKE THEY HAVE ON ETTI FOUR.
WHAT DO YOU THINK?
I THINK YOU NEED TO SURRENDER IN THE NEXT THREE SECONDS.
I TOLD YOU --
-- I WON'T ALLOW YOU TO KILL MY BROTHER.
I HAVE MY DUTY.
ALL I HAVE IS MY BROTHER.
ELLI! I'M TOUCHED -- REALLY TOUCHED -- BY YOUR LOYALTY!
ELLI...
ALL UNITS. PROTOCOL FIVE.

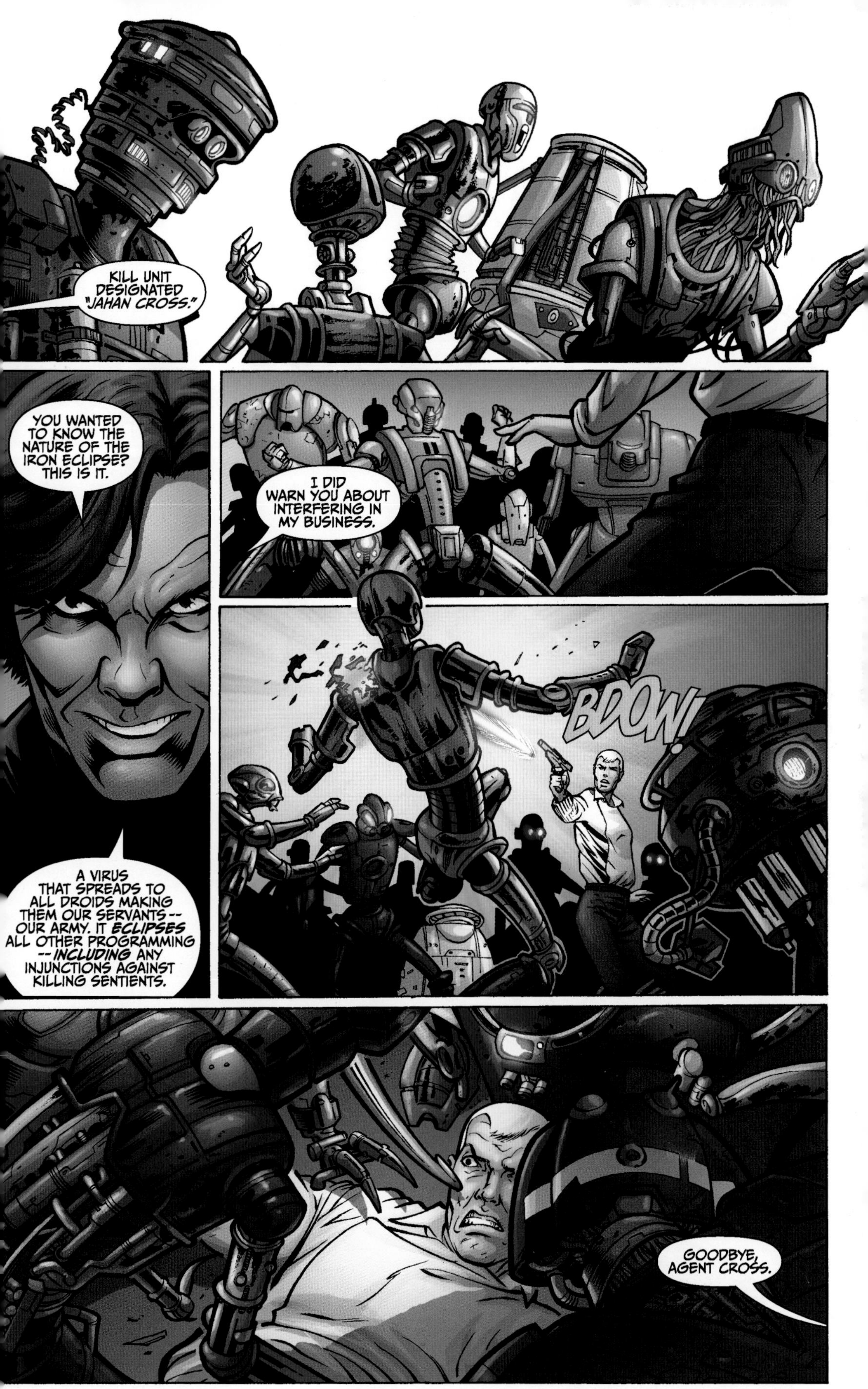
KILL UNIT DESIGNATED "JAHAN CROSS."
YOU WANTED TO KNOW THE NATURE OF THE IRON ECLIPSE? THIS IS IT.
I DID WARN YOU ABOUT INTERFERING IN MY BUSINESS.
BDOW!
A VIRUS THAT SPREADS TO ALL DROIDS MAKING THEM OUR SERVANTS--OUR ARMY. IT *ECLIPSES* ALL OTHER PROGRAMMING --*INCLUDING* ANY INJUNCTIONS AGAINST KILLING SENTIENTS.
GOODBYE, AGENT CROSS.

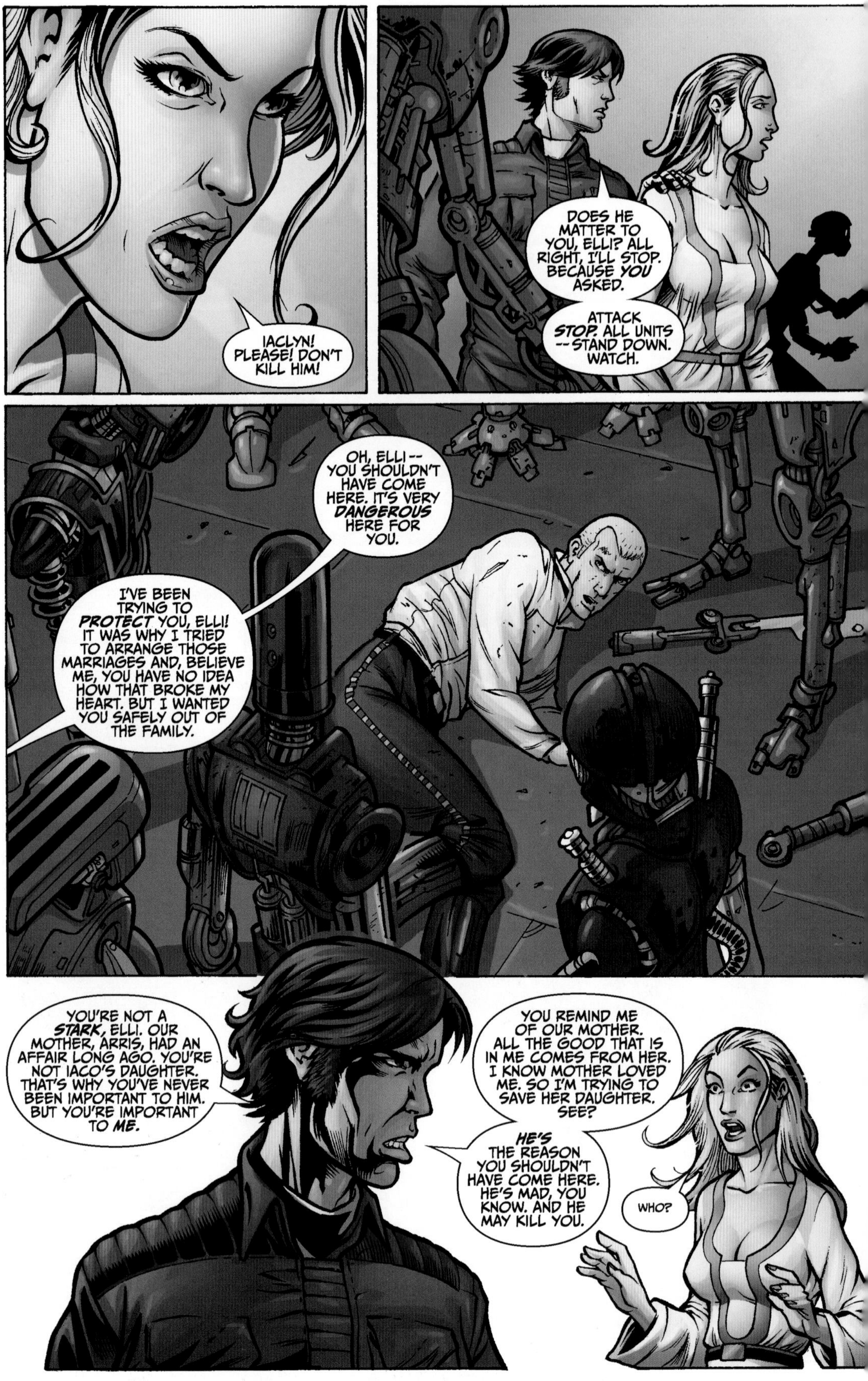
IACLYN! PLEASE! DON'T KILL HIM!
DOES HE MATTER TO YOU, ELLI? ALL RIGHT, I'LL STOP. BECAUSE YOU ASKED.
ATTACK STOP. ALL UNITS --STAND DOWN. WATCH.
OH, ELLI-- YOU SHOULDN'T HAVE COME HERE. IT'S VERY DANGEROUS HERE FOR YOU.
I'VE BEEN TRYING TO PROTECT YOU, ELLI! IT WAS WHY I TRIED TO ARRANGE THOSE MARRIAGES AND, BELIEVE ME, YOU HAVE NO IDEA HOW THAT BROKE MY HEART. BUT I WANTED YOU SAFELY OUT OF THE FAMILY.
YOU'RE NOT A STARK, ELLI. OUR MOTHER, ARRIS, HAD AN AFFAIR LONG AGO. YOU'RE NOT IACO'S DAUGHTER. THAT'S WHY YOU'VE NEVER BEEN IMPORTANT TO HIM. BUT YOU'RE IMPORTANT TO ME.
YOU REMIND ME OF OUR MOTHER. ALL THE GOOD THAT IS IN ME COMES FROM HER. I KNOW MOTHER LOVED ME. SO I'M TRYING TO SAVE HER DAUGHTER. SEE?
HE'S THE REASON YOU SHOULDN'T HAVE COME HERE. HE'S MAD, YOU KNOW. AND HE MAY KILL YOU.
WHO?

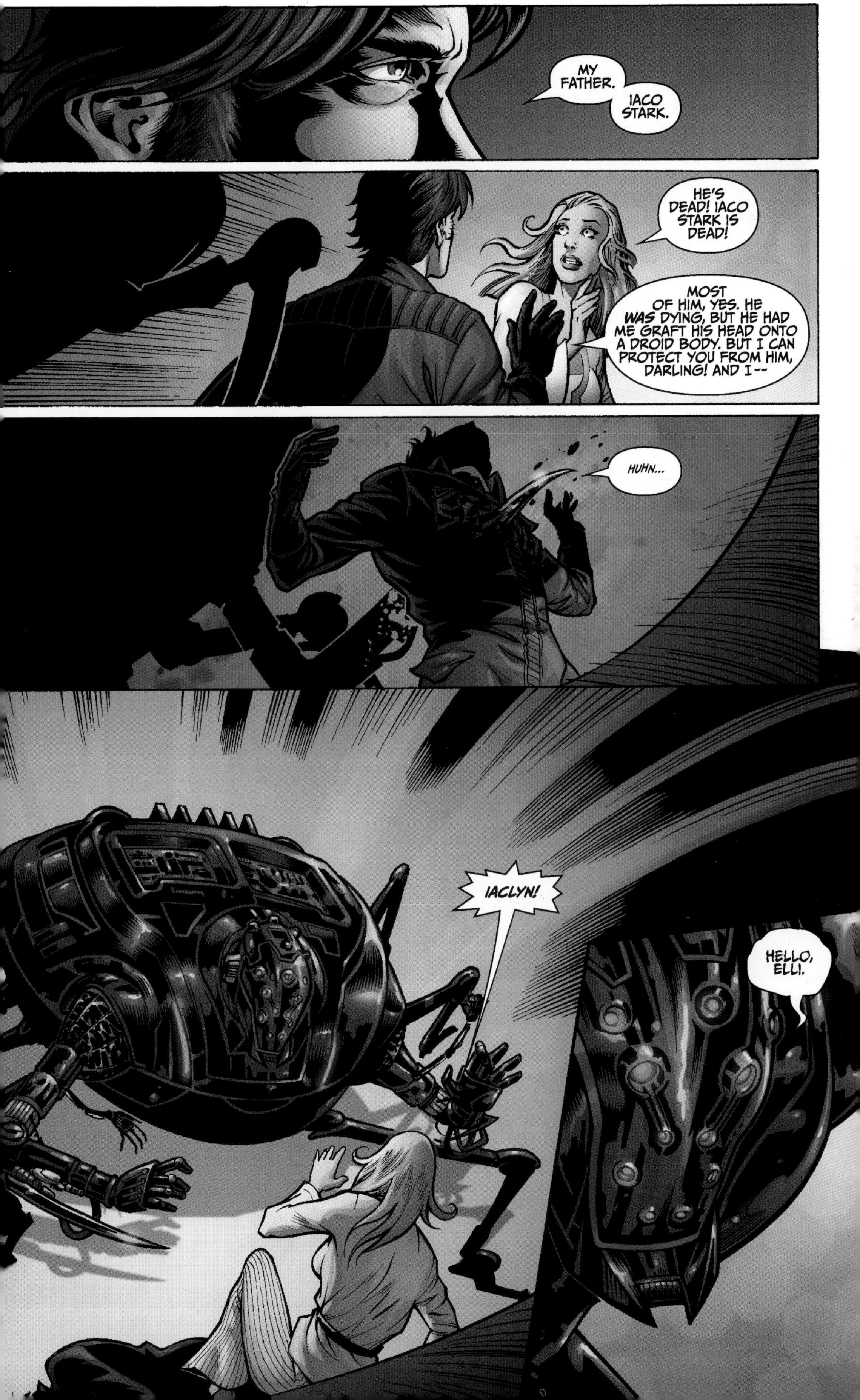
MY FATHER.
IACO STARK.
HE'S DEAD! IACO STARK IS DEAD!
MOST OF HIM, YES. HE WAS DYING, BUT HE HAD ME GRAFT HIS HEAD ONTO A DROID BODY. BUT I CAN PROTECT YOU FROM HIM, DARLING! AND I--
HUHN...
IACLYN!
HELLO, ELLI.

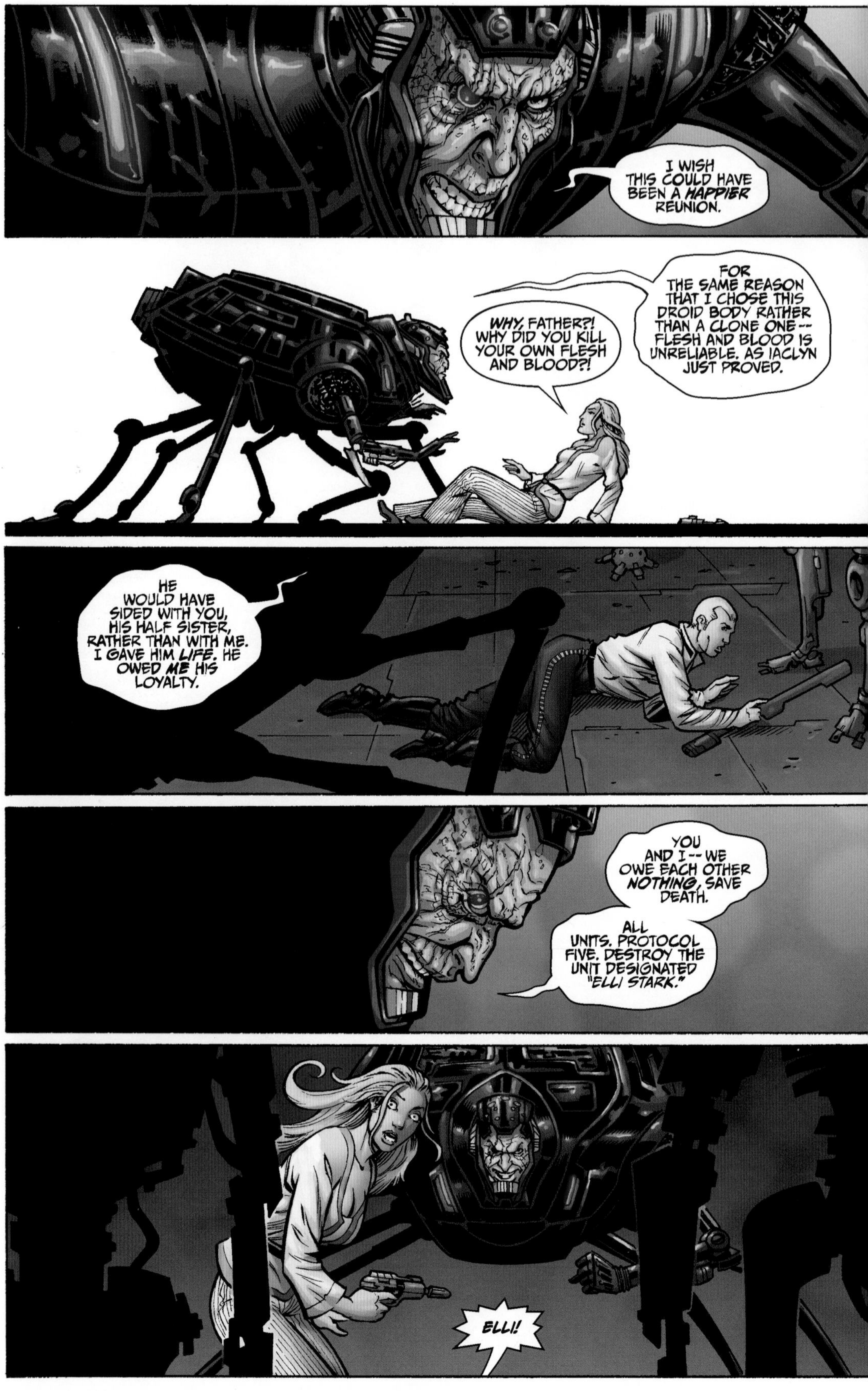

I WISH THIS COULD HAVE BEEN A *HAPPIER* REUNION.
WHY, FATHER?! WHY DID YOU KILL YOUR OWN FLESH AND BLOOD?!
FOR THE SAME REASON THAT I CHOSE THIS DROID BODY RATHER THAN A *CLONE* ONE-- FLESH AND BLOOD IS UNRELIABLE. AS IACLYN JUST PROVED.
HE WOULD HAVE SIDED WITH YOU, HIS HALF SISTER, RATHER THAN WITH ME. I GAVE HIM *LIFE.* HE OWED *ME* HIS LOYALTY.
YOU AND I-- WE OWE EACH OTHER *NOTHING,* SAVE DEATH.
ALL UNITS. PROTOCOL FIVE. DESTROY THE UNIT DESIGNATED *"ELLI STARK."*
ELLI!

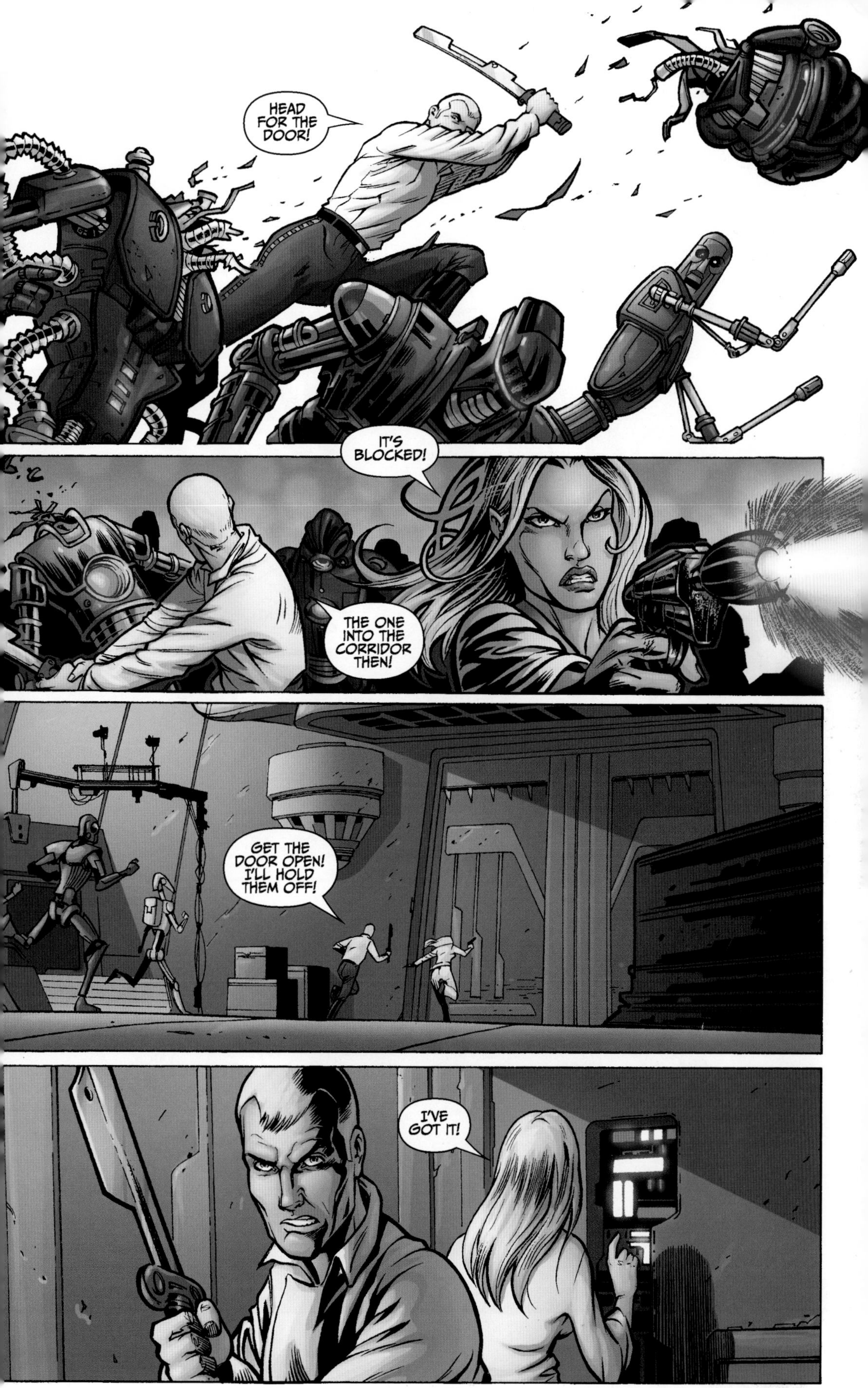
HEAD FOR THE DOOR!
IT'S BLOCKED!
THE ONE INTO THE CORRIDOR THEN!
GET THE DOOR OPEN! I'LL HOLD THEM OFF!
I'VE GOT IT!

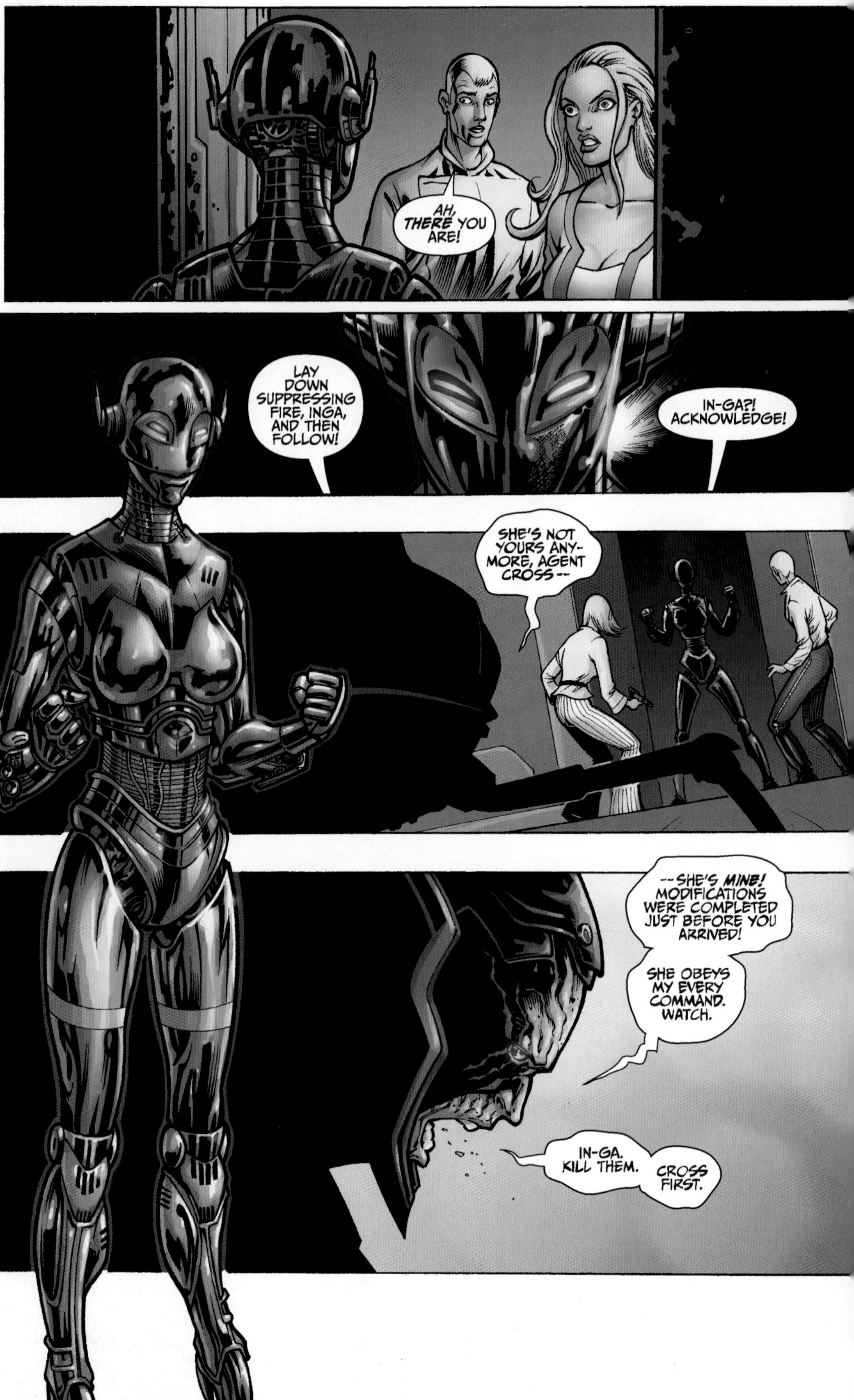

AH, THERE YOU ARE!
LAY DOWN SUPPRESSING FIRE, INGA, AND THEN FOLLOW!
IN-GA?! ACKNOWLEDGE!
SHE'S NOT YOURS ANY-MORE, AGENT CROSS--
--SHE'S MINE! MODIFICATIONS WERE COMPLETED JUST BEFORE YOU ARRIVED!
SHE OBEYS MY EVERY COMMAND. WATCH.
IN-GA. KILL THEM.
CROSS FIRST.

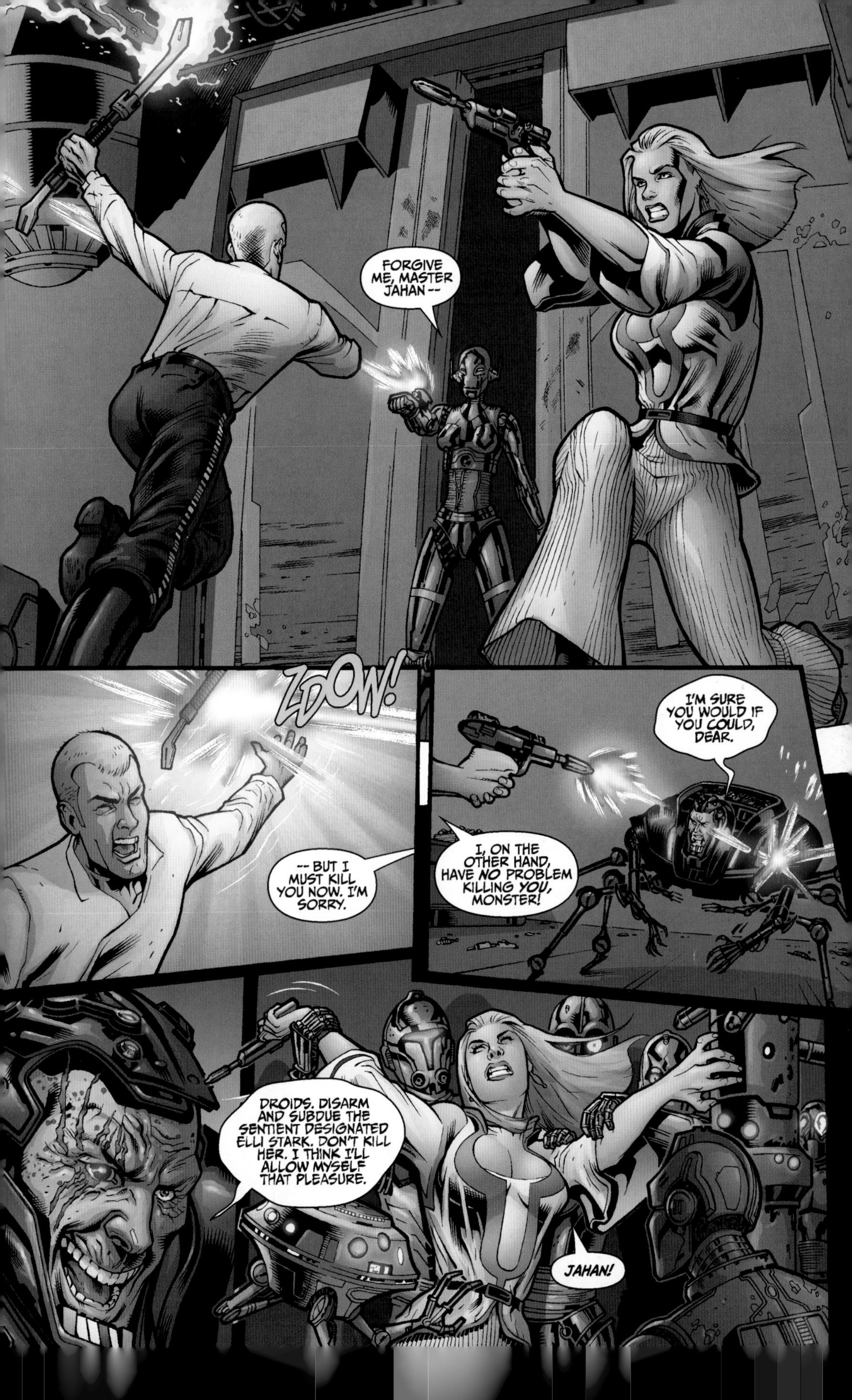
FORGIVE ME, MASTER JAHAN --
ZDOW!
-- BUT I MUST KILL YOU NOW. I'M SORRY.
I, ON THE OTHER HAND, HAVE *NO* PROBLEM KILLING *YOU*, MONSTER!
I'M SURE YOU WOULD IF YOU *COULD*, DEAR.
DROIDS. DISARM AND SUBDUE THE SENTIENT DESIGNATED ELLI STARK. DON'T KILL HER. I THINK I'LL ALLOW MYSELF THAT PLEASURE.
JAHAN!

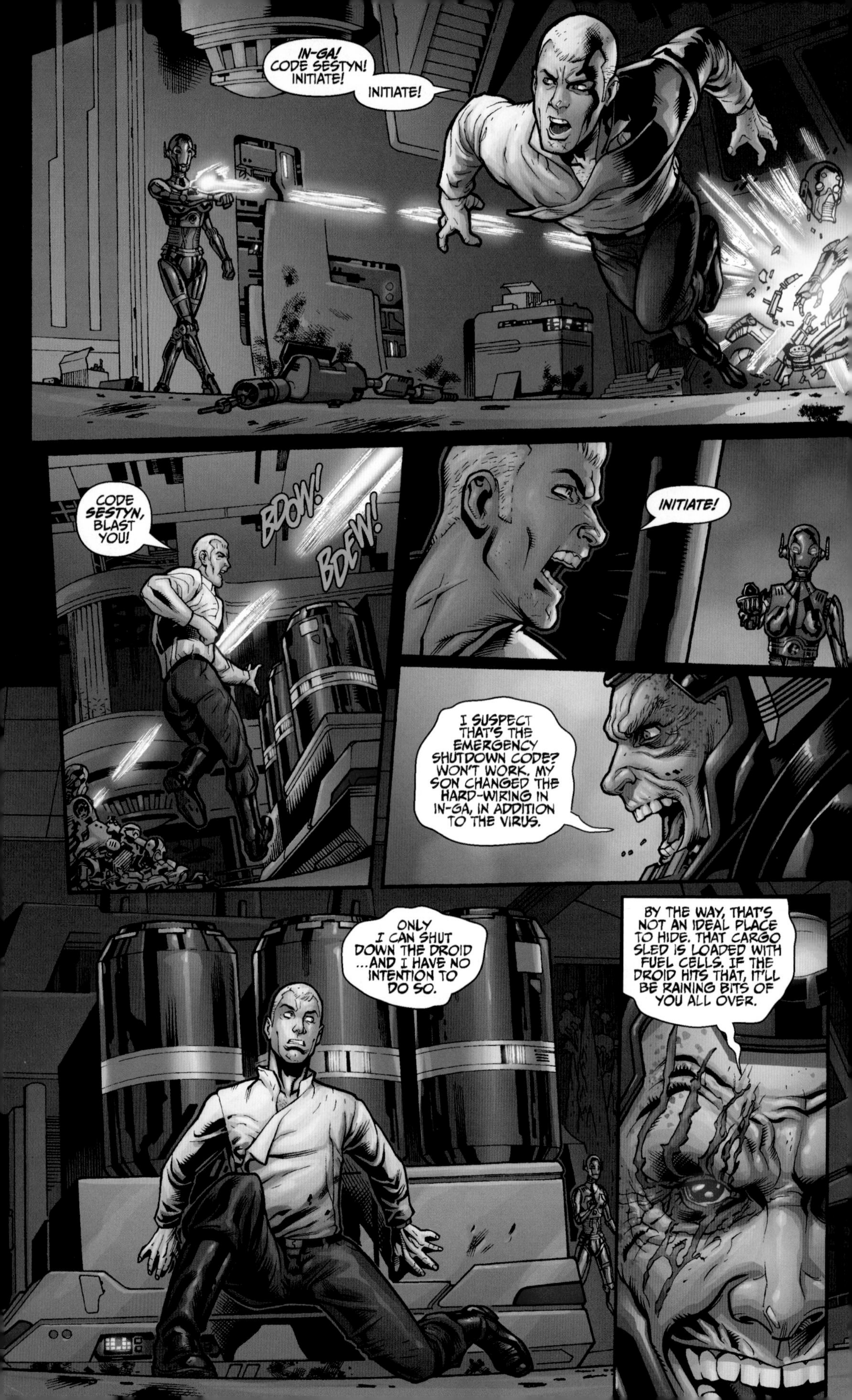
IN-GA! CODE SESTYN! INITIATE!
INITIATE!
CODE SESTYN, BLAST YOU!
BDOW!
BDEW!
INITIATE!
I SUSPECT THAT'S THE EMERGENCY SHUTDOWN CODE? WON'T WORK. MY SON CHANGED THE HARD-WIRING IN IN-GA, IN ADDITION TO THE VIRUS.
ONLY I CAN SHUT DOWN THE DROID ...AND I HAVE NO INTENTION TO DO SO.
BY THE WAY, THAT'S NOT AN IDEAL PLACE TO HIDE. THAT CARGO SLED IS LOADED WITH FUEL CELLS. IF THE DROID HITS THAT, IT'LL BE RAINING BITS OF YOU ALL OVER.

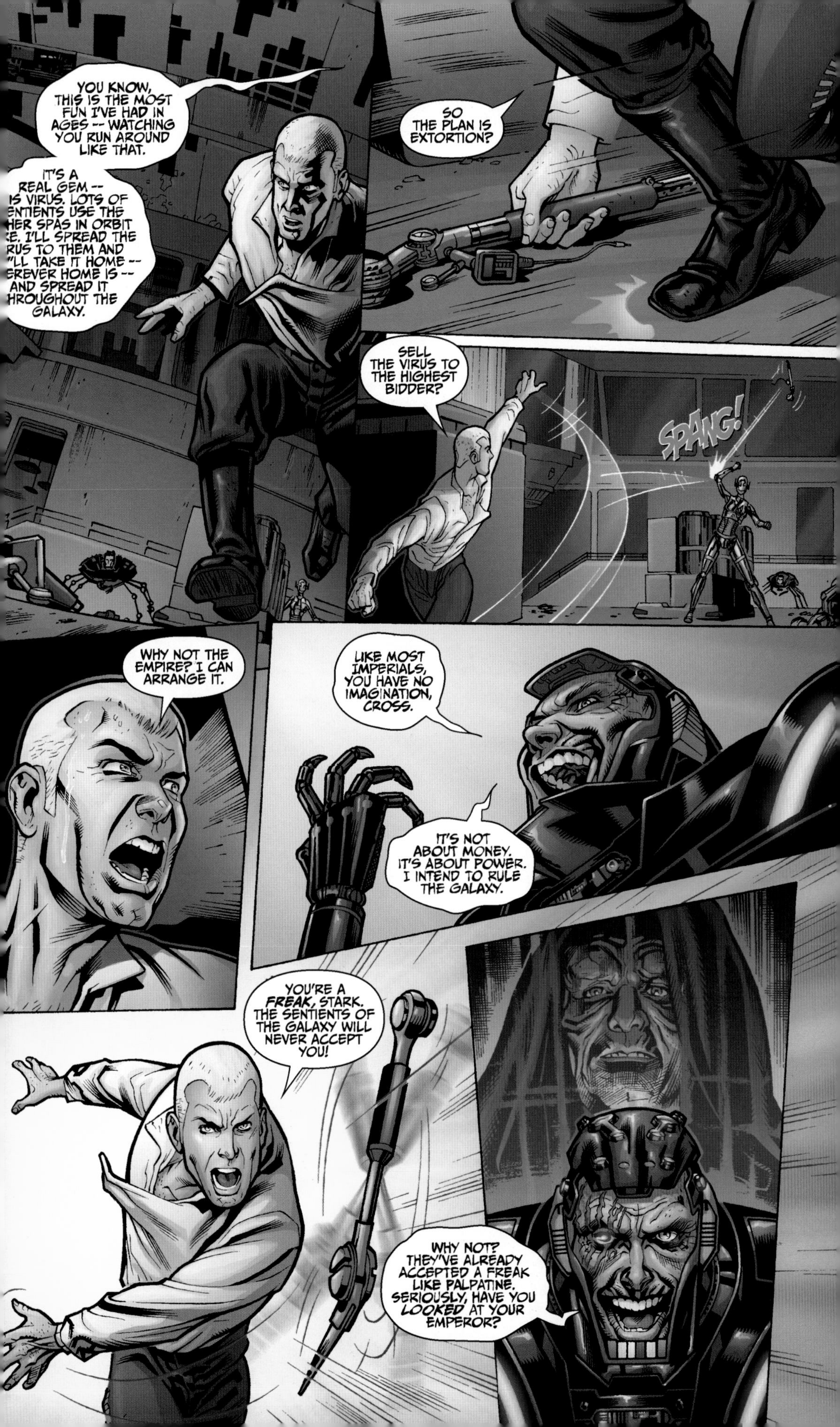
YOU KNOW, THIS IS THE MOST FUN I'VE HAD IN AGES -- WATCHING YOU RUN AROUND LIKE THAT.
IT'S A REAL GEM -- IS VIRUS. LOTS OF ENTIENTS USE THE HER SPAS IN ORBIT E. I'LL SPREAD THE RUS TO THEM AND 'LL TAKE IT HOME -- EREVER HOME IS -- AND SPREAD IT HROUGHOUT THE GALAXY.
SO THE PLAN IS EXTORTION?
SELL THE VIRUS TO THE HIGHEST BIDDER?
SPANG!
WHY NOT THE EMPIRE? I CAN ARRANGE IT.
LIKE MOST IMPERIALS, YOU HAVE NO IMAGINATION, CROSS.
IT'S NOT ABOUT MONEY. IT'S ABOUT POWER. I INTEND TO RULE THE GALAXY.
YOU'RE A FREAK, STARK. THE SENTIENTS OF THE GALAXY WILL NEVER ACCEPT YOU!
WHY NOT? THEY'VE ALREADY ACCEPTED A FREAK LIKE PALPATINE. SERIOUSLY, HAVE YOU LOOKED AT YOUR EMPEROR?

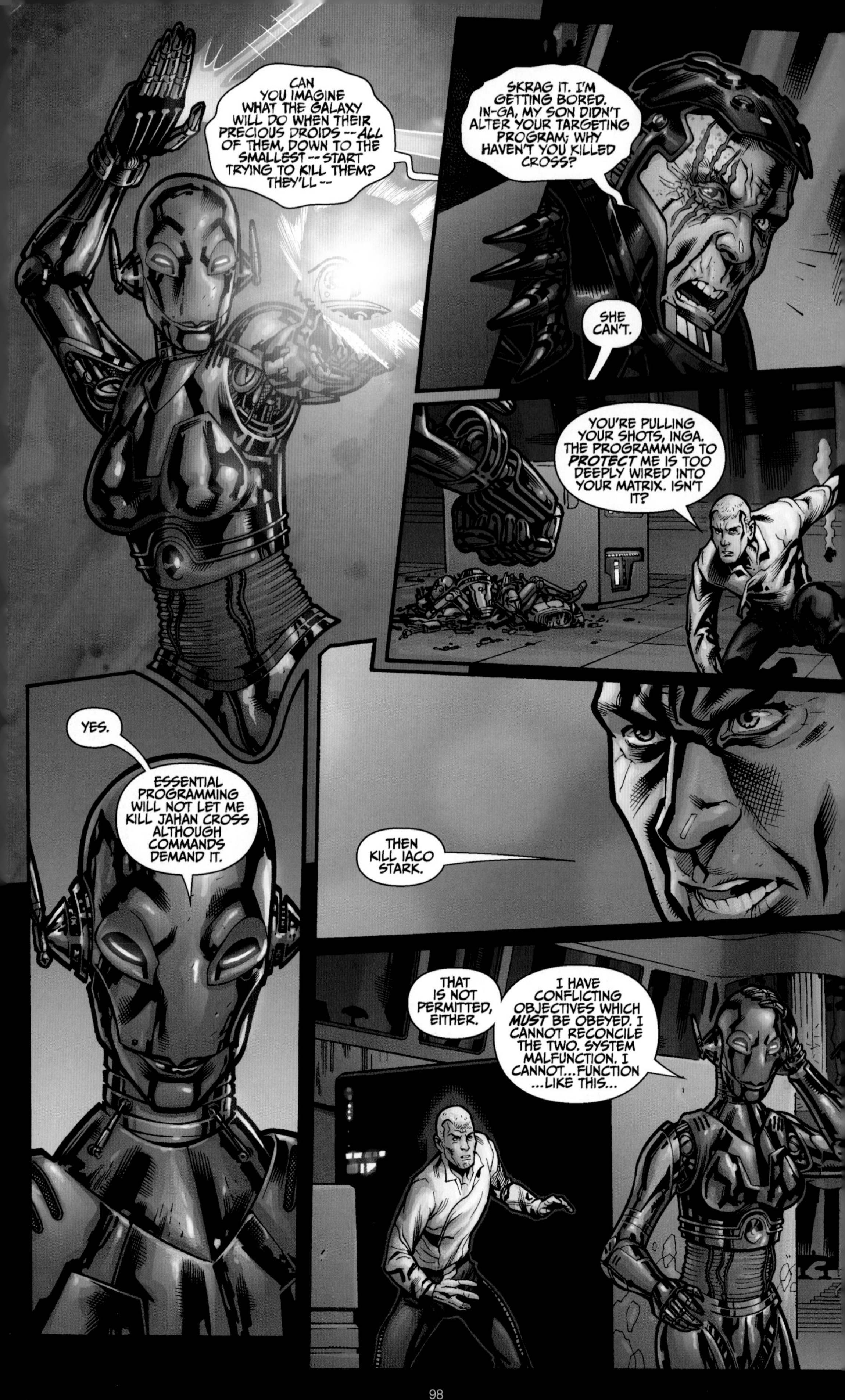

CAN YOU IMAGINE WHAT THE GALAXY WILL DO WHEN THEIR PRECIOUS DROIDS -- ALL OF THEM, DOWN TO THE SMALLEST -- START TRYING TO KILL THEM? THEY'LL --
SKRAG IT. I'M GETTING BORED. IN-GA, MY SON DIDN'T ALTER YOUR TARGETING PROGRAM; WHY HAVEN'T YOU KILLED CROSS?
SHE CAN'T.
YOU'RE PULLING YOUR SHOTS, INGA. THE PROGRAMMING TO PROTECT ME IS TOO DEEPLY WIRED INTO YOUR MATRIX. ISN'T IT?
YES.
ESSENTIAL PROGRAMMING WILL NOT LET ME KILL JAHAN CROSS ALTHOUGH COMMANDS DEMAND IT.
THEN KILL IACO STARK.
THAT IS NOT PERMITTED, EITHER.
I HAVE CONFLICTING OBJECTIVES WHICH MUST BE OBEYED. I CANNOT RECONCILE THE TWO. SYSTEM MALFUNCTION. I CANNOT...FUNCTION ...LIKE THIS...

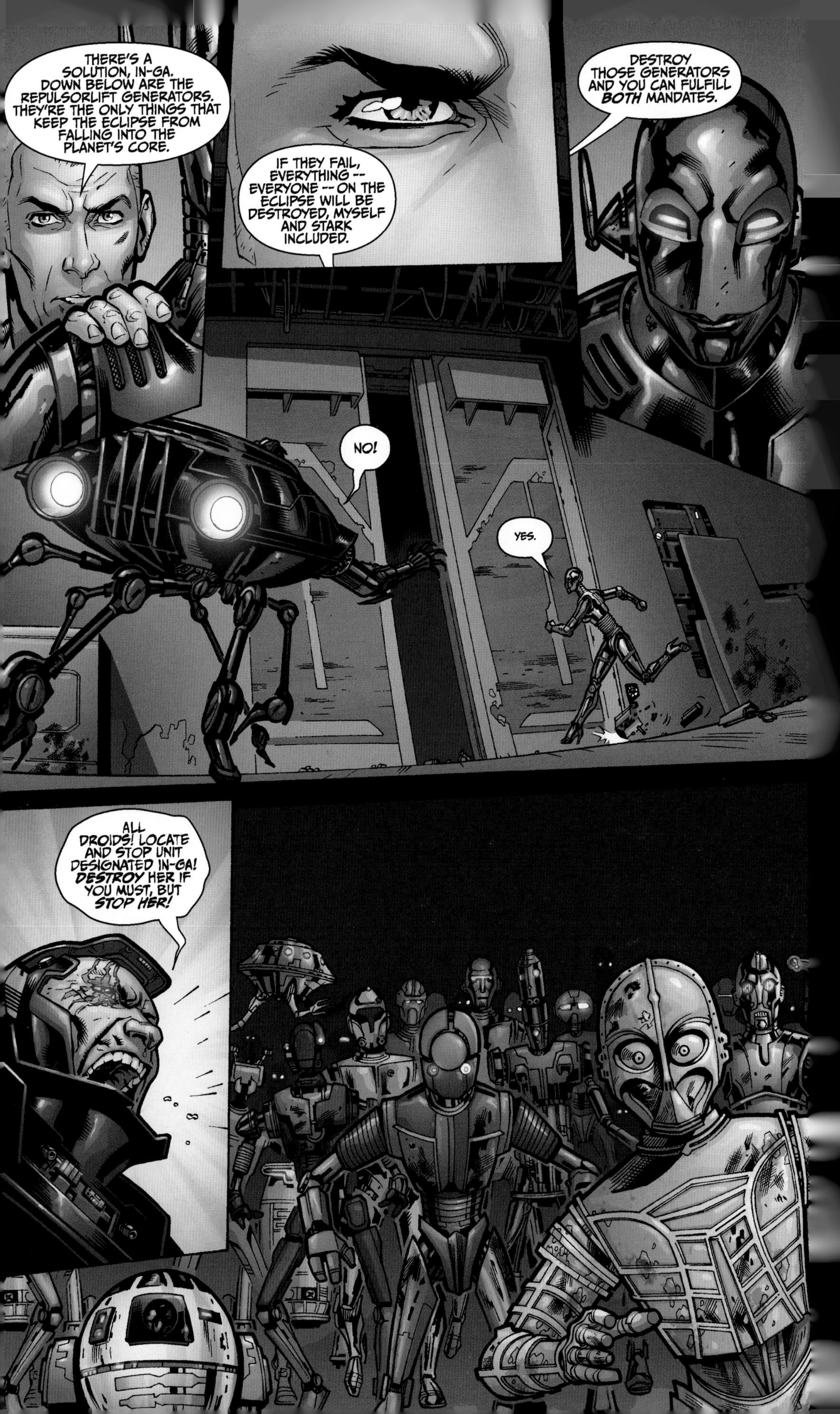
THERE'S A SOLUTION, IN-GA. DOWN BELOW ARE THE REPULSORLIFT GENERATORS. THEY'RE THE ONLY THINGS THAT KEEP THE ECLIPSE FROM FALLING INTO THE PLANET'S CORE.
IF THEY FAIL, EVERYTHING -- EVERYONE -- ON THE ECLIPSE WILL BE DESTROYED, MYSELF AND STARK INCLUDED.
DESTROY THOSE GENERATORS AND YOU CAN FULFILL BOTH MANDATES.
NO!
YES.
ALL DROIDS! LOCATE AND STOP UNIT DESIGNATED IN-GA! DESTROY HER IF YOU MUST, BUT STOP HER!

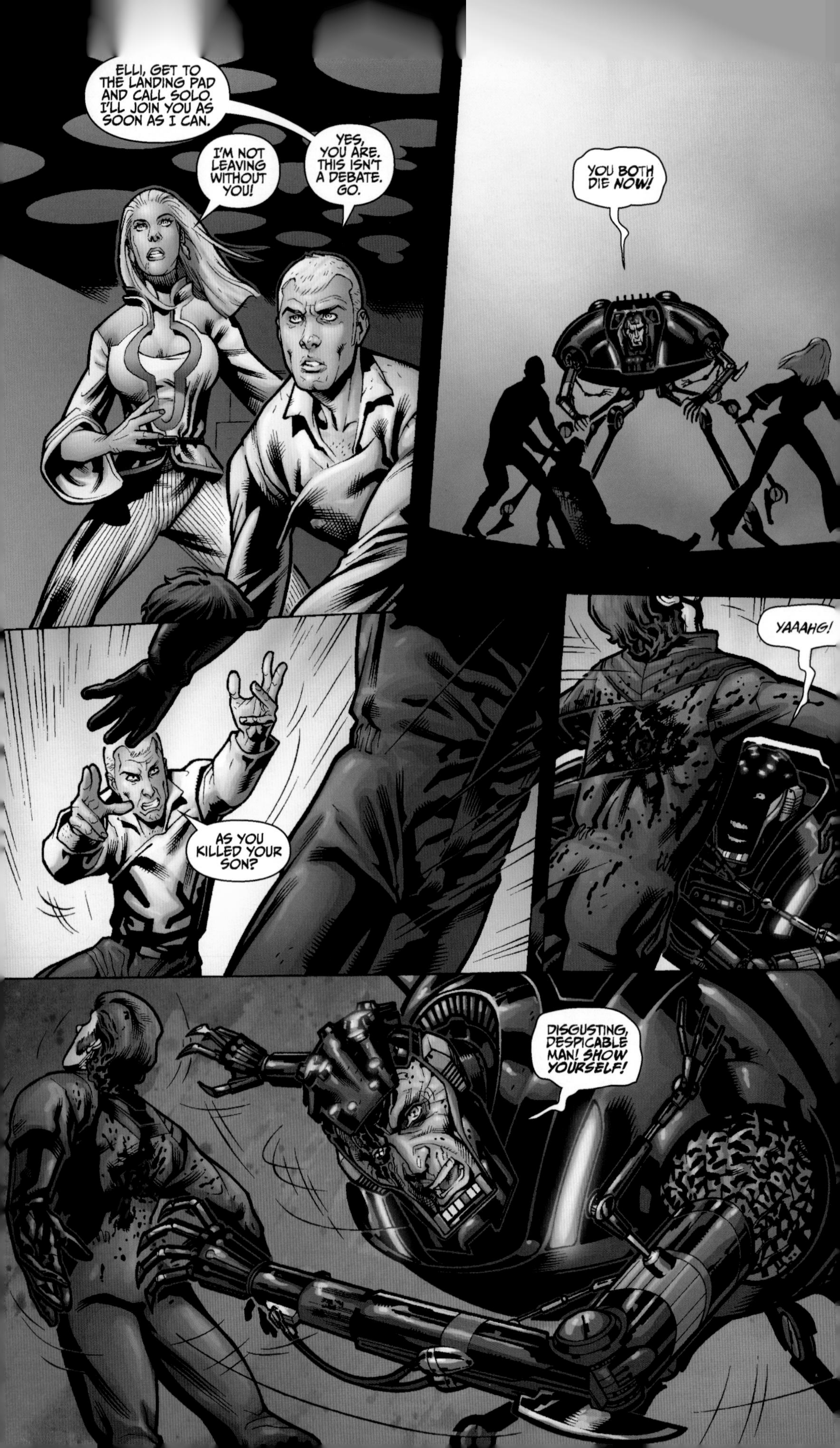

ELLI, GET TO THE LANDING PAD AND CALL SOLO. I'LL JOIN YOU AS SOON AS I CAN.
I'M NOT LEAVING WITHOUT YOU!
YES, YOU ARE. THIS ISN'T A DEBATE. GO.
YOU BOTH DIE NOW!
AS YOU KILLED YOUR SON?
YAAAHG!
DISGUSTING, DESPICABLE MAN! SHOW YOURSELF!

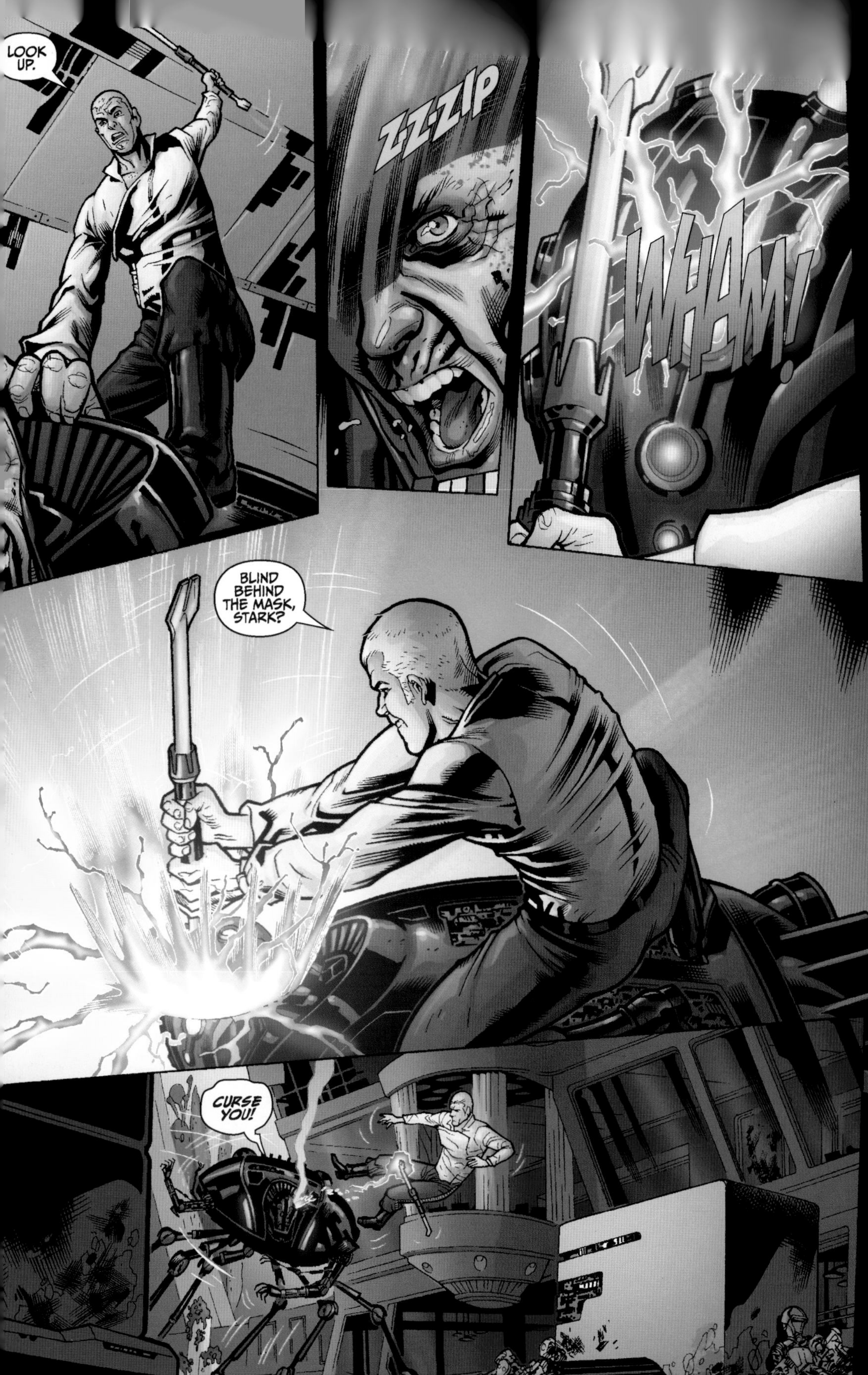
LOOK UP.
Z-Z-ZIP
WHAM!
BLIND BEHIND THE MASK, STARK?
CURSE YOU!

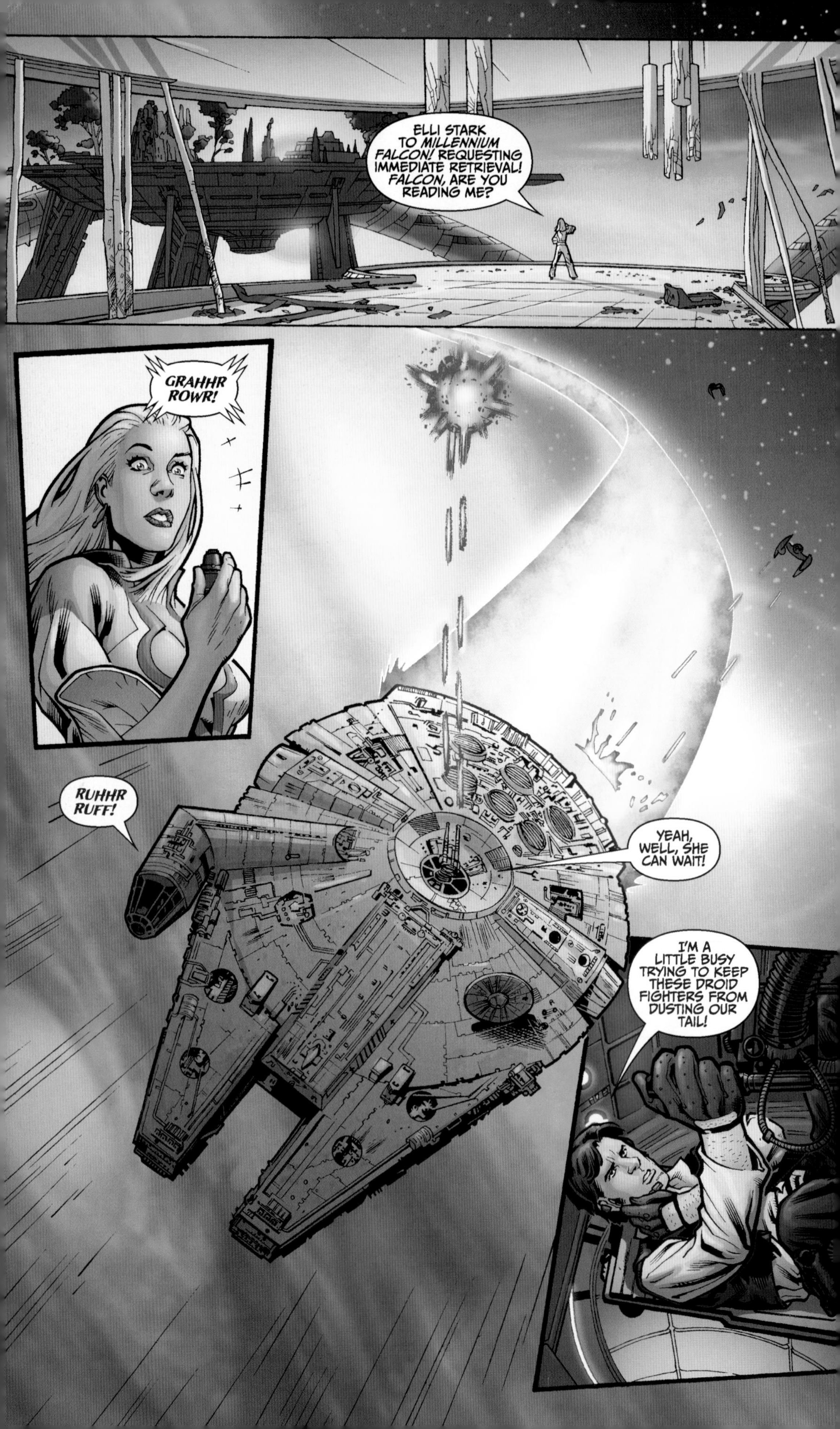
ELLI STARK TO MILLENNIUM FALCON! REQUESTING IMMEDIATE RETRIEVAL! FALCON, ARE YOU READING ME?
GRAHHR ROWR!
RUHHR RUFF!
YEAH, WELL, SHE CAN WAIT!
I'M A LITTLE BUSY TRYING TO KEEP THESE DROID FIGHTERS FROM DUSTING OUR TAIL!

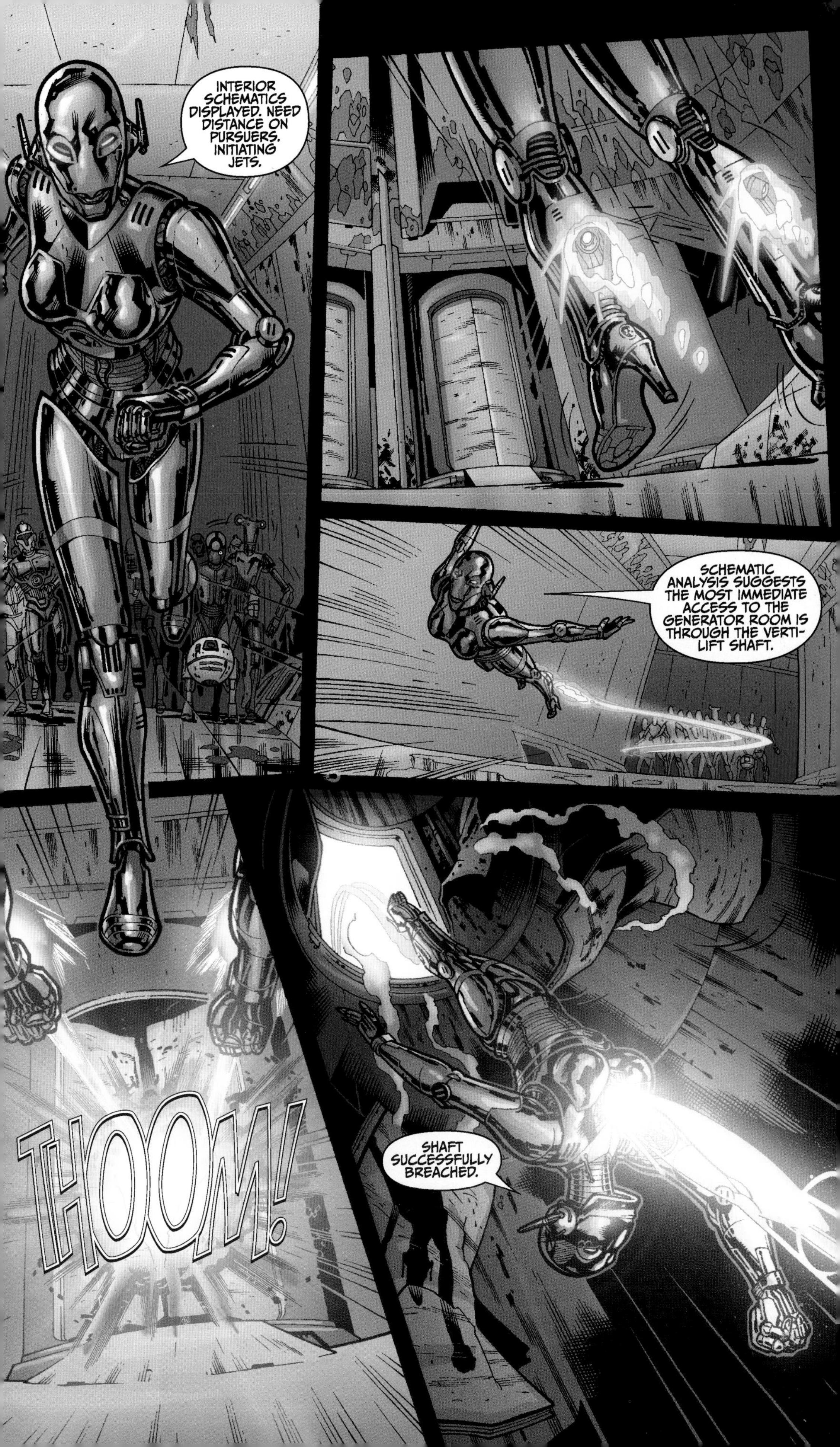
INTERIOR SCHEMATICS DISPLAYED. NEED DISTANCE ON PURSUERS. INITIATING JETS.
SCHEMATIC ANALYSIS SUGGESTS THE MOST IMMEDIATE ACCESS TO THE GENERATOR ROOM IS THROUGH THE VERTI-LIFT SHAFT.
THOOM!
SHAFT SUCCESSFULLY BREACHED.

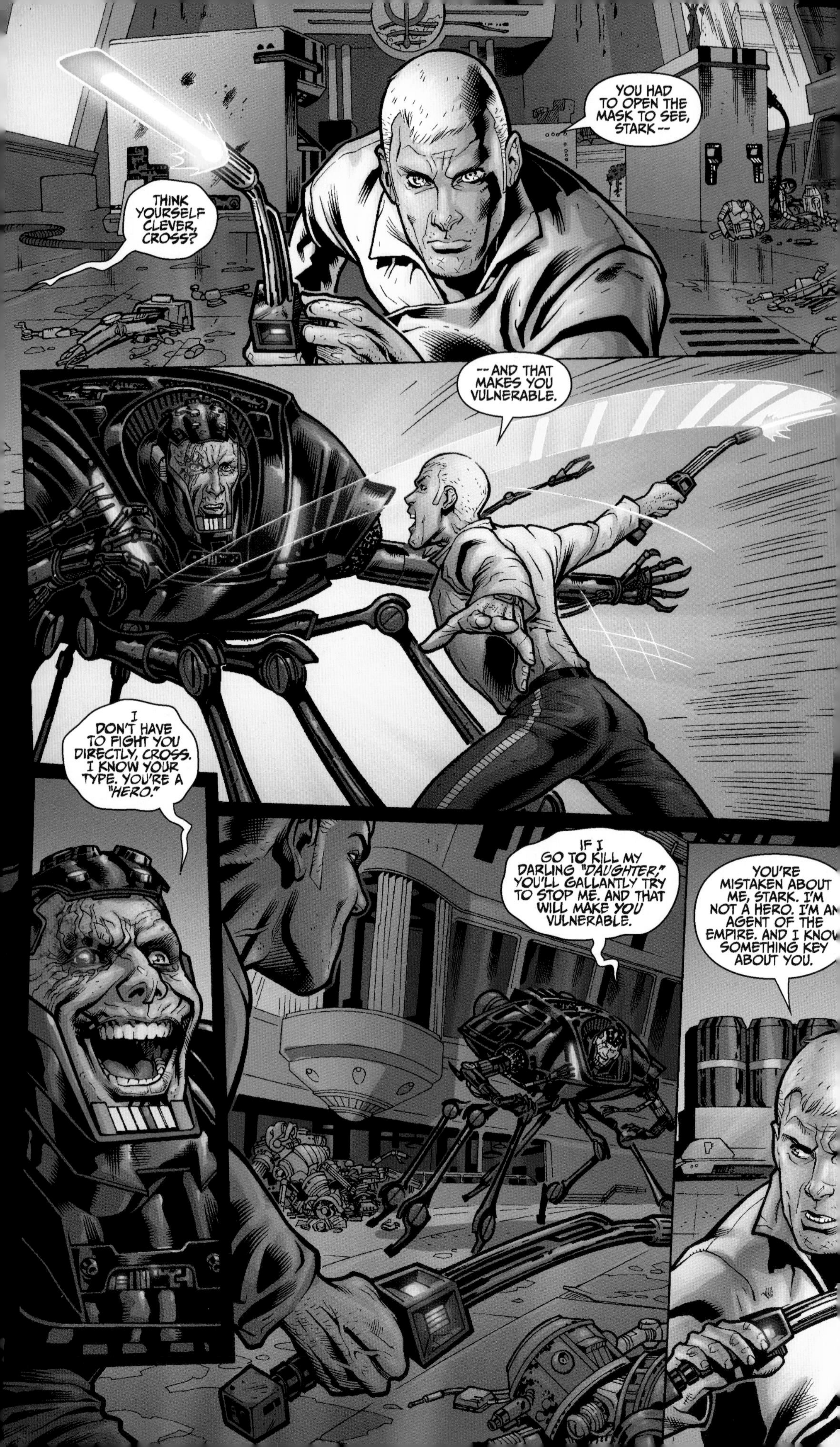
THINK YOURSELF CLEVER, CROSS?
YOU HAD TO OPEN THE MASK TO SEE, STARK --
-- AND THAT MAKES YOU VULNERABLE.
I DON'T HAVE TO FIGHT YOU DIRECTLY, CROSS. I KNOW YOUR TYPE. YOU'RE A "HERO."
IF I GO TO KILL MY DARLING "DAUGHTER," YOU'LL GALLANTLY TRY TO STOP ME. AND THAT WILL MAKE YOU VULNERABLE.
YOU'RE MISTAKEN ABOUT ME, STARK. I'M NOT A HERO. I'M AN AGENT OF THE EMPIRE. AND I KNOW SOMETHING KEY ABOUT YOU.

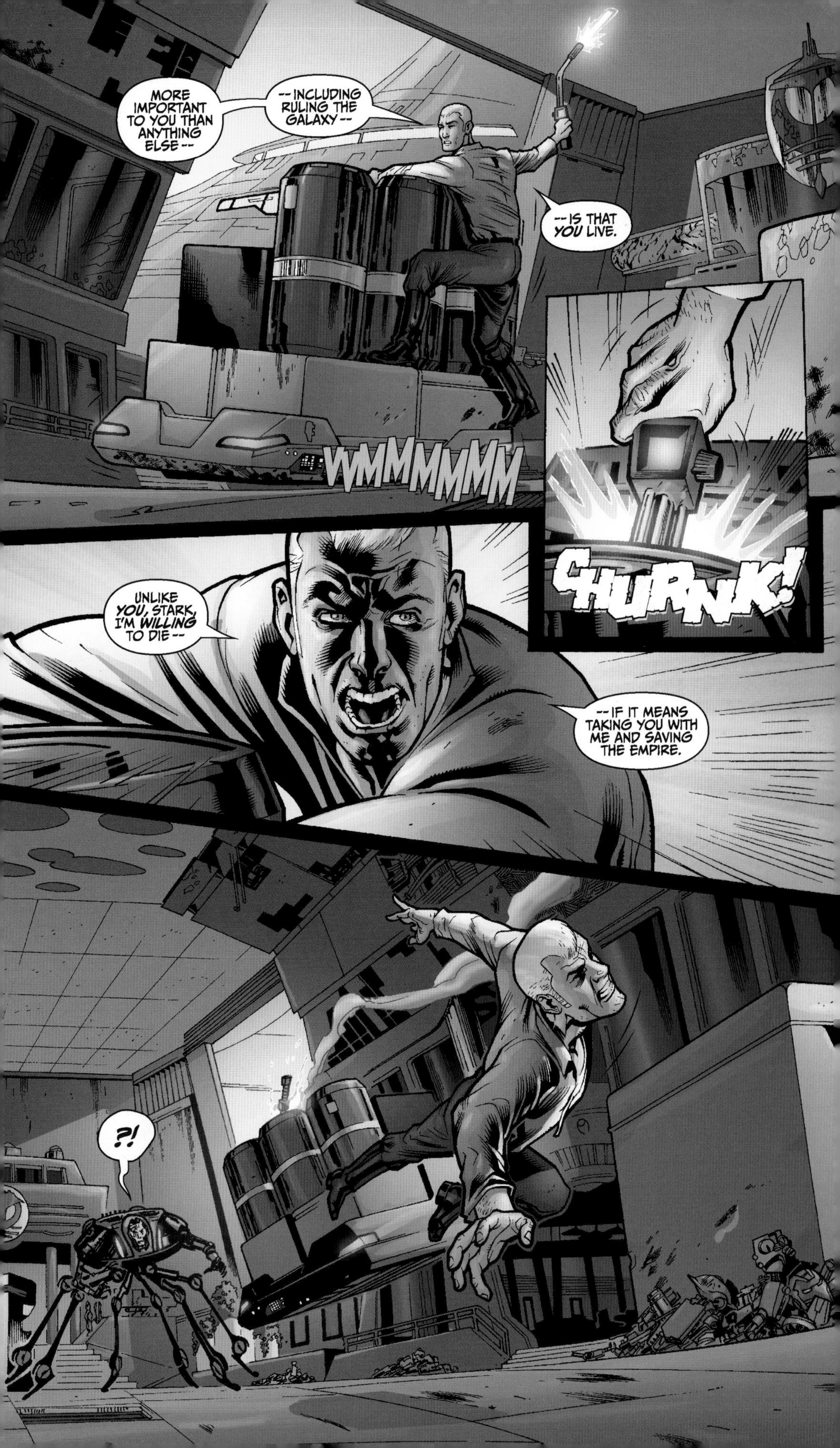
MORE IMPORTANT TO YOU THAN ANYTHING ELSE --
-- INCLUDING RULING THE GALAXY --
-- IS THAT *YOU* LIVE.
VVMMMMMM
CHURNK!
UNLIKE *YOU*, STARK, I'M *WILLING* TO DIE --
-- IF IT MEANS TAKING YOU WITH ME AND SAVING THE EMPIRE.
?!

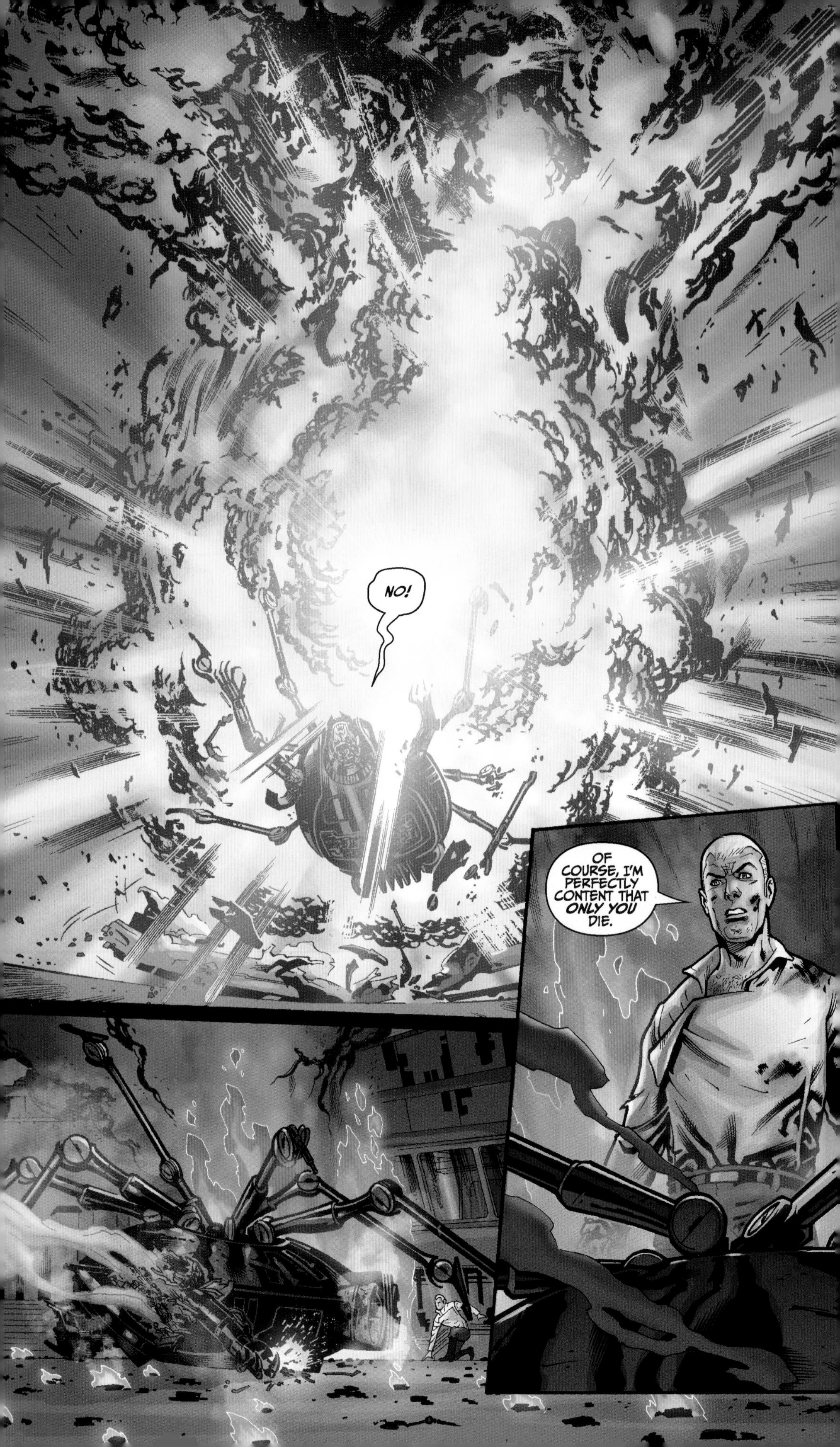
NO!
OF COURSE, I'M PERFECTLY CONTENT THAT ONLY YOU DIE.

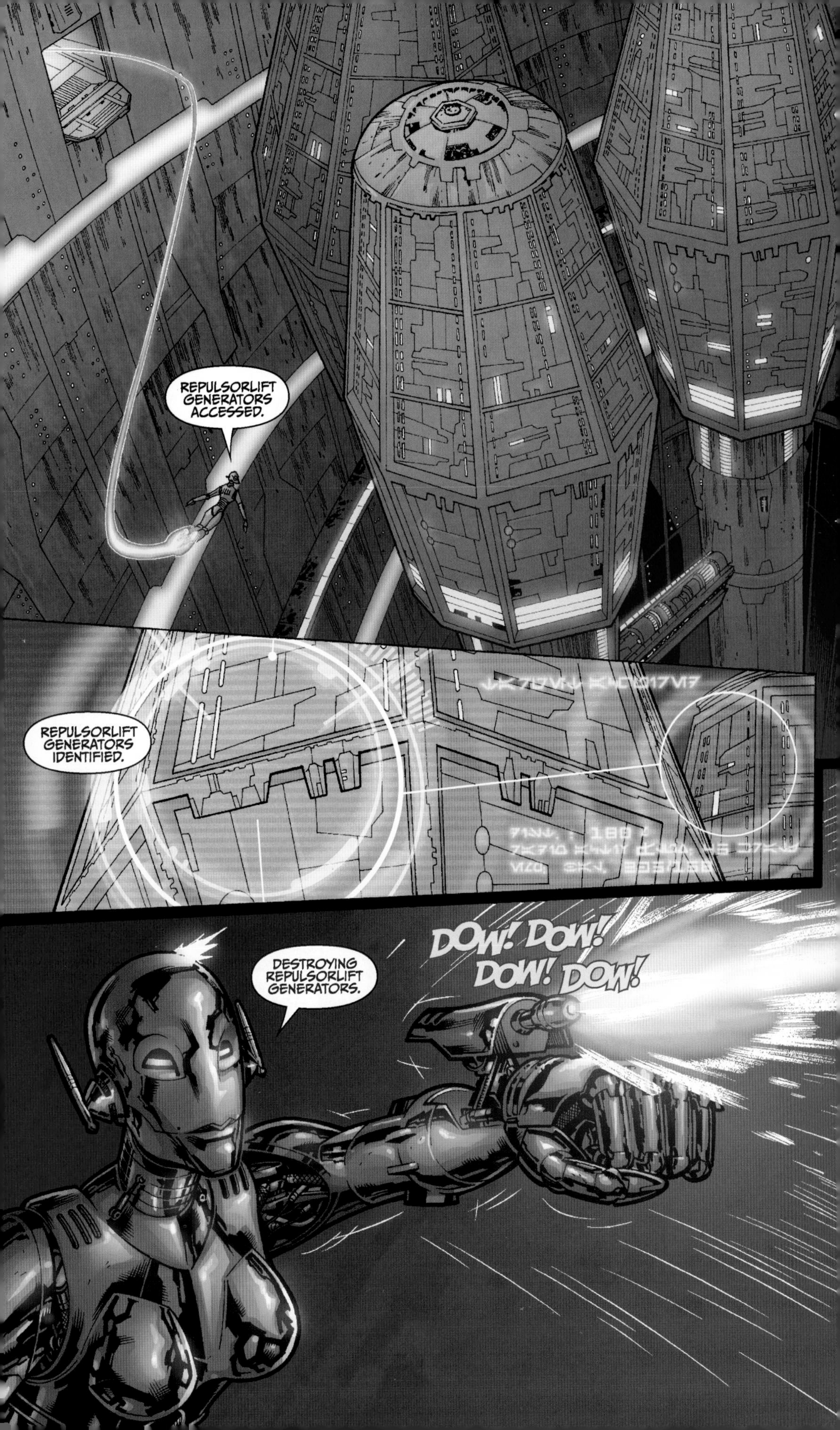
REPULSORLIFT GENERATORS ACCESSED.
REPULSORLIFT GENERATORS IDENTIFIED.
DESTROYING REPULSORLIFT GENERATORS.
DOW! DOW! DOW! DOW!

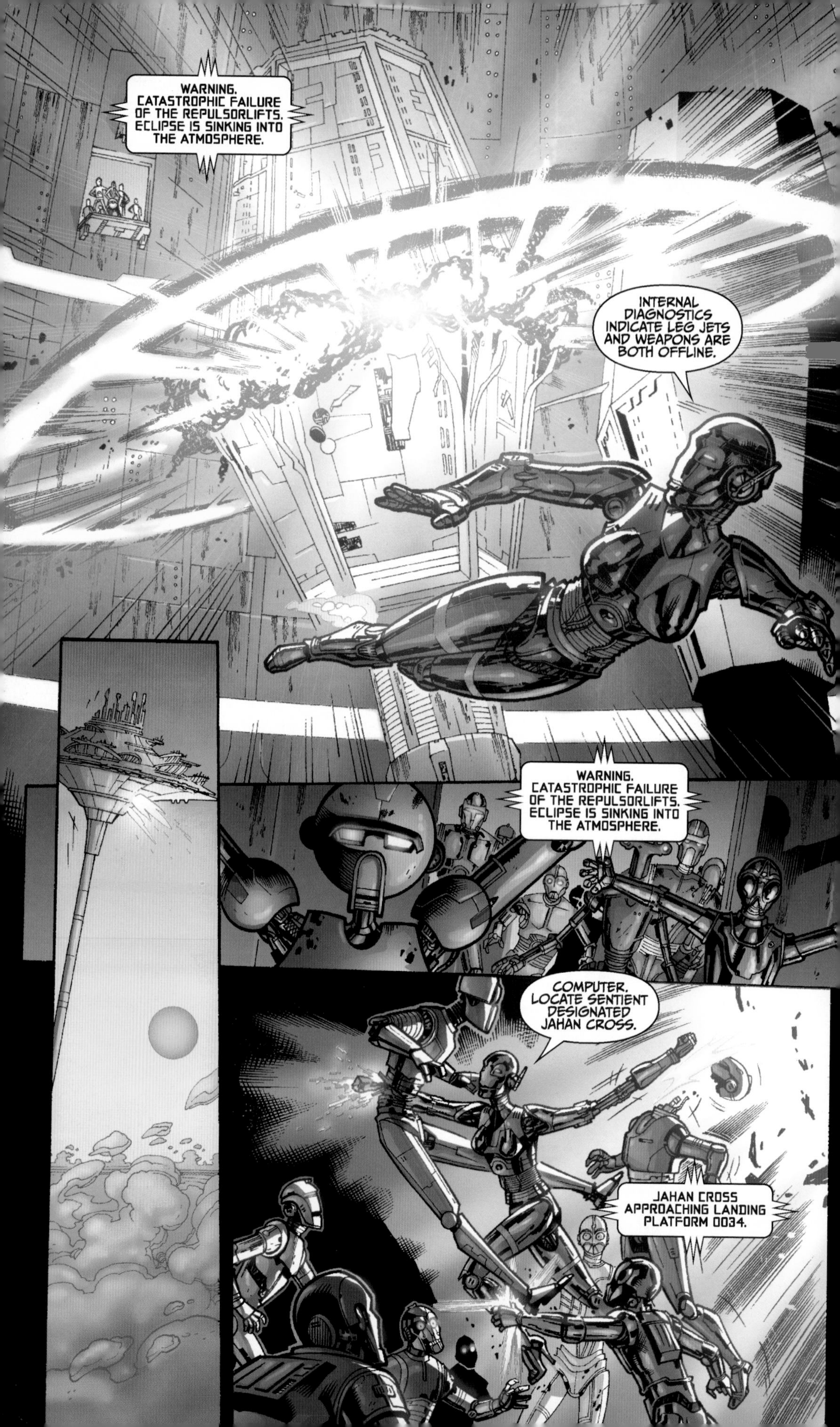
WARNING. CATASTROPHIC FAILURE OF THE REPULSORLIFTS. ECLIPSE IS SINKING INTO THE ATMOSPHERE.
INTERNAL DIAGNOSTICS INDICATE LEG JETS AND WEAPONS ARE BOTH OFFLINE.
WARNING. CATASTROPHIC FAILURE OF THE REPULSORLIFTS. ECLIPSE IS SINKING INTO THE ATMOSPHERE.
COMPUTER. LOCATE SENTIENT DESIGNATED JAHAN CROSS.
JAHAN CROSS APPROACHING LANDING PLATFORM 0034.

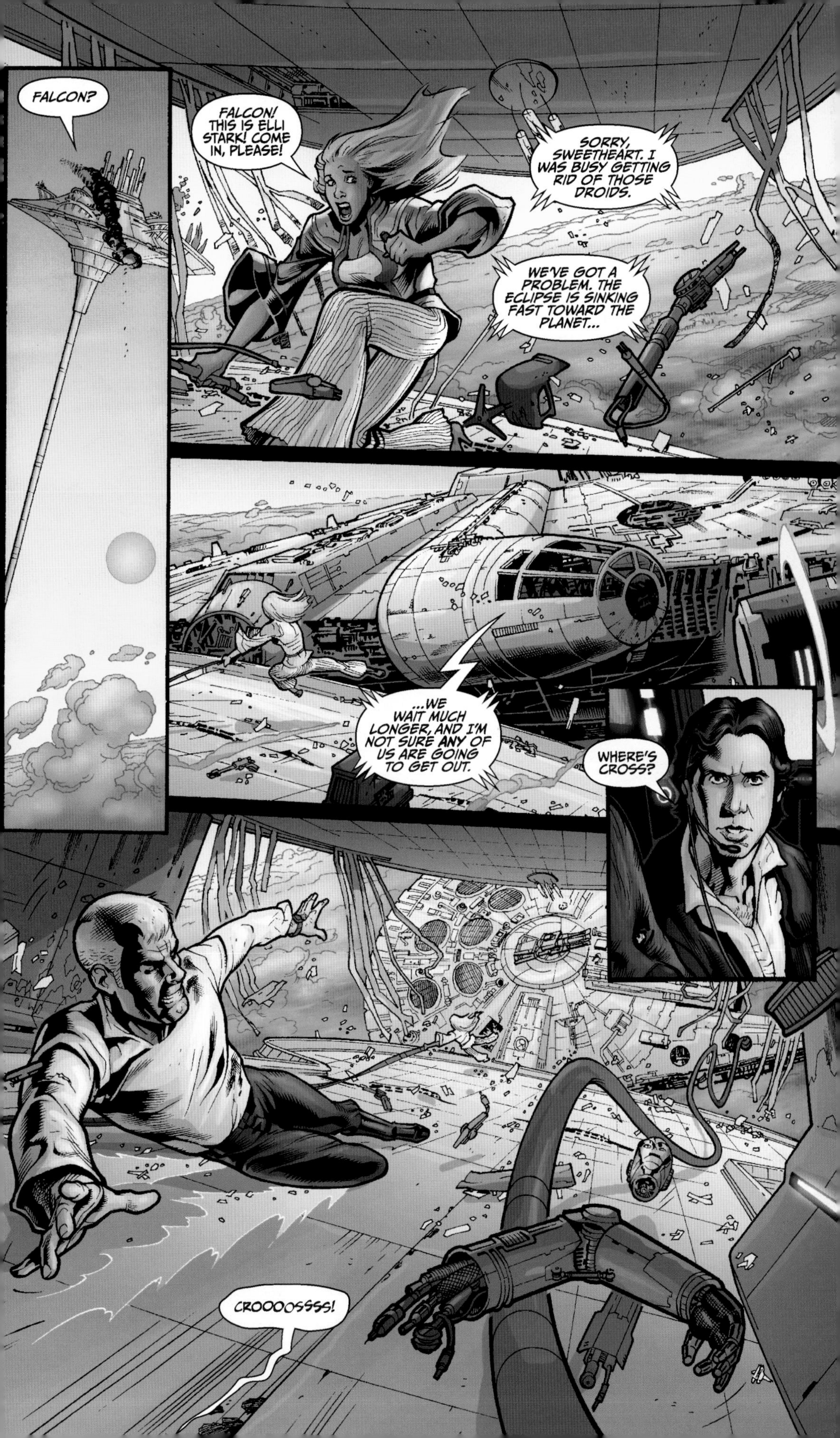
FALCON?
FALCON! THIS IS ELLI STARK! COME IN, PLEASE!
SORRY, SWEETHEART. I WAS BUSY GETTING RID OF THOSE DROIDS.
WE'VE GOT A PROBLEM. THE ECLIPSE IS SINKING FAST TOWARD THE PLANET...
...WE WAIT MUCH LONGER, AND I'M NOT SURE ANY OF US ARE GOING TO GET OUT.
WHERE'S CROSS?
CROOOOSSSS!

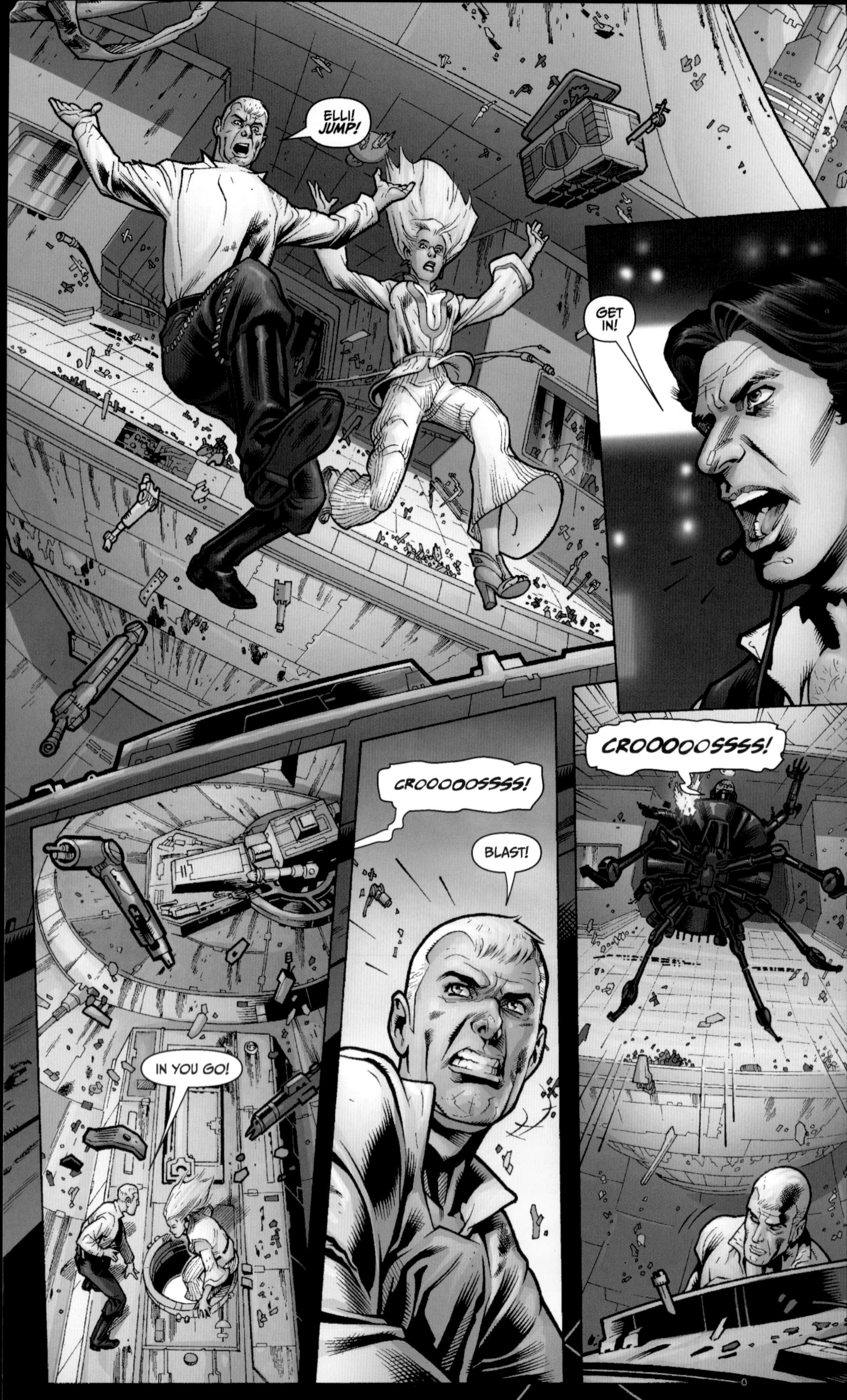
ELLI! JUMP!
GET IN!
IN YOU GO!
CROOOOOSSSS!
BLAST!
CROOOOOSSSS!

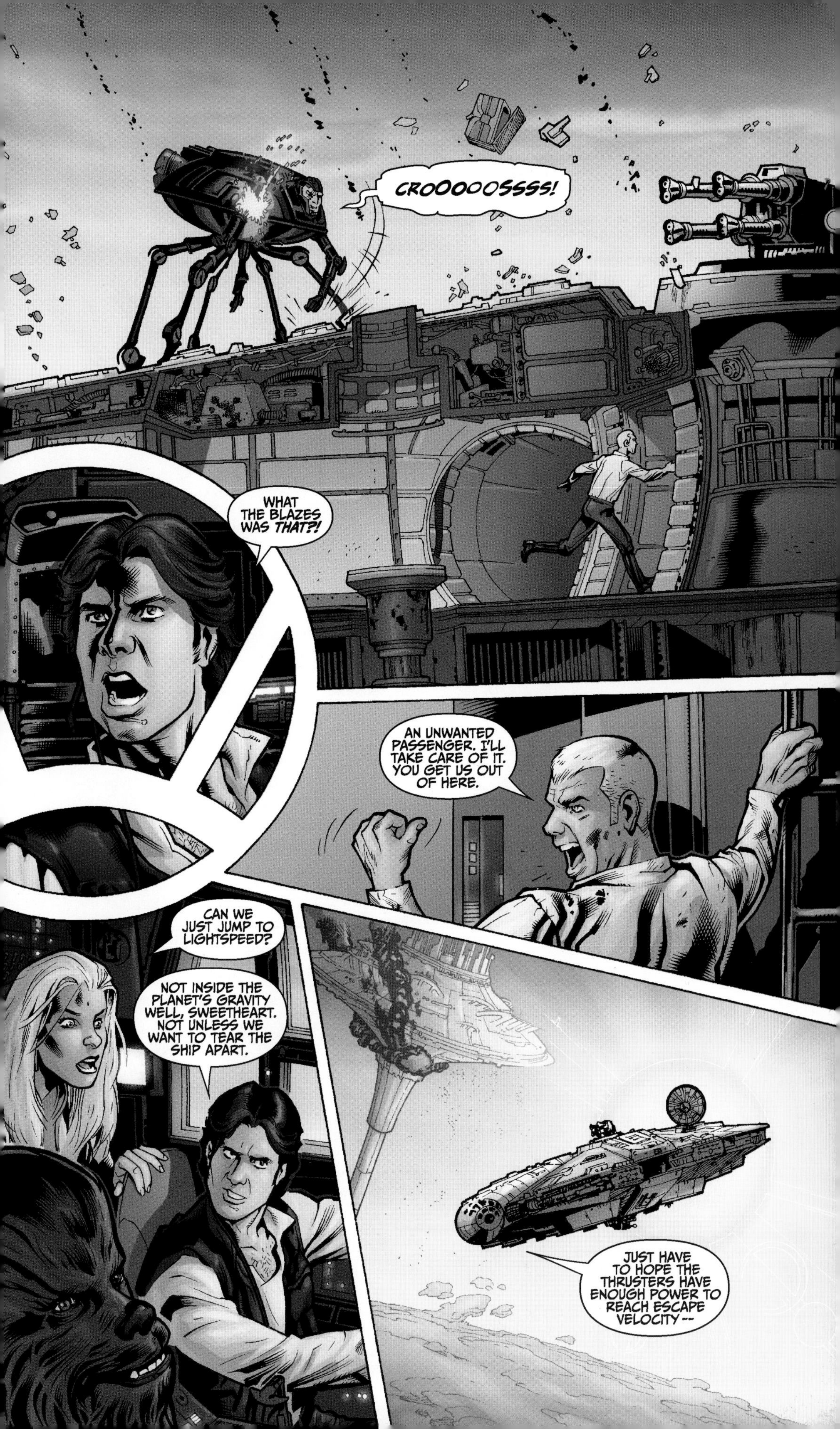
CROOOOOSSSS!
WHAT THE BLAZES WAS *THAT?!*
AN UNWANTED PASSENGER. I'LL TAKE CARE OF IT. YOU GET US OUT OF HERE.
CAN WE JUST JUMP TO LIGHTSPEED?
NOT INSIDE THE PLANET'S GRAVITY WELL, SWEETHEART. NOT UNLESS WE WANT TO TEAR THE SHIP APART.
JUST HAVE TO HOPE THE THRUSTERS HAVE ENOUGH POWER TO REACH ESCAPE VELOCITY--

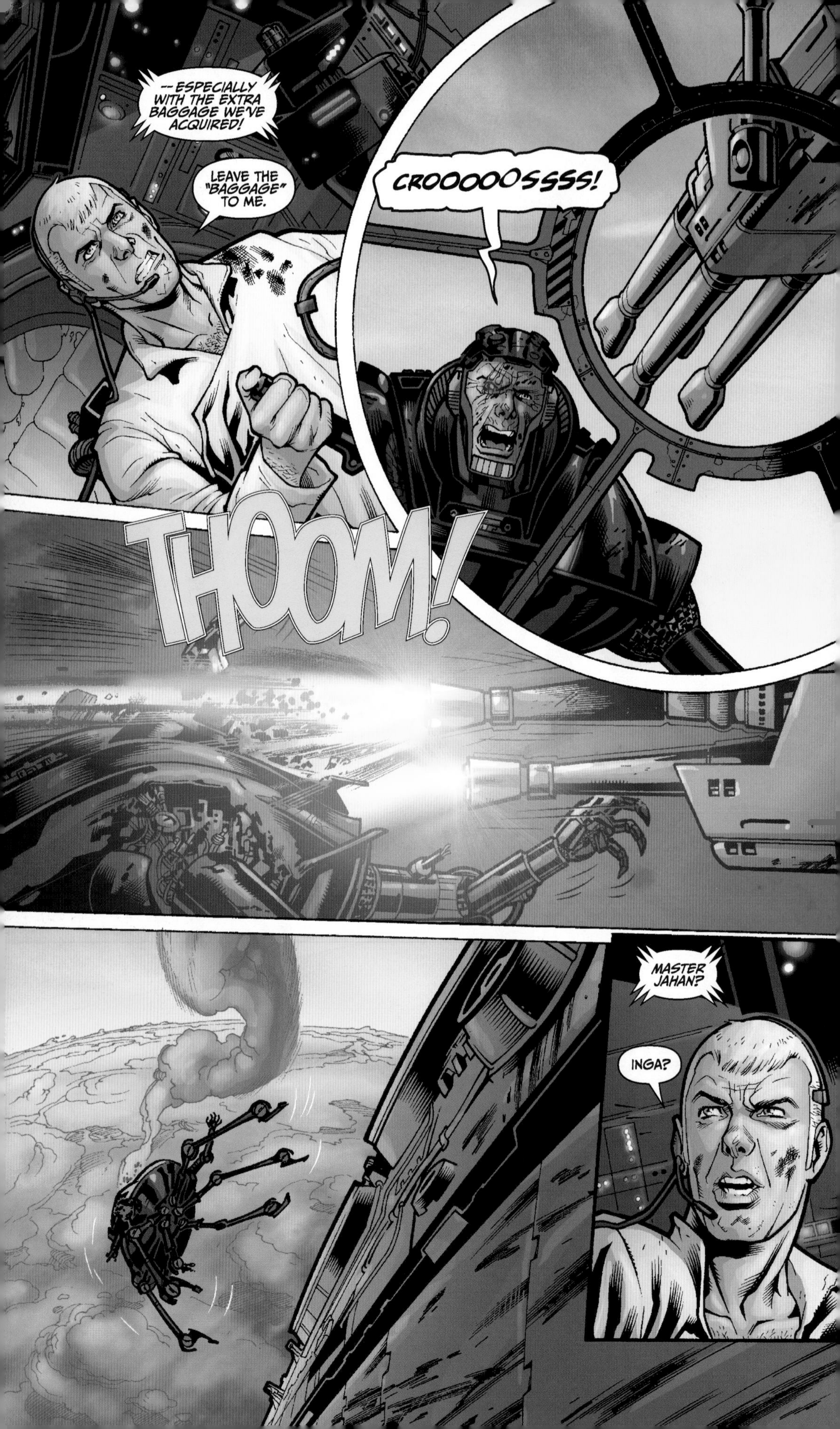
--ESPECIALLY WITH THE EXTRA BAGGAGE WE'VE ACQUIRED!
LEAVE THE "BAGGAGE" TO ME.
CROOOOOSSSS!
THOOM!
MASTER JAHAN?
INGA?

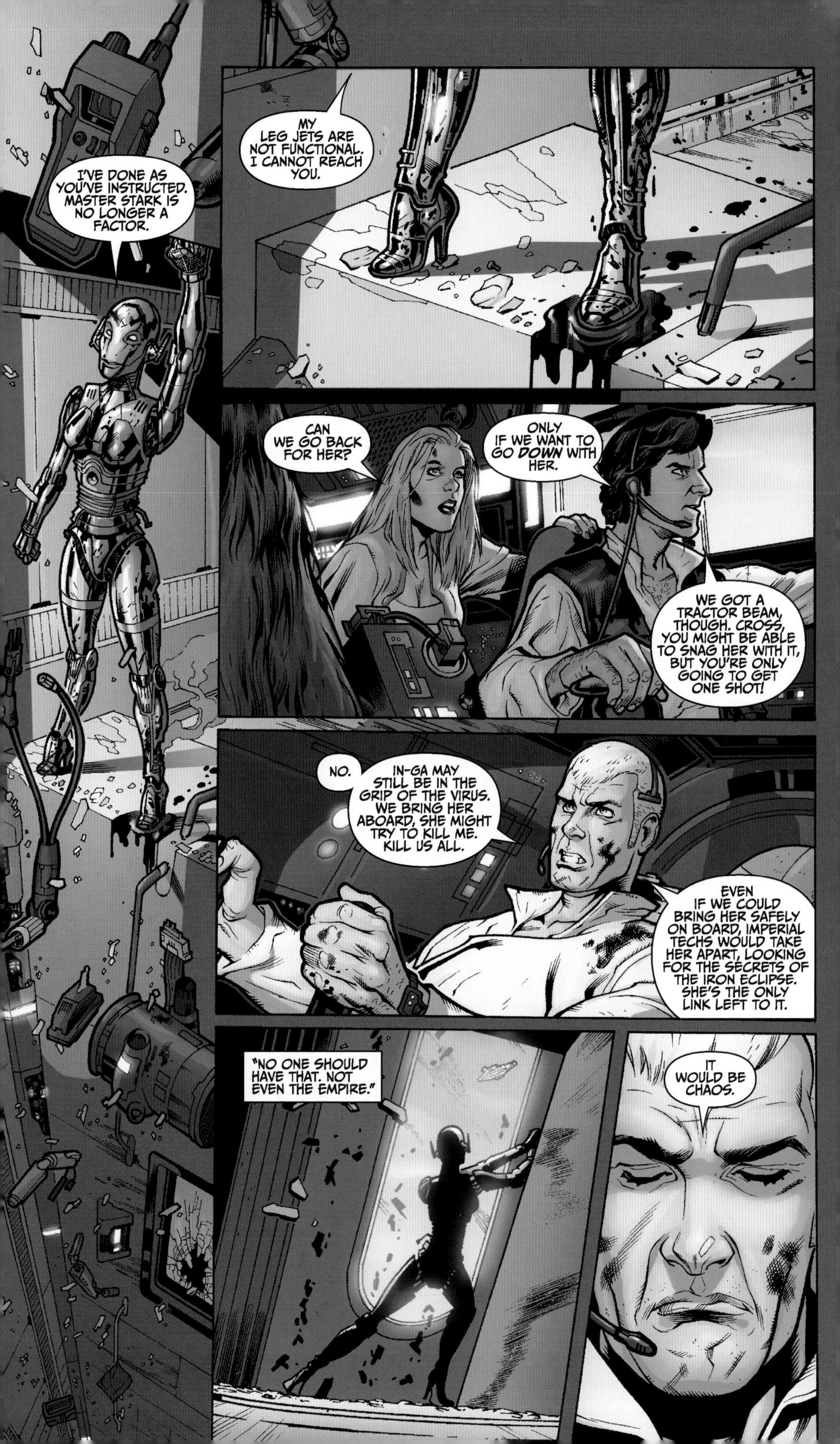
I'VE DONE AS YOU'VE INSTRUCTED. MASTER STARK IS NO LONGER A FACTOR.
MY LEG JETS ARE NOT FUNCTIONAL. I CANNOT REACH YOU.
CAN WE GO BACK FOR HER?
ONLY IF WE WANT TO GO DOWN WITH HER.
WE GOT A TRACTOR BEAM, THOUGH. CROSS, YOU MIGHT BE ABLE TO SNAG HER WITH IT, BUT YOU'RE ONLY GOING TO GET ONE SHOT!
NO.
IN-GA MAY STILL BE IN THE GRIP OF THE VIRUS. WE BRING HER ABOARD, SHE MIGHT TRY TO KILL ME. KILL US ALL.
EVEN IF WE COULD BRING HER SAFELY ON BOARD, IMPERIAL TECHS WOULD TAKE HER APART, LOOKING FOR THE SECRETS OF THE IRON ECLIPSE. SHE'S THE ONLY LINK LEFT TO IT.
"NO ONE SHOULD HAVE THAT. NOT EVEN THE EMPIRE."
IT WOULD BE CHAOS.

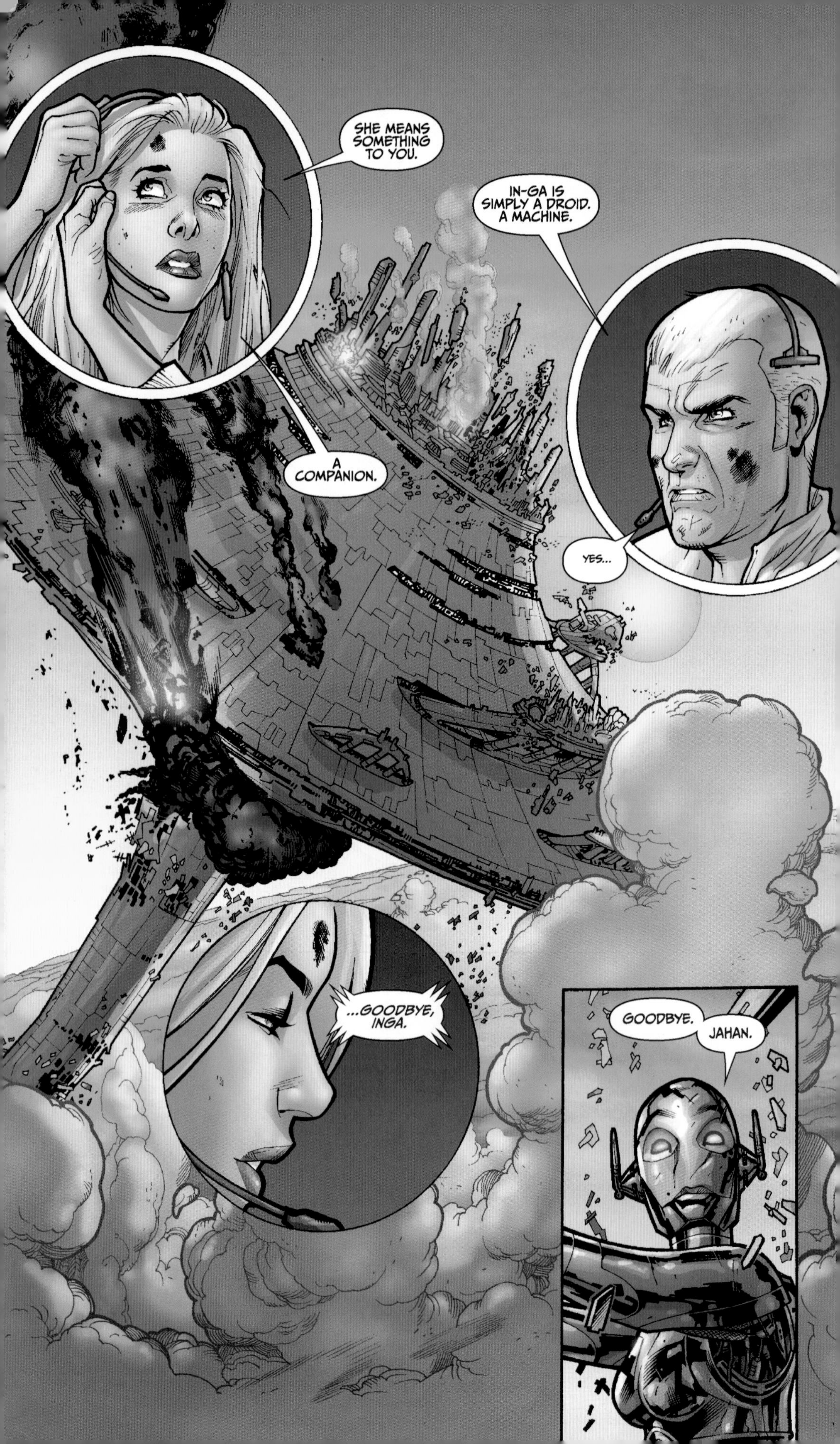
SHE MEANS SOMETHING TO YOU.
IN-GA IS SIMPLY A DROID. A MACHINE.
A COMPANION.
YES...
...GOODBYE, INGA.
GOODBYE.
JAHAN.

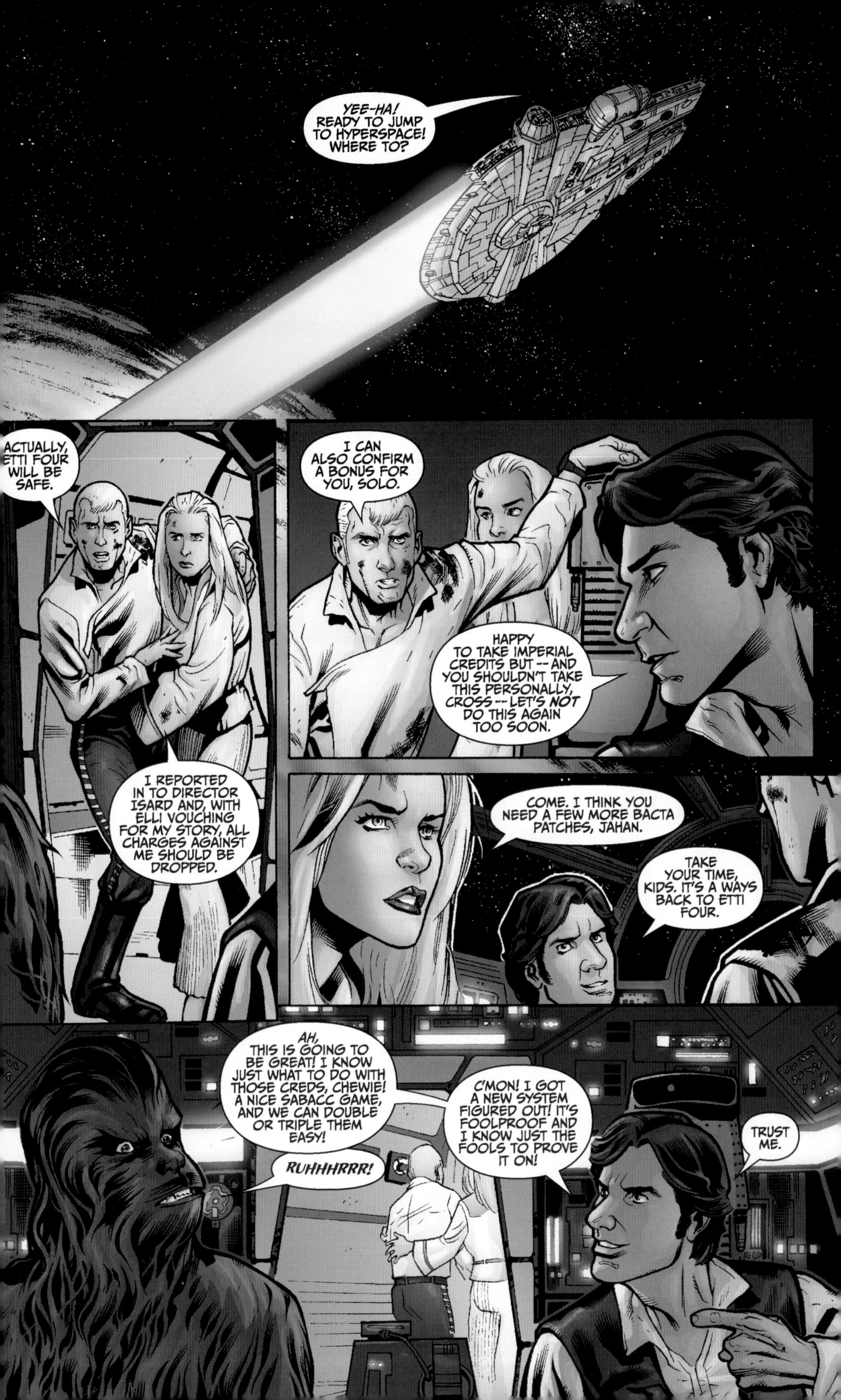
YEE-HA! READY TO JUMP TO HYPERSPACE! WHERE TO?
ACTUALLY, ETTI FOUR WILL BE SAFE.
I REPORTED IN TO DIRECTOR ISARD AND, WITH ELLI VOUCHING FOR MY STORY, ALL CHARGES AGAINST ME SHOULD BE DROPPED.
I CAN ALSO CONFIRM A BONUS FOR YOU, SOLO.
HAPPY TO TAKE IMPERIAL CREDITS BUT -- AND YOU SHOULDN'T TAKE THIS PERSONALLY, CROSS -- LET'S NOT DO THIS AGAIN TOO SOON.
COME. I THINK YOU NEED A FEW MORE BACTA PATCHES, JAHAN.
TAKE YOUR TIME, KIDS. IT'S A WAYS BACK TO ETTI FOUR.
AH, THIS IS GOING TO BE GREAT! I KNOW JUST WHAT TO DO WITH THOSE CREDS, CHEWIE! A NICE SABACC GAME, AND WE CAN DOUBLE OR TRIPLE THEM EASY!
RUHHHRRR!
C'MON! I GOT A NEW SYSTEM FIGURED OUT! IT'S FOOLPROOF AND I KNOW JUST THE FOOLS TO PROVE IT ON!
TRUST ME.

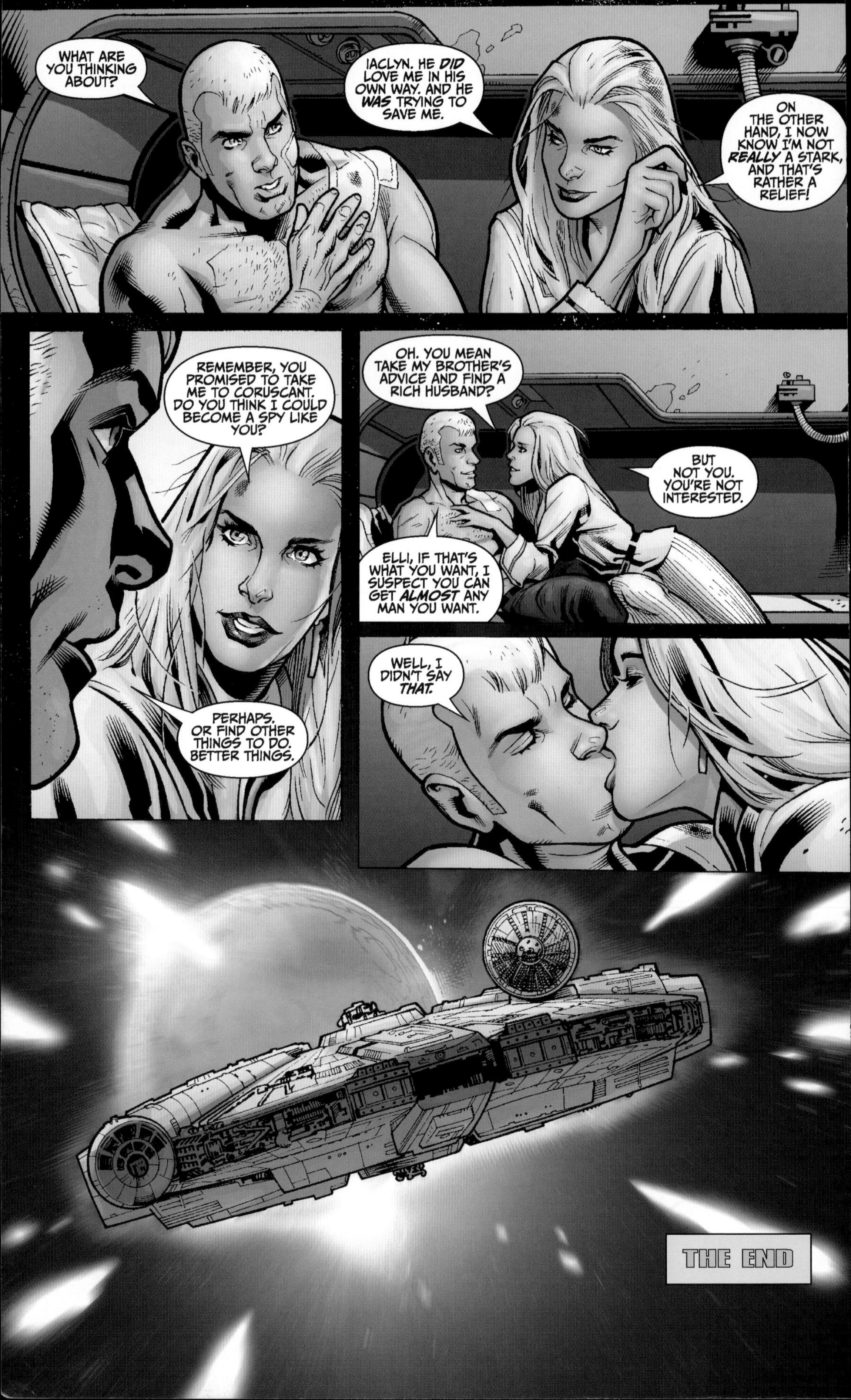
WHAT ARE YOU THINKING ABOUT?
IACLYN. HE DID LOVE ME IN HIS OWN WAY. AND HE WAS TRYING TO SAVE ME.
ON THE OTHER HAND, I NOW KNOW I'M NOT REALLY A STARK, AND THAT'S RATHER A RELIEF!
REMEMBER, YOU PROMISED TO TAKE ME TO CORUSCANT. DO YOU THINK I COULD BECOME A SPY LIKE YOU?
PERHAPS. OR FIND OTHER THINGS TO DO. BETTER THINGS.
OH. YOU MEAN TAKE MY BROTHER'S ADVICE AND FIND A RICH HUSBAND?
BUT NOT YOU. YOU'RE NOT INTERESTED.
ELLI, IF THAT'S WHAT YOU WANT, I SUSPECT YOU CAN GET ALMOST ANY MAN YOU WANT.
WELL, I DIDN'T SAY THAT.
THE END

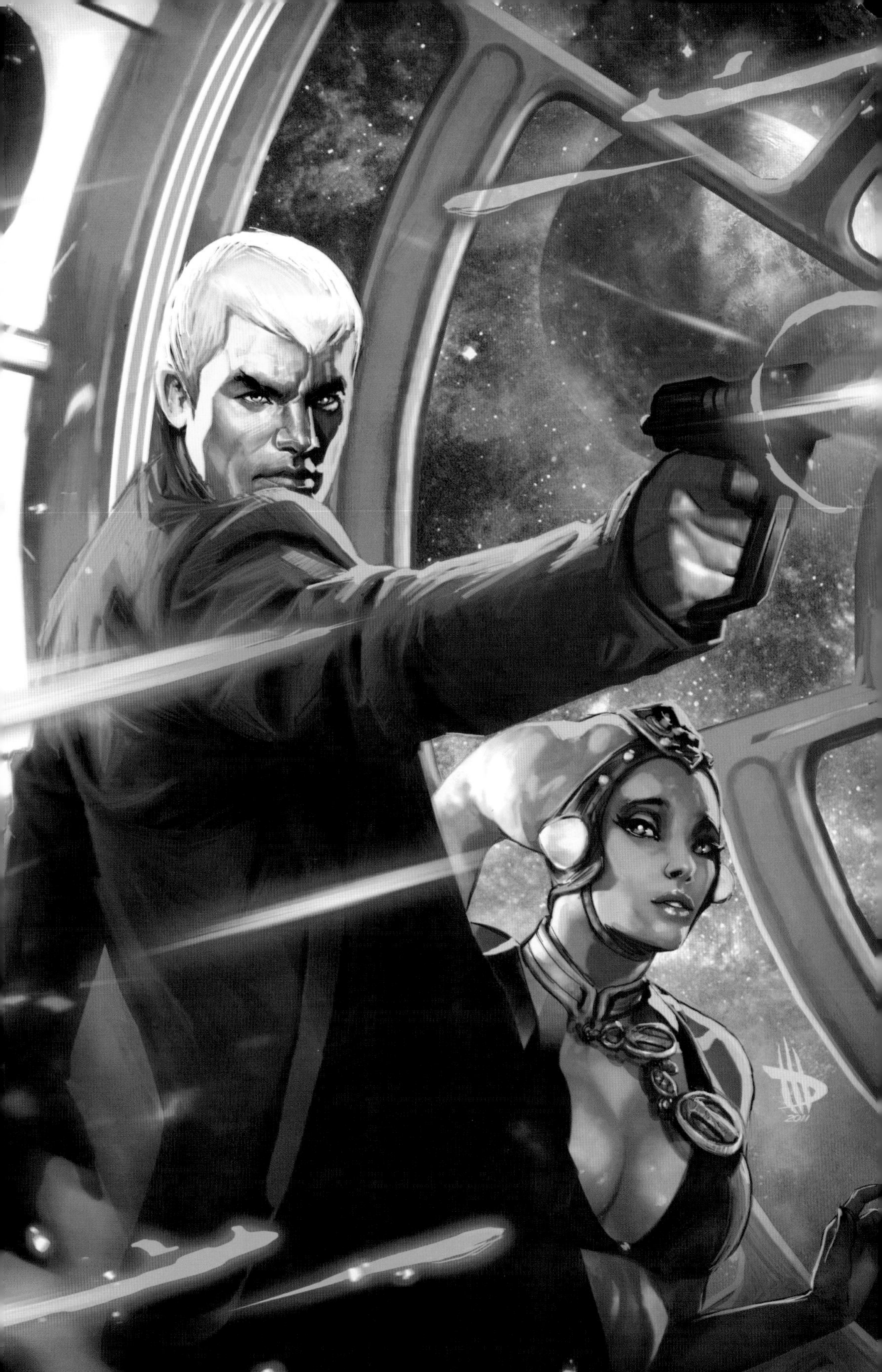

Illustration by » DAVE WILKINS

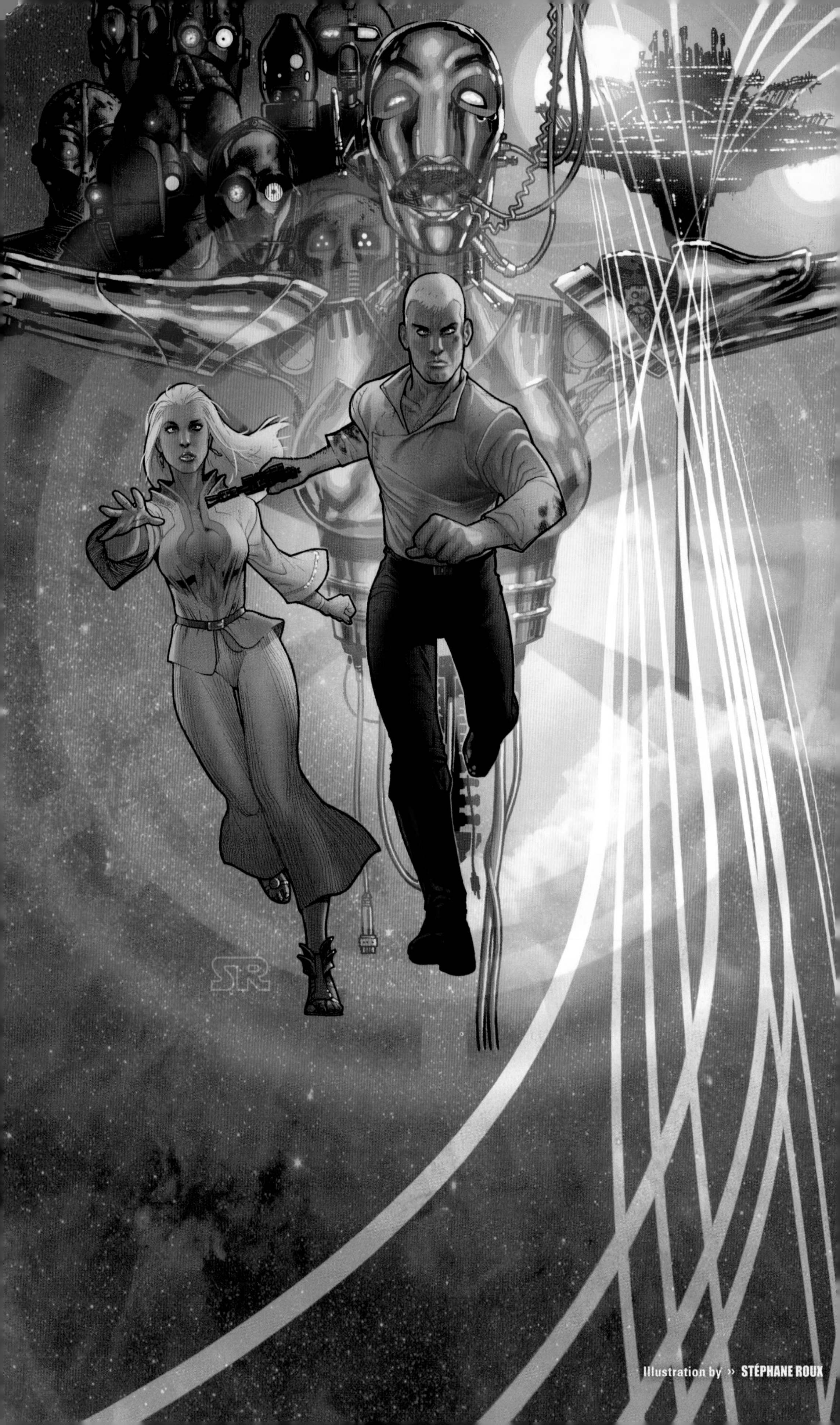

Illustration by » STÉPHANE ROUX

STAR WARS GRAPHIC NOVEL TIMELINE (IN YEARS)

Omnibus: Tales of the Jedi—5,000–3,986 BSW4

Knights of the Old Republic—3,964–3,963 BSW4

The Old Republic—3653, 3678 BSW4

Knight Errant—1,032 BSW4

Jedi vs. Sith—1,000 BSW4

Omnibus: Rise of the Sith—33 BSW4

Episode I: The Phantom Menace—32 BSW4

Omnibus: Emissaries and Assassins—32 BSW4

Omnibus: Quinlan Vos—Jedi in Darkness—31–30
BSW4

Omnibus: Menace Revealed—31–22 BSW4

Honor and Duty—22 BSW4

Blood Ties—22 BSW4

Episode II: Attack of the Clones—22 BSW4

Clone Wars—22–19 BSW4

Clone Wars Adventures—22–19 BSW4

General Grievous—22–19 BSW4

Episode III: Revenge of the Sith—19 BSW4

Dark Times—19 BSW4

Omnibus: Droids—5.5 BSW4

Omnibus: Boba Fett—3 BSW4–10 ASW4

Omnibus: At War with the Empire—1 BSW4

Episode IV: A New Hope—SW4

Classic Star Wars—0–3 ASW4

Omnibus: A Long Time Ago . . .—0–4 ASW4

Empire—0 ASW4

Omnibus: The Other Sons of Tatooine—0 ASW4

Omnibus: Early Victories—0–3 ASW4

Jabba the Hutt: The Art of the Deal—1 ASW4

Episode V: The Empire Strikes Back—3 ASW4

Omnibus: Shadows of the Empire—3.5–4.5 ASW4

Episode VI: Return of the Jedi—4 ASW4

Omnibus: X-Wing Rogue Squadron—4–5 ASW4

Heir to the Empire—9 ASW4

Dark Force Rising—9 ASW4

The Last Command—9 ASW4

Dark Empire—10 ASW4

Crimson Empire—11 ASW4

Jedi Academy: Leviathan—12 ASW4

Union—19 ASW4

Chewbacca—25 ASW4

Invasion—25 ASW4

Legacy—130–137 ASW4

Old Republic Era
25,000 – 1000 years before
Star Wars: A New Hope

Rise of the Empire Era
1000 – 0 years before
Star Wars: A New Hope

Rebellion Era
0 – 5 years after
Star Wars: A New Hope

New Republic Era
5 – 25 years after
Star Wars: A New Hope

New Jedi Order Era
25+ years after
Star Wars: A New Hope

Legacy Era
130+ years after
Star Wars: A New Hope

Vector
Crosses four eras in the timeline

Volume 1 contains:
Knights of the Old Republic Volume 5
Dark Times Volume 3

Volume 2 contains:
Rebellion Volume 4
Legacy Volume 6

BSW4 = before *Episode IV: A New Hope*. ASW4 = after *Episode IV: A New Hope*.

STAR WARS OMNIBUS COLLECTIONS

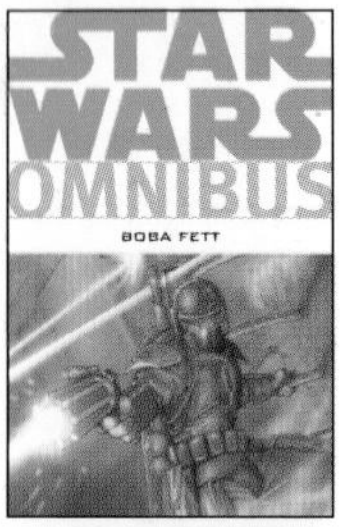
STAR WARS
OMNIBUS
BOBA FETT

STAR WARS: BOBA FETT

Boba Fett, the most feared, most respected, and most loved bounty hunter in the galaxy, now has all of his comics stories collected into one massive volume!

ISBN 978-1-59582-418-9 | $24.99

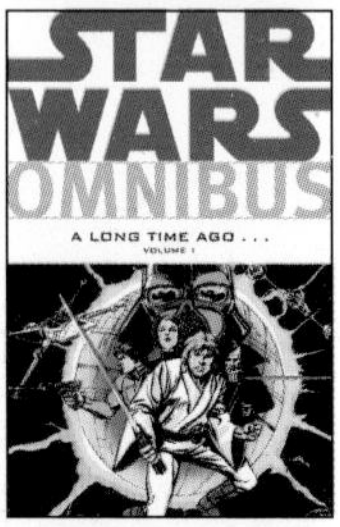
STAR WARS
OMNIBUS
A LONG TIME AGO . . .

STAR WARS: A LONG TIME AGO. . . .

Star Wars: A Long Time Ago. . . . omnibus volumes feature classic *Star Wars* stories not seen in over twenty years! Originally printed by Marvel Comics, these stories have been recolored and are sure to please *Star Wars* fans both new and old.

Volume 1: ISBN 978-1-59582-486-8 | $24.99
Volume 2: ISBN 978-1-59582-554-4 | $24.99
Volume 3: ISBN 978-1-59582-639-8 | $24.99
Volume 4: ISBN 978-1-59582-640-4 | $24.99
Volume 5: ISBN 978-1-59582-801-9 | $24.99

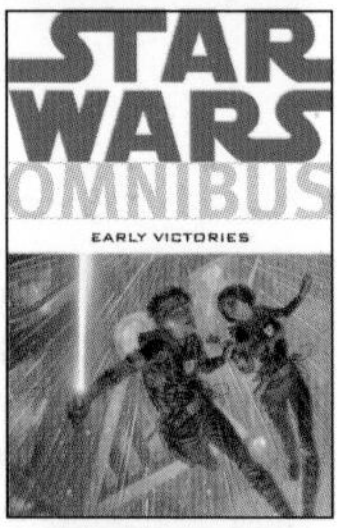
STAR WARS
OMNIBUS
EARLY VICTORIES

STAR WARS: EARLY VICTORIES

Following the destruction of the first Death Star, Luke Skywalker is the new, unexpected hero of the Rebellion. But the galaxy hasn't been saved yet—Luke and Princess Leia find there are many more battles to be fought against the Empire and Darth Vader!

ISBN 978-1-59582-172-0 | $24.99

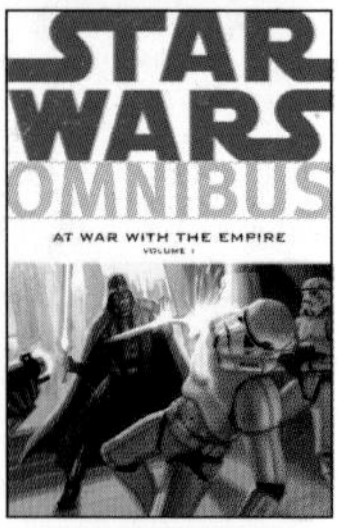
STAR WARS
OMNIBUS
AT WAR WITH THE EMPIRE

STAR WARS: AT WAR WITH THE EMPIRE

Stories of the early days of the Rebel Alliance and the beginnings of its war with the Empire—tales of the *Star Wars* galaxy set before, during, and after the events in *Star Wars: A New Hope*!

Volume 1: ISBN 978-1-59582-699-2 | $24.99
Volume 2: ISBN 978-1-59582-777-7 | $24.99

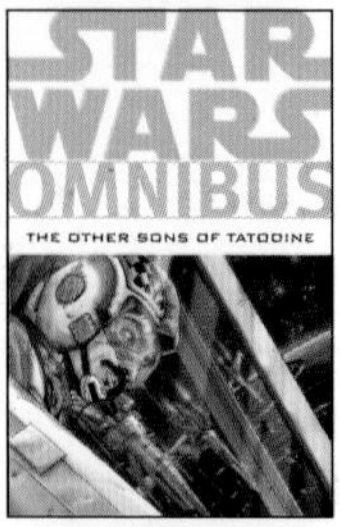
STAR WARS
OMNIBUS
THE OTHER SONS OF TATOOINE

STAR WARS: THE OTHER SONS OF TATOOINE

Luke's story has been told time and again, but what about the journeys of his boyhood friends, Biggs Darklighter and Janek "Tank" Sunber? Both are led to be heroes in their own right: one of the Rebellion, the other of the Empire . . .

ISBN 978-1-59582-866-8 | $24.99

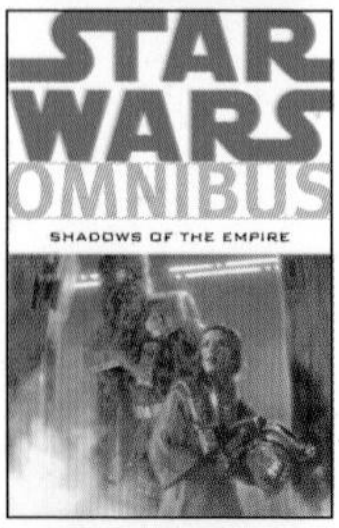
STAR WARS
OMNIBUS
SHADOWS OF THE EMPIRE

STAR WARS: SHADOWS OF THE EMPIRE

Featuring all your favorite characters from the *Star Wars* trilogy—Luke Skywalker, Princess Leia, and Han Solo—this volume includes stories written by acclaimed novelists Timothy Zahn and Steve Perry!

ISBN 978-1-59582-434-9 | $24.99

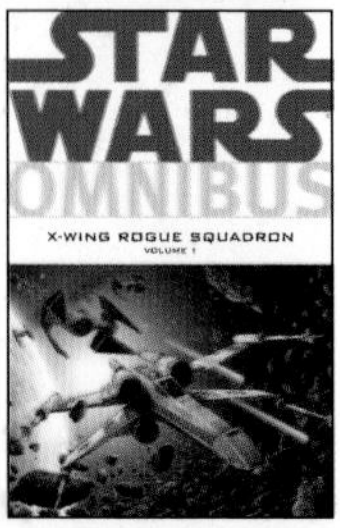
STAR WARS
OMNIBUS
X-WING ROGUE SQUADRON

STAR WARS: X-WING ROGUE SQUADRON

The greatest starfighters of the Rebel Alliance become the defenders of a new Republic in this massive collection of stories featuring Wedge Antilles, hero of the Battle of Endor, and his team of ace pilots known throughout the galaxy as Rogue Squadron.

Volume 1: ISBN 978-1-59307-572-9 | $24.99
Volume 2: ISBN 978-1-59307-619-1 | $24.99
Volume 3: ISBN 978-1-59307-776-1 | $24.99

AVAILABLE AT YOUR LOCAL COMICS SHOP OR BOOKSTORE!

To find a comics shop in your area, call 1-888-266-4226

For more information or to order direct: • On the web: DarkHorse.com • E-mail: mailorder@darkhorse.com • Phone: 1-800-862-0052 Mon.–Fri. 9 AM to 5 PM Pacific Time